DR. JOHN ODERO ONG'ECH- IN THE DREAMS OF MY FATHER:

From A Humble Beginning to an International Award Winning Medical Doctor

Publication jointly done by Wamra Technoprises, P.O. BOX 36665-00200, Nairobi, wamratechnoprises@gmail.com, and KDP, USA.

ISBN: 9798793424387

DR. JOHN ODERO ONG'ECH- IN THE DREAMS OF MY FATHER

Published on: 31st December, 2021

Prof. A O Afullo (Ed)

DEDICATION

I have dedicated this autobiography to my Late Father Jeremiah Ong'ech Ogola. My late father together with my mother Mama Sipora Achieng Ong'ech raised me from a humble beginning to an award winning Medical Doctor with Global Recognition. The dreams of my father started with him attending Usenge Primary School in 1935, when he was 11 years. The compound of the Usenge sector school he attended way back then later became the current Usenge High School where he later took me. This is the place that shaped my future. When I was 11-year-old, he told me he had a vision that I will be a great medical doctor, and indeed this came to pass. My father lived a life full of service to the community and helping others. A life of honesty, hard work and integrity. He set up for me a path that I have followed all my life. I believe I have lived in the dreams of my father.

ACKNOWLEDGEMENT

I acknowledge the editor of my autobiography Prof Augustine Otieno Afullo for inspiring me to do this at this time in my life. He did the same for my late father Jeremiah Ong'ech Ogola when he was alive and also after his death. I acknowledge my family-the Odero Ong'ech family for their support and encouragements. The great Ong'ech Ogola family led by Retired Mwalimu Ochieng' Ong'ech provided the foundation of my education and the necessary social support that shaped me and led to the wonderful journey in my life that is documented in this my memoirs.

I am very grateful to friends and relatives that have taken their time to make their contributions for this piece. Most of my entire career as a doctor was spent at Kenyatta National Hospital (KNH). I am therefore very grateful to this great institution for making me a great doctor. Finally, I am grateful to the USA Embassy Kenya that awarded me FullBright Scholarship (HHF) to study in USA that exposed me to the International Community thus changing my life history.

FORWARD- GERALD OKOLA

AUTOBIOGRAPHY FORWARD

Excerpts from the autobiography by Dr. Ongech is well thought out. These reflections through the corridors of medical service and various incidents in his tour of public service, service to society, immediate and extended family will motivate, encourage, and guide young professionals and the youth as these reflections are a rare treat. The reflections are a source of experiential knowledge acquired over many years. Experience is never taught in school.

As a man who hails from a humble background, Dr. Ong'ech is an alumnus of Usenge High School, Siaya County in Kenya where he passed through the tutelage of the late Moses Paul Warom who was the head teacher then. The head teacher had instilled in his students the value of hard work and he would tell his students that, "**the secret of playing a part is to think yourself into it.**" This meant that you could never keep it up unless you could manage to convince yourself that you were it. I happen to have been his senior in the same school.

Personally I know 'daktari' as passionate about his work. He pays attention to detail and thorough to the core. Dr. Ong'ech is kindhearted as evidenced from his service to nuclear family and to those that relate to him remotely. Being a perfectionist his temper is usually evident whenever he encounters mediocrity.

Besides his academic achievements in the field of medicine, he has made outstanding contributions through leadership in various boards and professional organizations. His dedication to medicine in both the public sector, private practice and service to society has inspired countless students in Kenya and beyond. The tributes written in the book by family, friends, colleagues, together with memorable photographs provide excellent summary of how he is viewed by others.

Dr. Ong'ech's autobiography presents his illustrious life history and shares precious experience and philosophy, resonating with attributes of others. This book apart from being enjoyable, it's also a source of inspirational reading to most people. I see his life history and experience as a reflection of the deep thoughts and aspirations of his late father whom I interacted with very closely in the past.

Here is a person whose life is inspiring. Life which is characterized by an enviable work ethic, unpretentious forthrightness. I would sum it as, 'from modest to complex.'

GERALD OKOLA (BA, MBA, CPS)
RETIRED DIRECTOR, ADMINISTRATIVE SERVICES, NATIONAL ASSEMBLY, KENYA

CEO, EASY LINK, BUSINESS ENTERPRISES

Preface: About the Book

This autobiography of a renowned award winning Obstetrics and Gynaecology (Obs/Gyn) specialist consultant in Nairobi, Kenya, gives highlights on how to change life fortunes from low to top society. It has 13 chapters, the last of which is purely photo gallery. In each of the remaining chapters is a progressive personality development in the various stages of education and training / practice (formation).

Chapter 1 sets the scene by outlining the roots of Dr Ong'ech, otherwise called Aruba by his father and close friends. He is the son of Jeremiah Ong'ech Ogola (Dola) of Kamhore, jakabondo and Mama Siporah Achieng Ong'ech NyaKowil. It's Kamhore; Karodi, from which Daktari and kin are called Jakabondo after their great grandfather, Rodi Abondo. The Karodi is a clan of heroes, from where the great Ogutu Kipapi (Kachwiji) the fighter who helped save Yimbo from frequent raids from Sakwa; the great Dr Walter Otieno who discovered the Malaria Vaccine; Melkazedek Andiki from Kagaya, the great pioneer Yimbo graduate teacher who brought schools to their top level achievement; Otip the great Nyamonye businessman (Okola); and of late a nephew who is a top Gor Mahia player.

Chapter 2 highlights the birth and early childhood of daktari, followed by education and training in chapter 3. Born some 55 years ago under a Kwogo tree, a birth overseen by a traditional birth attendant (TBA), Dr Ongech's father dreams on his 11th birthday of a son who would make a great doctor. His father, the late Jeremiah Ong'ech Ogola (Dola) dropped from Usenge Sector School in class three, but promising himself to come back to the same school big, now Usenge

High School (UHS). Over 4 decades later, Dola sends Odero to this same school where the son does not disappoint; he registers the second best KCE result in the entire history of the school, earning a place in the Prestigious Kericho High School where, alongside his top UHS classmates, he meets award winning colleagues such as Dr Odhiambo Odoyo. He passes KACE exams with flying colours, becoming possibly the first ever Jakamhore to become a medic; a top award winning one. Thus his father's dream of UHS rebounce and top medic both come to pass...and pass highly. At 55, he is a retired, yet not tired, award winning women's doctor with gifted hands, living his father's dreams in multiple ways.

Through the pupilage and mentorship by the great doctor, Willis Badia Jang'olo and Dr Hayanga, he specializes in Obstetrics and Gynaecology, later taking up a prestigious Hubert Humphrey Fulbright Scholarship to undertake an MPH degree. From the latter he rates highly in research, health systems, monitoring and evaluation. Chapter 4 of the autobiography is on marriage life, followed by parenting experience in chapter 5. It's in these two chapters that the spouse, Beatrice Adongo and the 5 children write very moving tributes to their loved one. He strives to give one-on-one parental care to each and every kid, taking them though the most competitive schools and colleges across the globe. In his shoes currently is Grace Obuya Odero, the second born daughter who by all standards is on the father's trail to become a top medic. As the saying goes, best fruit trees never drop their seeds far away from the mother.

Chapter 6 recognises the Dr Odero Ong'ech roots at nuclear level, by presenting the great Ong'ech (Dola) family in which Dr John falls in as number 5, alongside 2 brother and 4 sisters. Chapter 7 focuses on Dr Ong'ech's working life, promotion, culminating to an honour of a top national appointment as the CEO of Kenyatta National Hospital (KNH), an appointment he respectfully turns down in principle. Having grown through the ranks of KNH to the professionally top most position, Dr Ong'ech takes an early retirement to focus on his successful private priactise. These public and private work life experience are both well documented in chapters 7 and 8.

In chapter 9, there are highlights of Daktari's corporate social responsibility (CRS)- service to community and mankind. He initiated the Ogam Health facility, and gives professional support to Mary Goreti Nyamonye Catholic mission hospital, among others. In addition, he initiated a vey successful and active Jeremiah Ong'ech educational Kitty that to date has disbursed Kshs 1,000,000 largely from himself. In chapter 10, an extremely sad moment is registered in 2009: a gun-shot tragedy in a Usenge hotel that throws the entire family, the profesion, the Kamhore, the Yimbo and Siaya county friends and family into dep confusion. Backed by a rich network of professional friends, daktari miraculously fights for his life and makes major lifestyle change decisions that are working very well for him, the family, friends and the clients. To ashame the devil, the very reason - UHS BOM chairmanship suspected to have been behind his shooting, he bounces back to take up the patron position of the UHS alumni association.

Chapter 11 is spared for friends, relatives and professional colleagues' tributes on Dr Odero, followed by chapter 12 in which he gives his views on how a health sector needs to run. He borrows from the USA based training on health systems, drawing the 6 health systems pillars as core to theis critical sector. Chapter 13 comprises a rich photo profile of Daktari and family. It presents a faily good ending of a successful life which began on a low profile; humble beginning to an award wining medical doctor. Incidentally, other than the Fulbright (2001/2), The Fulbright Alumni of the year award (2009), The Company of the Year Award (COYA, 2013) award; the KNH CEO appointment (2018); Daktary triumphantly takes a top 3-year award as Safaricom's health advisor on his 55th Bithrday, aligned to the completion and release of this moving title '**in the dreams of my father**'. Safarocom is currently the top corporate in Kenya and the region, and rates among the top 100 glovbally. Let Daktari's star continue shining till he gets a top global award in his private practice in leadership, maternal and child health (MCH), and Obstetrics and Gynaecology where he continues to shine more than ever before.

Wamra Technoprises

ISBN: 9798793424387

DR. JOHN ODERO ONG'ECH- IN THE DREAMS OF MY FATHER

Published on: 31st December, 2021

Prof A O Afullo (Ed)

31.12.21: Dr Ongech on his 55th Birthday

Original Gangsta

Contents

DR. JOHN ODERO ONGECH-IN THE DREAMS OF MY FATHER:

From A Humble Beginning to International Award Winning Medical Doctor

Published 31st December 2021

ISBN: 9798793424387

Prof A Afullo (Ed)

CHAPTER 1: THE ROOTS:

1.0 THE LINEAGE OF MY FATHERS: THE RODI- KAMHORE CLAN GENEALOGY

1.1: The Karodi and the Kamhore clan

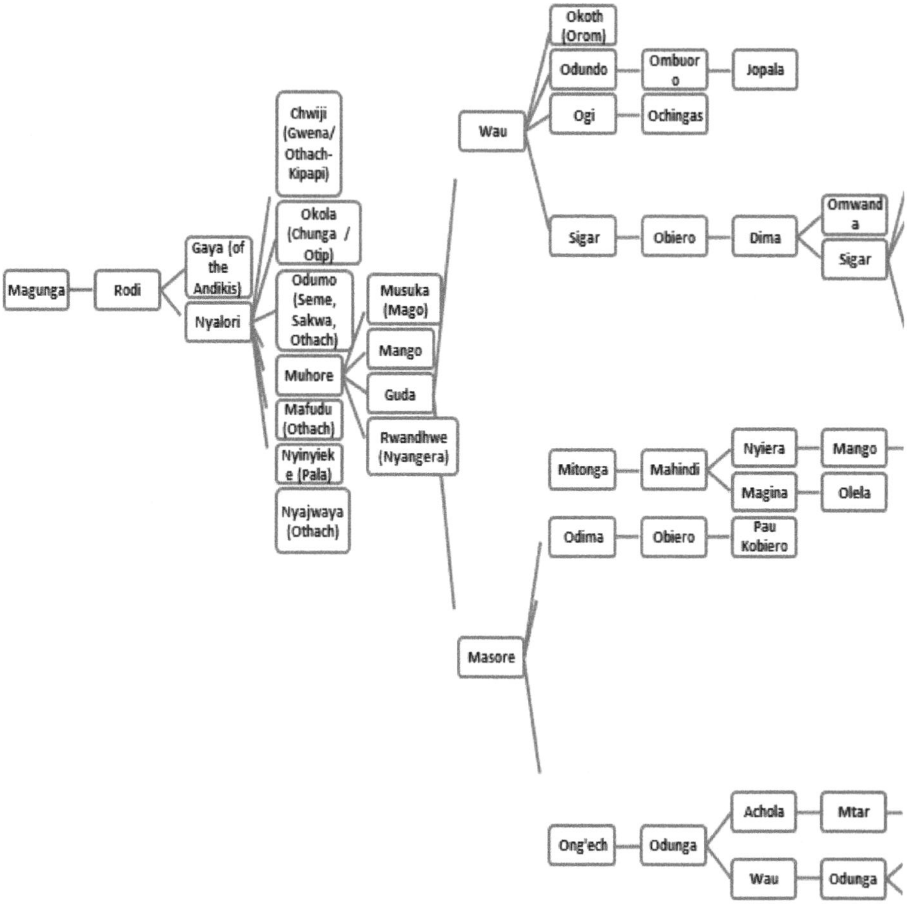

The Ancestor of the Kamhore was called Magunga, who migrated from Sudan and Uganda, and had a son called Rodi. Rodi gave birth to Gaya and Nyalori. The Andikis in Got Matar, including japuonj Melkazadek Juma

Andiki lineage fall in the Kagaya ancestry. Nyalori gave birth to seven sons, of whom one was Muhore. Others were Chwiji (who live in Othach, yimbo), Okola (the Otip family in Chunga, Yimbo), Odumo (in Seme, Sakwa and Othach), Mafudu (Othach, Yimbo), Nyinyieke (in Pala, Yimbo), and Nyajawaya (in Othach). It should be noted that one of the legendary heroes of the Luo, Ogutu Kipapi, was from the Chwiji sub-clan of this great Rodi clan.

1.2: Muhore

Muhore had 3 sons, namely: Musaka Mango, Guda and Rwandhwe (Nyangera). Guda gave forth 2 sons, Wau and Masore. Wau gave birth to 4 sons namely: Okoth (Orom), Odundo, Ogi and Sigar. The Sigar lineage is where the Obiero Sigars fit in; the Ogi is where the Ochingas fall, while Odundo's people include Ombuoro. Wau's brother, Masore, on the other hand gave forth Ong'ech, Mitonga and Obiero Kodima.

1.21: The Mitonga Manyala Kins

The extended Manyala family are the descendants of Mitonga, while the larger kobiero family based in Pau / Bar kObiero (the plains of Kobiero) are the descendants of Obiero. The Ong'ech family lineage is presented to details below.

1.3: The Ong'ech I and Ong'ech II family

Mzee Ong'ech II gave forth 3 sons: Dalmas Ogola, Joseph Ochieng and John Odero, who in turn have among them 22 children (nyikwa Mzee), comprising 9 boys and 13 girls. The Mzee also has four married daughters namely: Mary Atieno, Margaret Auma, Benta Aluoch and the late Grace Akoth, who have given forth 17 children comprising 8 okepe and 9 nyikepe.

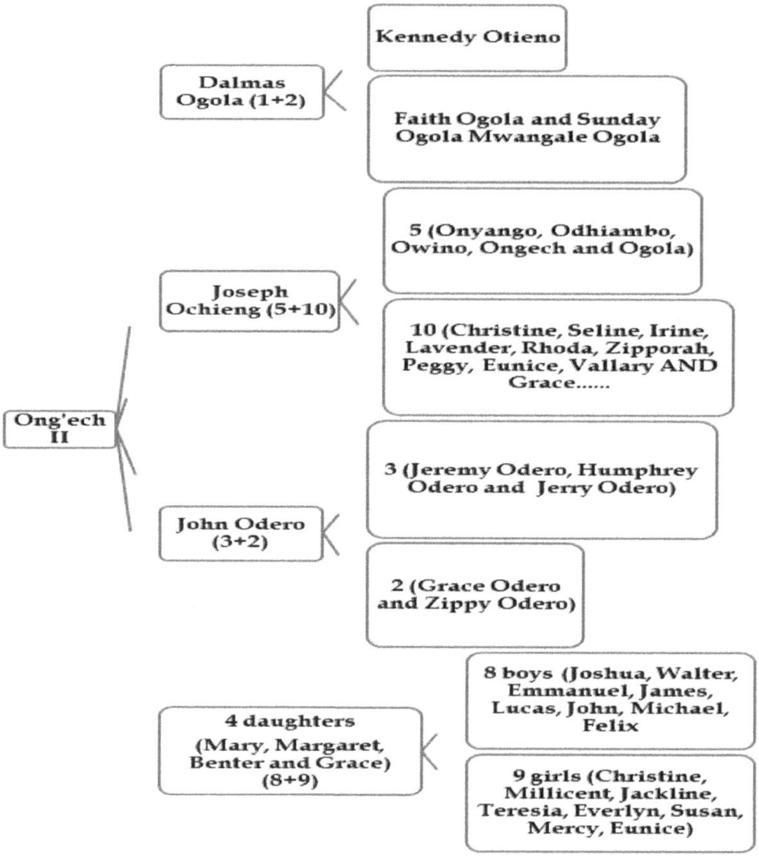

1.4: Full Kamhore and The great Ong'ech Dola (Ong'ech II) lineage tracking

Here Ong'ech Dola is thereafter referred to as Ong'ech II, as there is the 7th ancestor, the senior Ong'ech (referred to as Ong'ech I).With Jaduong Ong'ech Dola's children as the 1st generation, Mzee Dola the 2nd in line, there are 13 traceable generations within the wider Kamhore / Karodi /

Kamagunga clan. The lineage goes: Ogola k'Ong'ech; Ong'ech kogola[1]; Ogola ka Mtar; Mtar ka Achola; Achola ka Odunga; Odunga ka Ong'ech I; Ong'ech I ka Masoro; Masoro ka Guda; Guda ka Muhore; Muhore ka Nyalori; Nyalori ka Rodi; Rodi ka magunga. Dola is 2nd, Muhore is the 10th ancestor; Rodi is the 12th, while Magunga is the 13th. This is a rich lineage since for most clans, they hardly are able to trace beyond the 8th / 10th for the age mates of the Dola children.

The relationship table and the filial generations

Nth ancestor	13	12	11	10	9	8	7	6	5	4	3	2	1	0
Names of representatives	Magunga	Rodi	Gaya, Nyalori	Chwiji, Okola, Odumo, Muhore, Mafudu, Nyinyiek, Nyajwaya	Musuka, Mango, Guda, Rwandhwe	Wau, Masoro	Okoth, Odundo, Ogi, Sigar, Mitonga, Odima, Ong'ech I	Ombuoro, Obiero, Mahindi, Obiero, Odunga	Dima, Nyiera, Magana, Achola, Wau	Omwanda, Sigar, Mango, Olela, Mtar, Odunga	Akungu, Obiero, Spem, Nyiera, Ogola, Shem, Magana	Ong'ech II, Susan, Badia, Ouma, R Onyango	Ogola, Ochieng, Odero, Amina, Paul, Onyango	Dola grandchildren
	Magunga	Rodi	Nyalori	Muhore,	Guda,	Masoro	Ong'ech I	Odunga	Achola,	Mtar,	Ogola,	Ong'ech II	Ogola, Ochieng, Odero, Amina, Paul, Onyango	Dola grandchildren

1.5: The filial generations: who is a cousin to who in Kamhore?

In terms of relationships, the following are cousins:

Ong'ech II: Susan, Badia, Ouma and R Onyango;

Ogola: Akungu, Obiero, Spem, Nyiera, Shem and Magana

Mtar: Omwanda, Sigar, Mango, Olela and Odunga; Achola: Dima, Nyiera, Magina, Wau;

[1] Ong'ech Kogola means Ongech wuod Ogola, Ong'ech Arap Ogola; Ongech Ole Ogola; Ong'ech wa Ogola; Ong'ech son of Ogola

Odunga I: Ombuoro, Obiero Kodima, Mahindi, Obiero ka Sigar;

Ong'ech I: Okoth (Orom), Odundo, Ogi, Sigar, Mitonga and Odima;

Masoro: Wau; Guda: Musuka, Mango, Rwandhwe;

Muhore: Chwiji, Okola, Odumo, mafudu, Nyinyiek, Nyajwaya,

Nyalori: Gaya Rodi: None Magunga: None

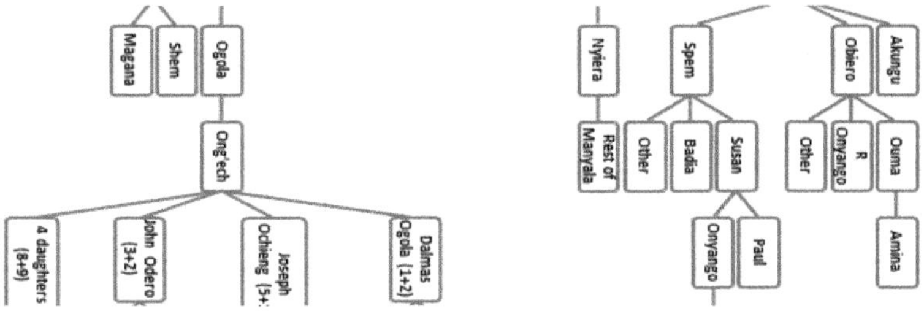

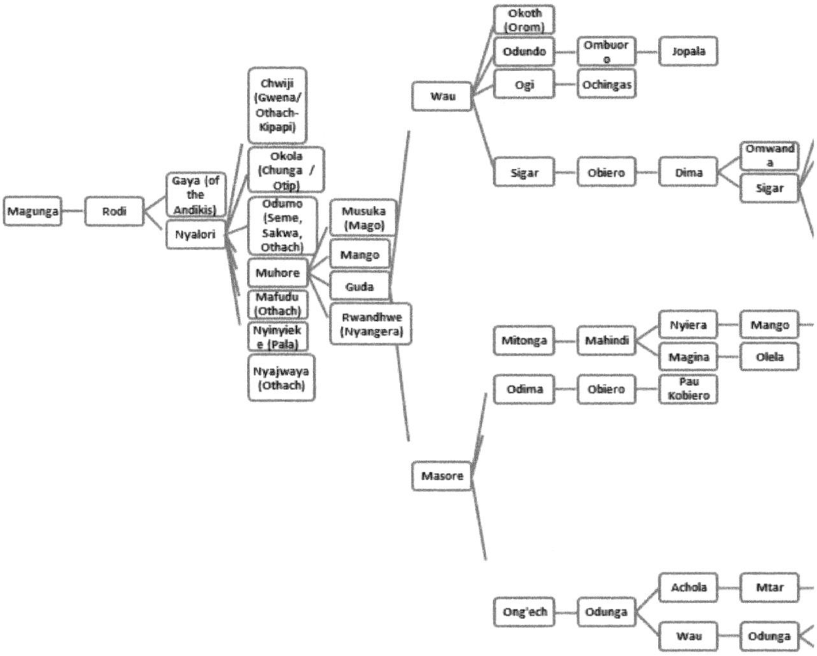

1.6 Kodunga, Kobiero, Ka mahindi:

The Kodunga has Achola and Wau. Wau bore Odunga, who bore Shem and Magana.Achola, on the other hand, bore Mtar, who bore Ogola, the father of Ong'ech II (Dola). The lineage of Obiero I is the wider Kobiero family residing in Pau Kobiero near Ogam. Mahindi bore Nyiera and Magina. Magina bore Olela, while Nyiera bore Mango, who in turn bore Nyiera II. Obiero II lineage comprises the current ka spem and kobiero as they stand. Obiero II bore Dima, who bore Sigar and Omwamda. Sigar bore Spem, Akungu and Obiero. The Ogi is where the Ochingas fall. Chief Margaret Ochinga Nyaseme is a powerful member of the family. She is the assistant chief of Barkanyango sub-location, and has acted as chief of North Yimbo many occasions in the absence of the substantive chief. She actually was a front runner in the chief North Yimbo when it became vacant, following the retirement of senior Chief Joseph Rajema Nengo, a Jakadimo of the Maganda sub-clan. However, Chief Vicliffe Opil carried the day and to date remains the chief of the location.

1.7: Other pictorials:

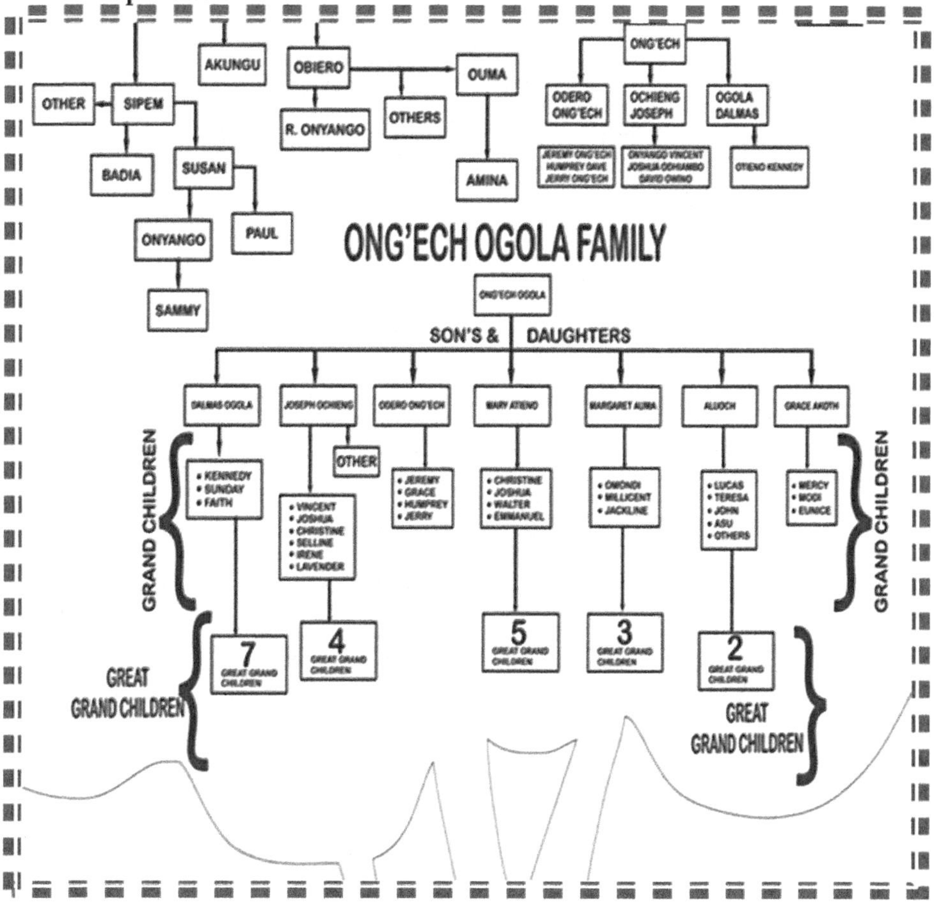

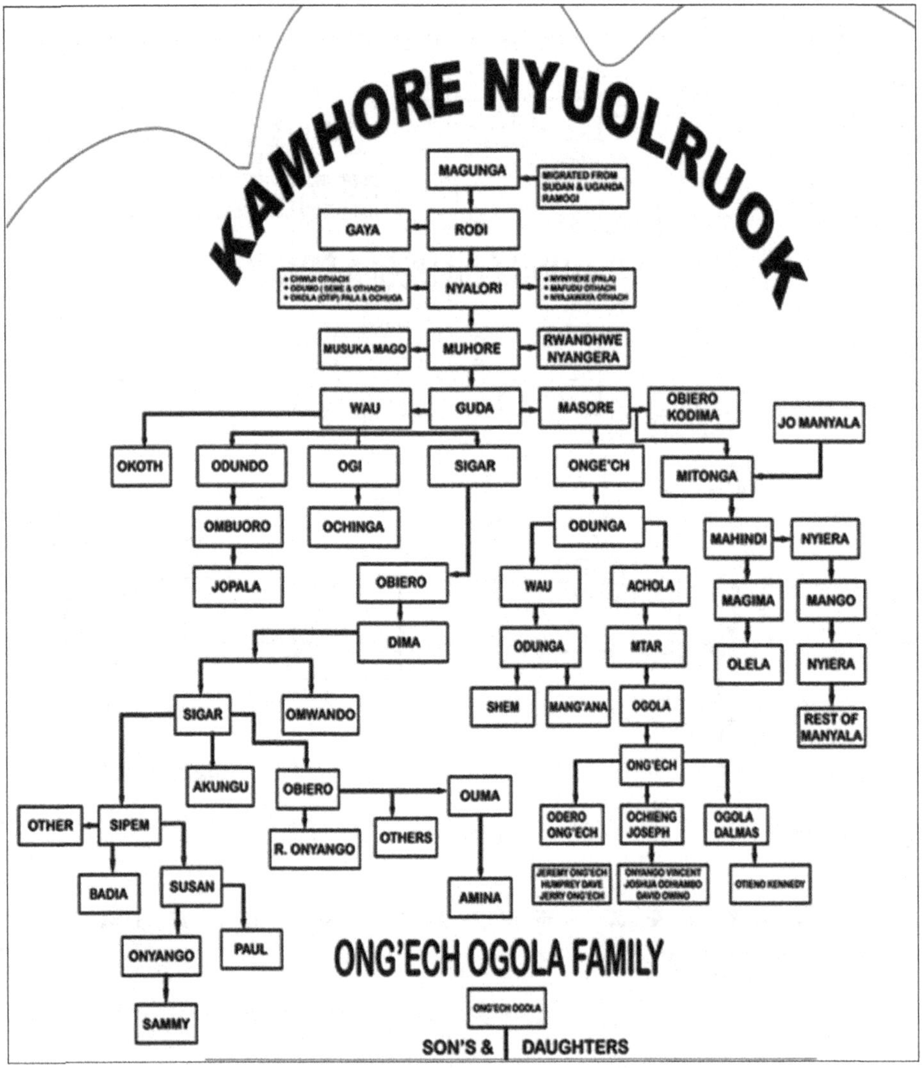
KAMHORE NYUOLRUOK
MAGUNGA
MIGRATED FROM SUDAN & UGANDA RAMOGI
GAYA
RODI
NYALORI
MUSUKA MAGO
MUHORE
RWANDHWE NYANGERA
WAU
GUDA
MASORE
OBIERO KODIMA
JO MANYALA
OKOTH
ODUNDO
OGI
SIGAR
ONGE'CH
MITONGA
OMBUORO
OCHINGA
ODUNGA
MAHINDI
NYIERA
JOPALA
OBIERO
WAU
ACHOLA
MAGIMA
MANGO
DIMA
ODUNGA
MTAR
OLELA
NYIERA
SHEM
MANG'ANA
OGOLA
REST OF MANYALA
SIGAR
OMWANDO
ONG'ECH
AKUNGU
OBIERO
OUMA
OTHER
SIPEM
R. ONYANGO
OTHERS
ODERO ONG'ECH
OCHIENG JOSEPH
OGOLA DALMAS
JEREMY ONG'ECH
HUMPREY DAVE
JERRY ONG'ECH
ONYANGO VINCENT
JOSHUA OCHIAMBO
DAVID OWINO
OTIENO KENNEDY
BADIA
SUSAN
AMINA
ONYANGO
PAUL
ONG'ECH OGOLA FAMILY
ONG'ECH OGOLA
SAMMY
SON'S &
DAUGHTERS

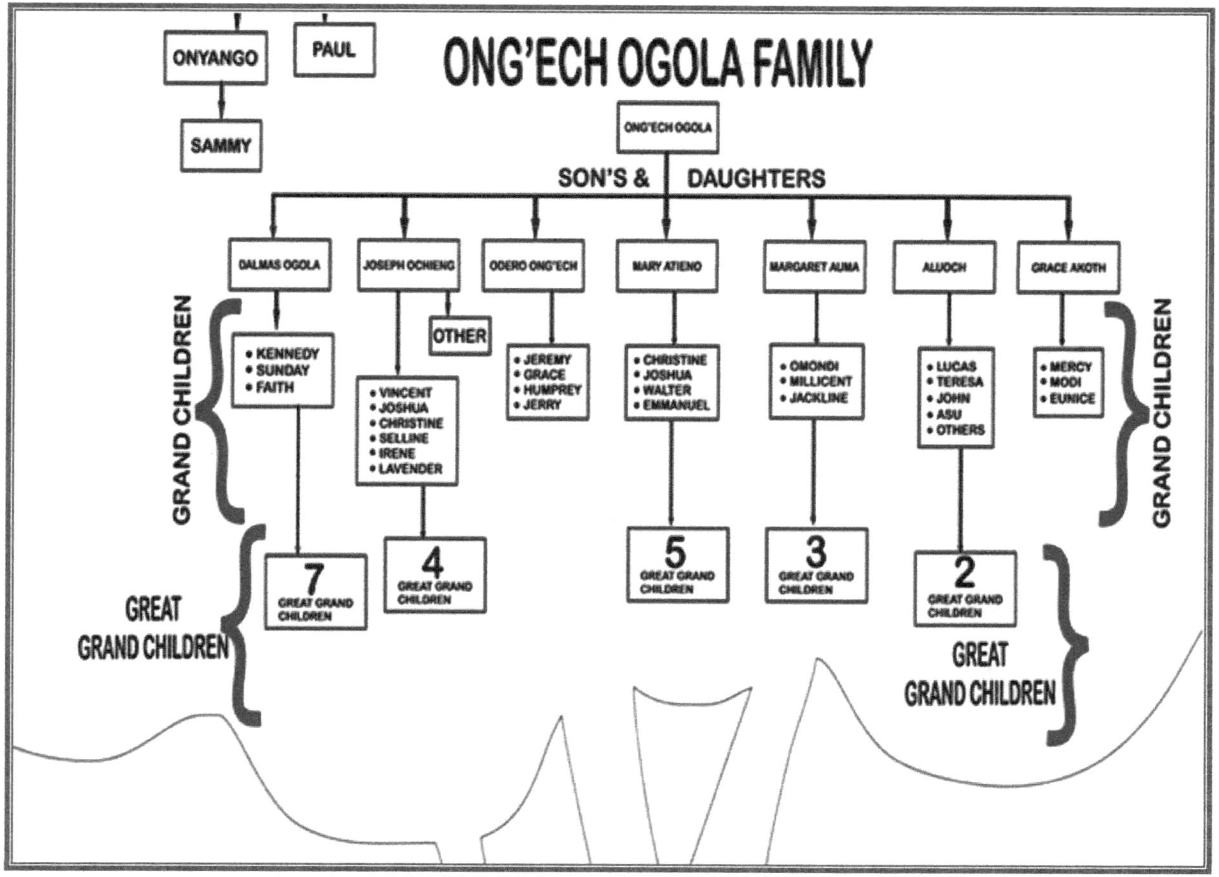
ONG'ECH OGOLA FAMILY
ONYANGO
PAUL
SAMMY
ONG'ECH OGOLA
SON'S & DAUGHTERS
DALMAS OGOLA
JOSEPH OCHIENG
ODERO ONG'ECH
MARY ATIENO
MARGARET AUMA
ALUOCH
GRACE AKOTH
OTHER
GRAND CHILDREN
KENNEDY
SUNDAY
FAITH
VINCENT
JOSHUA
CHRISTINE
SELLINE
IRENE
LAVENDER
JEREMY
GRACE
HUMPREY
JERRY
CHRISTINE
JOSHUA
WALTER
EMMANUEL
OMONDI
MILLICENT
JACKLINE
LUCAS
TERESA
JOHN
ASU
OTHERS
MERCY
MODI
EUNICE
GRAND CHILDREN
7 GREAT GRAND CHILDREN
4 GREAT GRAND CHILDREN
5 GREAT GRAND CHILDREN
3 GREAT GRAND CHILDREN
2 GREAT GRAND CHILDREN
GREAT GRAND CHILDREN
GREAT GRAND CHILDREN

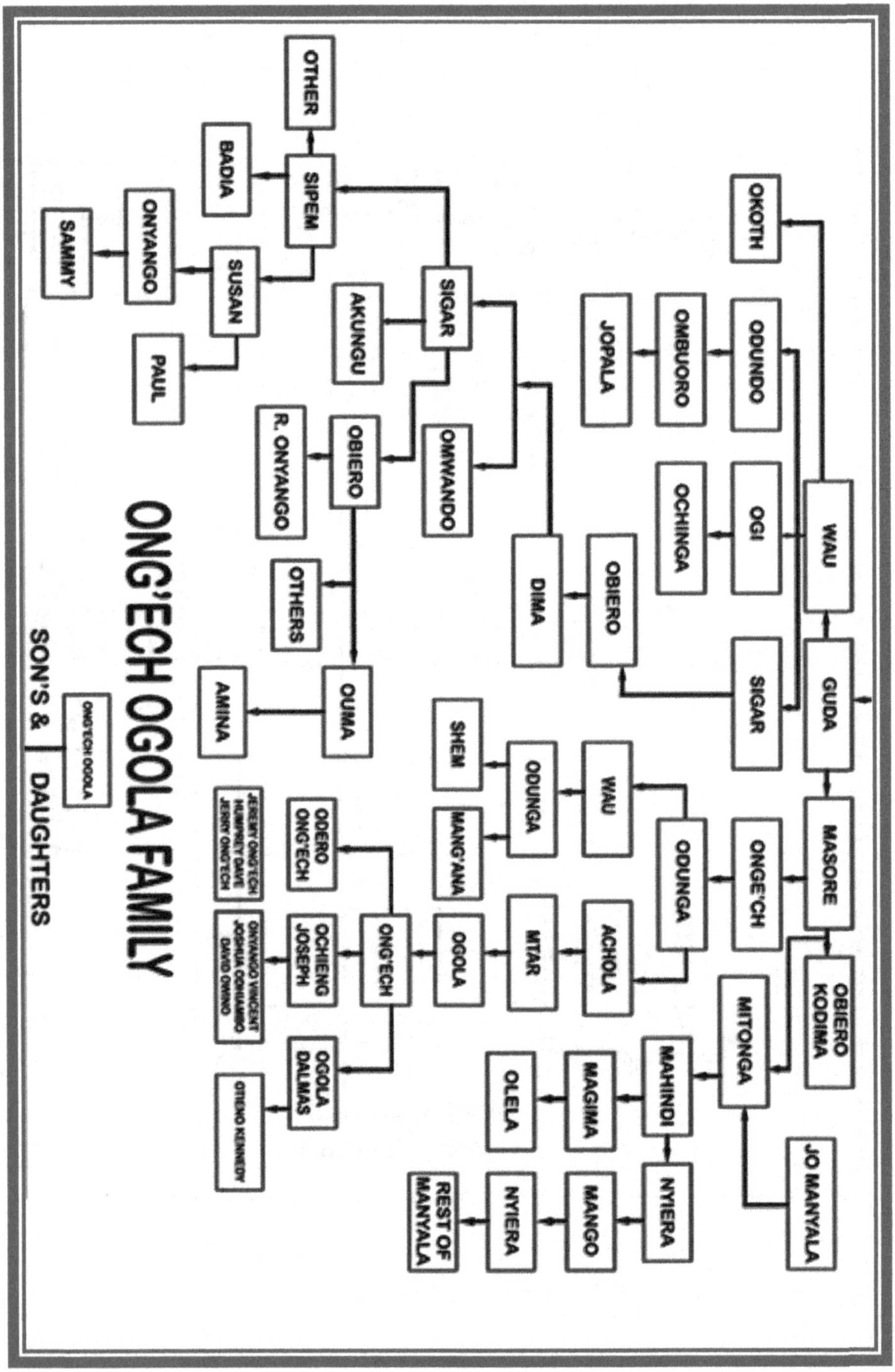
ONG'ECH OGOLA FAMILY
SON'S &
DAUGHTERS
ONG'ECH OGOLA
GUDA
WAU
OKOTH
ODUNDO
OMBUORO
JOPALA
OGI
OCHINGA
SIGAR
OBIERO
DIMA
SIGAR
SIPEM
OTHER
BADIA
SUSAN
ONYANGO
SAMMY
PAUL
AKUNGU
OMWANDO
OBIERO
R. ONYANGO
OTHERS
OUMA
AMINA
MASORE
ONGE'CH
ODUNGA
WAU
ODUNGA
SHEM
MANG'ANA
ACHOLA
MTAR
OGOLA
ONG'ECH
ODERO ONG'ECH
JEREMY ONG'ECH
HUMPHREY DAVE
JERRY ONG'ECH
OCHIENG JOSEPH
ONYANGO VINCENT
JOSHUA ODHIAMBO
DAVID OWINO
OGOLA DALMAS
OTIENO KENNEDY
OBIERO KODIMA
MITONGA
JO MANYALA
MAHINDI
MAGIMA
OLELA
NYIERA
MANGO
NYIERA
REST OF MANYALA

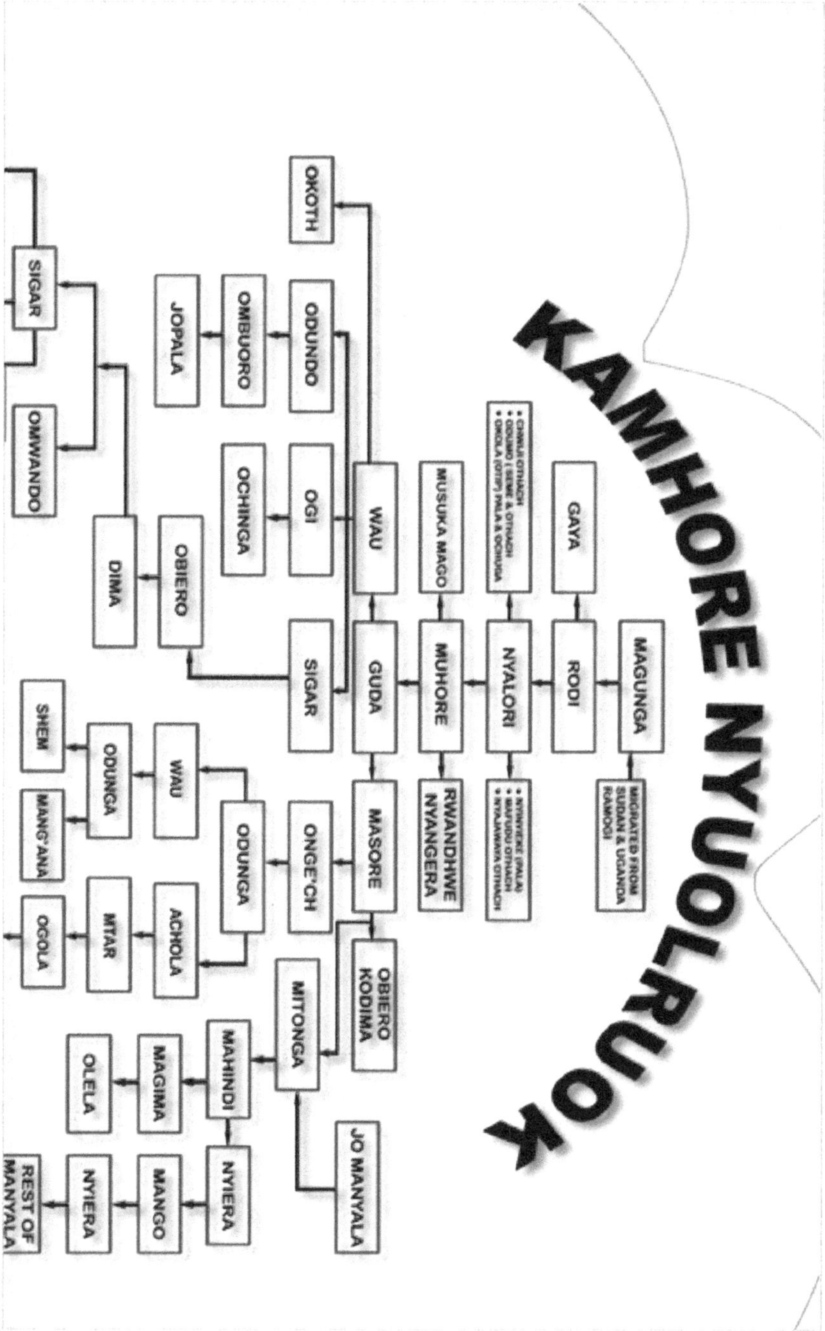
KAMHORE NYUOLRUOK
MAGUNGA
MIGRATED FROM SUDAN & UGANDA RAMOGI
GAYA
RODI
NYALORI
MUSUKA MAGO
MUHORE
RWANDHWE NYANGERA
WAU
GUDA
MASORE
OBIERO KODIMA
JO MANYALA
OKOTH
ODUNDO
OGI
SIGAR
ONGE'CH
MITONGA
OMBUORO
OCHINGA
ODUNGA
MAHINDI
NYIERA
JOPALA
OBIERO
WAU
ACHOLA
MAGIMA
MANGO
DIMA
ODUNGA
MTAR
OLELA
NYIERA
SIGAR
OMWANDO
SHEM
MANG'ANA
OGOLA
REST OF MANYALA

1.8 The Great Yimbo Migration:

This is a version adopted from: Anna von Sury (2016) Ethnography of Land Deals- 'Dominion has the biggest shamba now': Local Perceptions of the Dominion Farms Project in Western Kenya. Master of Arts in Social Anthropology, Institute of Social Anthropology, University of Berne, August 2016

Luo in western Kenya

Today, Luo people dominate the Kenyan part of the Lake Victoria Basin, which lies in former Nyanza Province in western Kenya (Shipton 2007: 45). Having their origins in the Bahr el Ghazal region of the Sudan, oral records suggest that Luo have been migrating South in small waves and on different routes over the past 450 to 500 years (Ogot 1967: 28, 41). The mythical origins of Luo society take us back to Podho, the forefather of all Luos, who was created by a divine being and settled at Ramogi hill in Uganda. The legend continues that one of Ramogi's sons, also called Ramogi I, went further south into today's Nyanza Province and settled on a hill in Kadimo, which is now known as Ramogi Hill, or Got Ramogi in *Dholuo*, the local language (Berg-Schlosser 1984: 117, cited in Anna, 2016). Indeed, Got Ramogi has been claimed to be the place of origin of the people living around the swamp, as this young villager describes:

"Since this time the Got Ramogi, meaning 'Ramogi's Hill', is a holy hill for all Luo people. It is the hill where our founding father fought against our enemies. His sons were Dimo, Alego, Gem, Samia and Ugenya, among others. They all settled here in Siaya County. Women cultivated the soil while men reared the cattle. Alego was married to Aloo, their sons were Seje and Kadenge. That's the reason why the village is called after the sons of the sons of Ramogi. This is the land of my forefathers........"

Therefore, Luo identify with a shared past as descendants of Ramogi (Geissler and Prince 2010: 44). Not far from Got Ramogi lies Kadenge sublocation, the area where Anna did her Research. It must be remembered that The Kadimo had a sojourn in Alego, and even after settling in their Kadimo home, they later went back to Alego in large numbers to escape the Dreaded sleeping sickness that nearly swept the Dimo descendants. So Kadenge is as good as Kadimo.

Map of Nyanza showing the Luo Counties

Further reference is made to: **Dimo entry into Yimbo: an account by Mzee Ong'ech Ogola and Obumba Otieno). Largely adopted from chapter 12 of Mzee Jeremiah Ong'ech book: An Autobiography- Documenting the undocumented).**

1.81: Dimo Journey from Sudan through Uganda

(Mzee Ong'ech, Jeremiah)

The killing of Julu foretold and foreseen

Prior to the arrival of Dimo in Yimbo, the land of Yimbo was occupied by many clans, including the Kanyinek, Kalam, Jogoma, Ureje, Walwanga, Nyiywen, and Wasenje. Dimo came to Yimbo with a number of his sons: Julu, Mnyenye (renamed Oyugi), Bith, Were (renamed Nyathuon), and Ajong'o. Maganda was born in Kadimo when Dimo was a ripe old man. It had been foretold by the foreseers that for Dimo to capture Yimbo, his eldest son would be killed there by one of the clans already living there. Indeed when they reached Yimbo, Julu Waregna was killed by the Walwanga. His fulfilled the belief. 'Waluwanga nonego wuod Dimo manene obirogo, mane Dimo korogo piny', says Mzee Ong'ech. This is how Dimo managed to capture Yimbo and either scattered or made agreements with the people they found in Yimbo.

According to Mzee Ong'ech, Dimo was a jakowiny. Ramogi is the one who first came to Yimbo, with his son Jok, displacing the original occupants believed to have been Luhya and Kalenjin (Lango). Dimo came later. According to Mzee Ong'ech, the jopadhola of Uganda are the descendants of Adhola, a brother to Dimo, who remained in Uganda because he had a wound (Adhola) which could not allow him to continue with the walk during the migration. Dimo therefore left him in Uganda as he proceeded to Kenya. Adhola and Dimo were jokowiny (sons of Owiny), the son of Kisodhi, who was the son of Ramogi Ajwang', the father of all Luos. However, according to Obumba Otieno, Adhola was Dimo's brother in law, married to Dimo's sister, Mdama. They lived in Uganda, and when Dimo was on his way to Kenya from Sudan, he stayed there for some time.

The Arrival of Dimo in Got Ager in Alego

As Dimo walked from Sudan to Kenya, he met many different groups of people, some of whom were subdued, and assimilated. For instance the Mnyejra is one such a clan, originally a Bantu clan which is believed to have been picked on the way, and was fully assimilated by Dimo. They literally fully adopted, embraced and proclaimed Dimo's Luo origin and culture. . When Dimo came from Ujwang'a, Ruoth (now Karuoth) had come earlier to Got Ager (Ager Hill) in Alego. He found Ager (now jokager, Alego, Siaya), Ruoth (now Karuoth, Alego, Siaya), Ogelo (now Kogelo, Alego, Siaya), Nyingoro (now kanyingoro, Asembo) and Nyakwar (Now kanyakwar, Kisumo). (NB: Kanyakwar and Ogelo don't marry one another). When Dimo arrived, Ruoth objected to their settling there since both Dimo and Ruoth were royal clans with leadership crowns (Mula). No two royal families were allowed to live in the same place. As such, Dimo could not settle there and had to leave. He was a livestock farmer, as well as a hunter. So he had lots of livestock, but did hunting at daytime.

Dimo settlement in Mur Malanga in Ng'iya

(Account by Mzee Ong'ech)

Dimo therefore moved with his livestock on to Mur Malanga in Ng'iya where he was allowed to settle by Mur. To be allowed to settle meant he requested, and was given fire by the host clan. He settled with his livestock, but also used to go far in his hunting adventures. As far as Yimbo. It was during these adventures that it is said he once saw and fell in love with the Kadimo bay, Misori in Yimbo. He vowed to settle there. It is reported by a number of elderly key informants that Dimo might have married and left one of his senior wives, Nyang'idia, somewhere at the hills around Misori. She reportedly used to beg for food from the neighbours, eventually died and turned into a snake-a friendly snake that is gentle and harms nobody. This is akin to the Omieri of Nyakach.

The dehorning or bull slaughter ordeal

(Account by Mzee Ong'ech)

However, as a settler (jadak), there were belief systems guiding the relationship with the land owner (Mur). He had no full rights and some things were simply an abomination. Dimo's bull injured Mur's by the horns (*dhere nochwoyo dher Mur*). As a tradition, a settler's (jadak) cattle cannot injure that of the land owner (*wuon lowo* / Jo Alego). As a tradition, the settler's cattle which caused the damage / injury was to be dehorned by the land owner, Jo Alego. Dimo reluctantly agreed to the dehorning. But the activity had its procedures, such as season and time of execution. Dimo allegedly convinced Mur that they do it after the harvest when there was plenty, to make it a memorable and worthwhile ocasion. However, deep in his heart, he knew it was never to be, as he was making an escape plan. According to Mzee ong'ech, this was between evening and morning. However, other key informants say the plans took weeks, moving upto harvest time. Even then, between the day of the incident and the morning of executing the dehorning was a long time.

Dimo Crossing of River Maina (Now River Yala)

(Account by Mzee Ong'ech)

On the day the procedure was scheduled to happen, the kaDimo youth went as usual with the livestock to graze. As usual, they crossed River Yala to enable the livestock feed on the lush vegetation on the foot of Got Magombe. Except that this time, they were not meant to come back....walk, walk and walk after crossing. The women were also supposed to go to the river - a number of trips-to bring water for the ceremony. However, only a fraction were to come back for every water trip. Some were even carrying household items. Those who remained behind at the river were to cross and never to come back. Eventually, the last group of women went, with none to come back. After the last group of the Dimo women went, Mur people asked why the bull was not yet there for slaughter. Dimo offered to go and bring the bull himself. The Mur people never suspected anything all along. And Dimo also crossed River Maina. His people had escaped with the livestock and crossed river Maina (former name of River Yala) to Bar Nyang where his drum was heard beating. Bar Nyang was next to the foot of Magombe hill.

Ongech quoted this as follows:

'While the Mur people were busy, as hosts, drinking the local brew, the Kadimo women, pretending to be going to the river to fetch water, were in the meantime carrying the rest of the Dimo household goods'.

The Team waruowo, comprising Owil, Mnyejra and Dimo crossed the river together, with the Kowil leading the way. It is believed that a lot of Kowil died while leading the river crossing. Upon entering Bar Nyang', Dimo joined forces with Owil and Minyejra. However, he settled them, promising one another to join forces whenever alerted of danger facing Dimo, who was still on a journey towards his preferred home, Misori. Mnyejra were settled at the foot of Ramogi Hills as Dimo proceeded to Misori. According to Mzee Ong'ech, at Misori, Dimo found Kanyiywen already settled there. The Kanyiywen told Dimo they cannot give him fire for his home unless they were given a cow.

According to traditions, newcomers never started their own fire; Fire was given to newcomers by the hosts albeit with some conditions which were often set by the host. Dimo obliged, gave a cow to Nyiywen, and they were settled in Misori. However, other views are that Dimo refised, as he did not intend to be a jadak. He decided to fight his way through to conquer the land. The battle began, with Walwanga, supported by the Wareje and the Wagoma on the front line. Dimo's allies were the Karodi, the Wanyejra and the Kowil. They fought for two days, with no particular side having an obvious edge over the other. On the third day, Julu was killed by the Waluanga. And the Wagoma hanged his body on the cross.

Photographer: Edward Evan Evans-Pritchard

The Dimo departure from Alego-Nelson Mganda Osunga

Dimo departure from Mur / Kogelo

Dimo lived among the Kogelo people in Mur Malanga for some time, as their ally and brother, Ruoth, settled in boro. While in Mur, Dimo had a special power bull…nene nigi Ruadh Bilo…ae ruadhno gineno ka dhawga gi maggi to onge maloye….gikone to odhaw gi ruadh Jokogelo ma bende nene gingeyo ni tek kendo ger, ma onge ruath moro amora madilo. To dher Dimo noloye, kendo ochuowe. Mae nomiyo Jo Mur / Kogelo oramo ni nyaka ng'ad tung dhiang'. …The Dimo special bull hurt Ogelo / Mur's most powerful bull, injuring it. The Alego host therefore demanded that the Dimo bull be dehorned. Dimo, knowing this was where his powers lie, opted the diplomatic route, as he was also aware that his hosts were majority and they could not fight…..they would all be killed. Dimo nongeyo ni tekogi ne ni e dhereni, non'geyo ni ok onyal Ngado tunge, to bende ok onyal dhau gi Jog jokogelo / Mur, nikech joge tin kendo yot mondo Jo Alego oneggi tee ka dhaw owuok. Koro nene otemo mana yor mbetre…yor mbaka maler…yor dhok mayom. Nene owinjore go Mur/ Kogelo ni giyang odieching ma gingade tung dhereno. Ka nochopo kanyo, to kongo olos, kendo dhano ochoko metho ka girito nyasi maduong mar Ngado tung dhiang. Jo Dimo nene metho e agunchgi, to Jo Mur / Kogelo bebde metho e aguchgi mopogore. To e aguch Jo Kogelo to Dimo odhi okete yath moro ma memo jok mamadho, kendo gikia gima timore. To oyudo ka Dimo nosewinjore gi joge ni sa ma imetho, to jokwath wuok gi Jamni ka gima gidhi mama kwath, to gidhi mana nyago aora Yala. Mine bende nene onego odhi e aora gi dapi, to nus ema duogo, jomodong Ngado aora. To kuom jodongo modong, gin be nene onego giwuog mos mos….ka giwuondore no gidhi rango jokma olewo kelo dhiang' ongad tunge, to ok giduog….ma nene otimre nyaka gikone Dimo owuon ema owacho ni kara en powuon ema koro odhi okel dhiamg, nikech ero joge ogalre, kata dipoka masira moro omakogi. Ae en bende odhi, to ka Obudho to jo Alego ma pok nometho ahinya atang, ka gifwenyo ni aguch Dimo mar kongo koro onge kata ngato achiel mamethe. To yo aora, to rawere moko moa e miel kod kisera Sakwa bende oyudo ka koro duogo dala, to gineno ka jod Dimo duto osengado aora. Ae giringo gitero wach e dala, to saa mar luwo Dimo gi lange nosekalo. Mao e kaka Dimo nowuok Alego, kokalo Sakwa eka ochopo Yimbo.

To kuom jokor Dimo, Nene giwinjre ni Owil kod Mnyejra nowuog motelo, ka pod Dimo gi lange pod galo Mur / Jokogelo. Koro ji ariyogi notelo, ma gin bende ema nene gidhi dwaro kama inyalo ngadoe aora ma ok ohinyoji. Iwacho ni kame nene giteme dwaro yor nam maber ma digilu, moko kuomgi bende nene aora oywayo. Bange to yo maber noyudre, ma ka ne koro Dimo biro bange, to yo nene oselosre maber.

The coming of Dimo to Yimbo

(An account by Mzee benard odol)

Dimo was a leader of the team warwowo. This was the trio of Kowil, Mnyejra and Dimo. Whereas the first two crossed River Yala and moved to Yimbo much earlier, Dimo remained behind in Alego. The Wanyejra and Kowil resided at the foot of Got Ramogi, but the trio were in constant touch and remained one anothers' keeper. Dimo had a lot of cattle and women, which were envied by their host in Alego. Here there are various versions of the cause of Dimo leaving Alego. Whereas Mzee Ong'ech say that **Dher Dimo nochwoyo Dher Jalego**, and had to be dehorned, and this made Dimo escape, Mzee Odol presents no reason for disagreement, but agree that there was a disagreement. Whereas it does not explain the disagreement in details, it led Dimo to plan an escape. Livestock used to be taken all the way to Sakwa, across river Yala, to graze. Water was fetched from River Yala by women. The cattle alongside the herds boys were safely out, and there was a secret plan not to cross back to Alego. However, the women were there, doing daily chores. On that particular day, they were all to go to fetch water (in preparation for the ceremony). However, only some were to return, and others cross the river never to return. Of those who returned, only a few would remain behind while others went for 'another water trip'. This continued until the Alego people realized there was nobody left in the Dimo residence. He had crossed to Sakwa through Mahira…just next to Magombe / othach, a story section of the River that could allow safer crossing and climbing of the other side. He was on his way to Yimbo. Dimo arrived in Yimbo and settled at Misori the home of Onyango wuon Munda. Here is lake shore where his son 'JULU' was killed by the people Dimo found there-the Waluanga. It had ben prophesied that Dimo would find land in the place where his son, Julu, would be killed by the enemies.

The settling of the Yimbo clans

(An account of Mzee Paul Oyoro)

According to Paul Oyoro, the original Yimbo residents were the Kanyiywen and Jogoma, later joined by Wareje (the Oyoro/ Wambura/ Oduma/ Odoro family lines) who lives in Urima (current Got Agulu). Urima was a name of the Wareje forefather called Rima. Therefor Got Agulu rightfully belongs to the Wareje. They fought and crossed Dho Goye (the Goye Bridge).at the time Kadimo was living in Alego. When the Dimo bull fought the Alego bull....the cutting of the horns had to be done. This led to the Dimo night escape from Alego and came to Yimbo (Check Ong'ech book). The Dimo, Kowil and Wanyejra (the team Waruowo, or team we came together) arrived together in Yimbo from Alego. The Kowil went ahead, but unfortunately many died as they crossed River Yala. Their many dead bodies on the river formed a bridge (Olalo) which Dimo and Mnyejra used to cross the river. Before leaving Alego, Dimo had sought the wisdom of the foreseers who had prophesied that they were going to a place already inhabited by some people, and they were bound to face some resistance. However, in the battle, if one of the Dimo heroes is killed, with his head facing them, that is where they would get land, make a new home and settle. On arrival in Yimbo, Dimo first got hold of Misori, at Odero wuon Munda. This is, to date, considered the original home of Dimo. At the time, Wareje and Walwanga, being closely related by blood, were working together. Ureje (now Wareje) was a younger blood born brother of Wanga (Waluanga).

Just after crossing dho Goye (the goye bridge), the two met the Dimo warriors killed Dimo's son (Julu), and hanged him on a tree. Wareje were bad in battles. At that time, the Dimo team divided into two. One group was to face the battlefront and pretend they were fighting, while another group went behind, burning houses and granaries as they approached Ururi and Usigu. On realizing their houses and granaries had been burnt down, the

Walwanga and the Wareje retreated to Osieko, Manyala. The Kanyiywen were few and did not actively join the fights. The Goma people were more friendly and coped well with the Dimo. That is how Dimo conquered Yimbo, almost the entire stretch up to Osieko. On settling, however, Dimo realized something was amiss. Despite the fertile soils, there was no food, as there were no rains. They went to seek medicine man intervention, and they were told to seek the original land dwellers (Wareje / jokarima) to cleanse the land. The Wareje accepted on condition that they be given a land of their own, bearing their name, in return. This was acceptable to Dimo, and the jokarima were given the land at Ureje at the foot of Got Ramogi, which bears their name to date. The Walwanga on the other hand, protested arguing that they could never go back to a land where they had been massacred. To date, the Walwanga have no land in Yimbo bearing their name. The Jokarima condition met, they came, cleansed the land and it was soon productive again.

The Kadimo truce with Goma

At the peak of the Kadimo conquest of various clans of Yimbo, they had felt uneasy, and had to do some soul searching and reflection. These were critical for the future well-being of the entire community. They recognized that the Dimo men must get women to marry from other Yimbo clans they are not blood related to. As much as the neighboring Alego, Sakwa, Asembo and Uyoma were there and had, and would continue serving the role well, the Kadimo felt there was need to have within Yimbo itself a community from where their own men would marry. As such, they reached a pact, a truce, and an agreement with the WaGoma, with the two vowing never to fight again for posterity. The Dimo would get ladies from Goma to marry. This truce and agreement remains true to date. The two have lived as good neighbours, respecting the conditions and boundaries that were set in the truce. Since that time, the Goma ladies when married by Jokadimo prosper at family level, while unfortunately, the reverse has been the vice versa. It is believed that calamities easily trike a family of Goma whose uncles are Kadimo. There are lots of example, which would be unethical to mention in this book. The advice it's for the young ones who are not aware of this pact.....'Goma being source of ladies for Kadimo to marry'.

According to Mzee Ndai, Dimo arrival in Yimbo followed the following scenario: From Alego, Dimo, Owil and Mnyejra entered Yimbo through the foot of Magombe hill. They found Goma and Sakwa people already living in Yimbo. At the time the Kagwa people lived in utonga (Sakwa). Kagwa came in to help Dimo in the battle. Kagwa entered Yimbo through pap Uloma (Called Wath Gwa) near Got Winyo. The fighting team therefore was Dimo/ Kagwa/ Wanyejra/ Kowil on one hand VS other teams (Walwanga, Wareje/ Goma) on the other hand. It's the wars that scattered the Kagwa from the Uloma area to Barkanyango, and later to otherr areas. To successfully fight the enemies especially Sakwa, the three heroes: **Ogutu Kipapi** (Ogutu Thuon / Ogutu Raruoch) from kachwiji, **Obonyo Manyonge** (from Kachwiji) and **Jang'olo Kwach** from Kamhore led the battle. The story of Ogutu Kipapi is well explained elsewhere in this book.

1.82: Alternative View of Dimo Migration and Conquest.

Prior to the arrival of the Luo in the Kadimo area, now called Yimbo, Bantu and Highland Nilotic groups extended over the area between Lake Victoria and the Nandi escarpment but retreated inland (Fredrick Z A Odede et al, 2009). The Luo intrusion into western Kenya from Uganda displaced earlier groups such as Early Iron Age Bantus, thus hastening human encroachment into the forested highlands (Leakey et al., 1948; Ogot, 1967; Soper, 1969, cited in Fredrick Z A Odede et al, 2009).

Dimo Brief Sojourn in Soroti and Alego

Dimo was a Nilote from the Anyolo clan of Southern Sudan. Coming from Southern Sudan, he briefly stayed with the family of his sister, Mdama, the wife of Adhola, in their kingdom of Budama, Soroti, Uganda. From Budama, he was following his kin, Owiny Sigoma who had migrated earlier and settled in Alego Karuoth. He arrived safely with his livestock and his people, who included Owil, Ramogi and Mnyejra. Whereas Owil and Ramogi, who were brothers, were part of his team from Sudan, it is believed that he picked Mnyejra along the way, and assimilated him. Mnyejra became a loyal part of his team, and was responsible for carrying his Rapogi- the tool for sharpening his spear. While living at Karuoth, one of Dimo's favourite bulls seriously injured Owiny's bull. As per tradition, a settler's cattle harming the land owner's was an abomination, and had either to be dehorned or slaughtered. Dimo pretended to have agreed to the deal, knowing well that it was never to happen. And he planned that meticulously.

He first convinced Owiny that they needed to take time to organize a proper celebration, which could only happen after harvest to enable them brew beer in plenty. Owiny agreed. Meanwhile Dimo was planning with his people to leave in bits and cross river yala. On the material day, the local brew was indeed made as planned. People started drinking it, with Dimo and a small number of his people being part of the team. Dimo had made a plan with his people to pretend they are active on the ground working, while ensuring that they create enough errands to take them towards the river. The agreement was that of any team that moved to the river for whatever activity…fetching water for brewing, for cooking, and for young men, taking livestock to the river to drink, only a handful should come back while the rest cross.

As per expectation, the bull had also to be slaughtered to make the celebration worthwhile. When Sigoma asked Dimo why the bull had not been slaughtered. Dimo also pretended to be dismayed by the delay, and left the celebration with his small remaining team to go and bring the bull with them. They stayed for too long, and Sigoma and his people smelt a rat. Sigoma's sons tried to pursue Dimo, but were restrained by their father reasoning that Dimo was a uniquely strong man who could easily kill all of them if they dared pursue him. So Dimo crossed Rived Yala at Magombe hill, reaching Yimbo. Soon they heard Dimo's UDEKO drum beating across the river. However, it is believed that Dimo lost quite a number of his people through drowning and being trampled on as they crossed the River.

The Luo also found the Highland Nilotes occupying Yimbo Kadimo location as indicated by the oral traditions of the Terik (Nyang'ori) of western Kenya who are related to the Nandi. Luo oral traditions also indicate the presence of Maasai groups during their arrival in the region. The Kamagambo and Kakraw clans in South Nyanza were originally Maasai people who accompanied the Luo from northern Nyanza and were later assimilated or incorporated by the Luo. Therefore, the pre-Luo settlers of northern Nyanza during the historic period comprised both Bantu and Nilo-Hamitic groups (Ogot, 1967, cited in Fredrick Z A Odede et al, 2009).

The first southern Bantu groups or clans who moved into western Kenya from Bunyoro and Congo through Buganda include the Ababubi, Abasiyemba, Abakuwana and Abamalenge who settled on Sigulu Island, the Ababulu who occupied Mageta Island, both in Lake Victoria (Kenya territory); and the Abalusere, Abalwani, Abakholo, Abatsipi, Abenge, Abalungo, Ababasi, Ababambw, Abakhweri and Abakaala who settled in Yimbo at Ugoye in Bondo District (Fredrick Z A Odede et al, 2009).These early Bantu immigrants preceded the Luo in Nyanza and did not have much contact with them until the 19th century (Ogot, 1967, cited in Fredrick, 2009). Other pre-Luo Bantu groups who were later assimilated by Luo invaders are today repsented by the **Kagwa in Uyoma** peninsula (Madiany Division) in Bondo District, the **Kanyibule in Rusinga** Island and **Waturi in South Nyanza**. Kagwa, Kanyibule and Waturi oral traditions indicate they were the first inhabitants of Usenge Hill in Kadimo location, Bondo District, where the first Luo immigrants settled from Uganda and assimilated them. (Fredrick Z A Odede et al, 2009)

The Dimo-Bantu Encounter

After Dimo arrived in Kadimo, he quickly embarked on his mission. Being adventurous, he continued to go for many hunting adventures during which he was making his exploration of where he would go next, even as he lived in the foot of Magombe hills. A medicine man had told him that along his way, he would met many people who would try to stop his advance. Whereas he would generally overcome these, his final place to establish his kingdom would be the place where one of his best soldiers would be killed, and fall facing down. So he had been on the lookout for this sign all along. Even before he finally crossed to Yimbo, he had identified a beautiful beach land at Misori (Near Uhanya) where he wished, and was determined to settle in. During his hunting adventures to these areas, he had established some rapport with some of the people already living there such as the Wasihongo from Mageta. Some had not minded, for he was simply a hunter. For the few who feared, he even used his charming ways to endear them to him. However, on reaching Yimbo, it was a different ball game, for he needed to settle, as his own master, and not anybody's slave or jadak. He had assisted his team members and allies, Ramogi and Owil to settle along the way, as he proceeded to Misori and made his own fire. When the communities living there, led by the Walwanga, Wareje and Goma saw him, they protested and told him to put it off so that instead they give him fire. He refused. He could not even give them a cow in lieu of putting off his fire, but he could hear none of this either.

A war inevitably broke. They fought for 2 days, with no side showing any signs of winning. On the third day, unfortunately, Dimo's eldest son, Julu Waregna was killed by the Walwanga. Then the Goma people took his body and put it on a cross. All along, Mnyejra, Owil and Ramogi were fighting on his side. Even Rodi was on his side.

The death of Julu

Prior to the arrival of Dimo in Yimbo, the land of Yimbo was occupied by many clans, including the Kanyinek, Kalam, Jogoma, Ureje, Walwanga, Nyiywen, and Wasenje. Dimo came to Yimbo with six of his sons, Julu, Oyugi Waregna, Bith, Were Nyathuon and Ajongo. Maganda was the only Dimo son born in Kadimo. It had been foreseen by the foreseers that for Dimo to capture Yimbo, his eldest son would be killed there by one of the clans already living there. Indeed when they reached Yimbo, Julu was killed by the Walwanga. His fulfilled the belief. **'Walwanga nonego wuod Dimo manene obirogo, mane Dimo korogo piny',** *says Mzee Ong'ech.* This is how Dimo managed to capture Yimbo and either scattered or made agreements with the people they found in Yimbo (Afullo, 2018).

A war inevitably broke. They fought for 2 days, with no side showing any signs of winning. On the third day, unfortunately, Dimo's eldest son, Julu Waregna was killed by the Walwanga. Then the Goma people took his body and put it on a cross. All along, Mnyejra, Owil and Ramogi were fighting on his side. Even Rodi was on his side.

After Julu's killing, Dimo sought to know how he fell. His soldiers confirmed that he fell facing down. This was good news to Dimo, for it was the sign he had been looking for. It was in Yimbo where he would establish his kingdom, and Misori where Julu died would be its centre. From the fourth day onwards, the battle was too easy for Dimo; he easily subdued the enemies and killed them in masses. The Walwanga ran towards Manyala (promising never to ever come back), while the Wareje run to Udimbe and Manyala.

The Goma-Dimo peace pact

As the battle progressed, Dimo saw a compromising face of the Goma. On his side, Dimo realized that even after the battle, his descendants would need girls to marry. And these needed not come from very far. As such, if a few clans could co-exist with him, the better.at that time, the Goma, tired of battle with Dimo, also approached him. They reached an agreement, and accepted the the Goma surrender and offer of a girl to marry to mark the end of fight between the two. This was done, and Goma gave a girl called Maende to KaDimo. It would seem that Dimo may have been very old, or may have died by now, as Maende was married to Dimo's grandson, Hajula, the son of Were, the son of Dimo. This lady gave forth to twins, Wamra and Adongo, both sons of Hajula, and grandchildren of Were, the son of Dimo. Over and above the bridal offer, it is believed to have been an oath stating that from then henceforth, Goma would be source of ladies to Dimo, but the Goma should not marry Dimo daughters because there became his blood by their issuing ....to Dimo for marriage. To date, Goma ladies make very strong homes in Kadimo.

The famine and cleansing of the land

After the battle phase settled, Dimo was keen to produce food for his people. But there was a devastating famine. The rains had not rained for too long to keep the clan going. On seeing a medicine man, Dimo was advised to bring back at least one of the clans they found on the land to live alongside them as a way of participate in land cleansing. The Walwanga completely refused to come back, reasoning that they could not settle in eland in which nearly all their people had been killed.

The founding of the Ureje Nation

On trying the Wareje, they accepted on one condition: they need to be shown a place that would be of their own. Dimo had no difficulties implementing this condition, and the Wareje were shown the current Ureje at the foot of Ramogi hills, which has remained their land ever since. Walwanga, on the other hand, have no place they can associate even with the name of their clan, as they refused to play ball. Key informant interview of at least 30 elders indicate that most clans which faced Dimo head-on in the fight hardly survived. Later to ensure peaceful co-existence, Ureje also gave Dimo a girl for reconciliation, for having been involved in the killing of Julu. Goma people were also given a girl by Dimo as a pay so that they could remove Julu's body from the cross where they had hanged him after his killing.

Dimo arrival in Yimbo

Upon their arrival, they found many clans already settled in Yimbo , including Wamuri, Wanyejra, Wawamba, Nyinek, Goma, Kagwa, Wareje, kamreme, wasenje, Walwanga, Karodi (including Kachwiji, Kamhore, Kagaya, Kola), Nyibok, Walowa, among others. The Dimo Bilo, however, covered them from being seen or noticed by bthe host communities even as they walked past, in their hundreds, alongside their livestock…nene gikalo e kind mier to ok negi nikech bilo.... As they settled, they were able to quickly scatter some clans, some offered no resistance and were subdued. Dimo met the worst resistence in Misori.

The first Dimo battle in Yimbo:

Upon Dimo arrival in Misori, he put up his own fire. The neighbouring clans noticed smoke from Dimo's new settlement after some time, and called upon one another to see for themselves and debate on the best way out. They apppreoched Dimo and ordered him to put off his fire, so that they can give him their instead. They agreed on a date to do this.....gimoko mach, ae iro gineno ka dum e dho nam. Ae gichiwo order ni Dimo mondo oneg mae, eka gimiye margi. Giwinjore e chieng' ma onego gitimie ma. To mae nene omiyo Dimo thuolo mar ikre maber. Mokwongo, nodhi onyiso Owil gi Mnyejra mondo giikre gimong jogi kapok Chieng chiwo mach k ochopo. Mar ariyo en be nochako gero Ohinga aluora Dalane...koaUhanya nyaka Kamreme (near hayanga's home), mondo wasigu kik bed noi nyalo nene ei dalane kendo goye kokia. ...However, Dimo got time to mobilize his Owil, Mnyejra allies to ambush the would-be aggressors before the agreed day. He started building a wall (called Ohinga) around his homestead ...from Uhanya to kamreme...so that nobody would see the inside from whatever point. This was serious strategy, because before any attack, the enemies would normally identify a vantage point from where they could see the entire home and movement of the enemies. And they agreed with Mnyejra and Owil to attack their enemies before the Fire issue date.

On their agreed attack day, Dimo beat the Dimo UDEKO drum, and their allies followed suit with theirs...and the battle began. Dimo starting it off from Misori towards Usenge/ Goye/Ulowa/ Usigu/ Goma; Owil attacking from their base in Nyamonye towards Lela/ Bur Iro, while Mnyejra attacked from Ramogi towards Goma/Ndiwo. They killed the enemies in their thousands, and surrounded some, who were all killed. During the war, Julu was killed, but this gave them even more energy to pursue their enemies even deeper and further, as the Julu death had been foretold as the indicator that the land would be Dimo's. The Goma people tried fighting, but quickly paused, opting to cooperate with Dimo instead....Jo Goma to ok nodhaw alanda, negiting badgi, ae giyie ni giti atiya gi Dimo. Dimo's bilo had revealed that one of his closest and strongest warriors would be killed,...'... to ae nopodh Ataro, korango jogi....', he would fall down facing up, with the head facing the Dimo team. This is what happened, and Dimo knew it was the Promised Land, and required only a little extra effort and the lad would be theirs. And it came to pass after Julu killing by Walwanga.

The second Yimbo Kadimo battle- fighting Sakwa:

Once Dimo had settled in Yimbo, it was renamed Kadimo...the land of Dimo. It was so prominent, that to date, there is Kadimo Bay in the Map. Once settled, Dimo let Were occupy the eastern side which had more potential enemies (because he was deemed as 'Thuon'- the brave one), while Ajongo was left to the western side, alongside some members of the eldest house. Bith reamijed in his father's home in Misori, but also spread to Nyangera and ururi.

Even though they settled and agreed to co-exist in their diversity, there was one common and notorious aggressor- Josakwa. Jo Sakwa nene oloyo Yimbo, ma nene gibiroga saa ma gineno to gipeyo dhog Joyimbo ma gitiek, to Joyimbo mangeny bende ginego. Nene gimonjo Joyimbo, gikawo dhogi duto e pap Ndiwo (a long stretch from Mago to Kalejo Abora, to Nyamboyo to

Ndiwo). By then even Nyamboyo swamp was still just a plain ground for livestock grazing. Jokadimo nene oneno ni ma ok nyalre. Joyimbo laid a trap for them by assembling al their livestock in one point where they could easily be seen from Usire hill (Got Usire in Sakwa), the prominent vantage point from where Sakwa people used to do their survey and plan on where to go and get livestock from. The Dimo Bilo already made the Yimbo people aware of when the invasion was to take place. On the day of their ambush, the Sakwa people walked, but observed something unusual....even though they had seen a lot of livestock in Pap Ndiwo, individual homesteads would normally have their own livestock...but they were seeing none. They walked a long distance towards pap Ndiwo...in the meantime, the Yimbo people were observing them come, from the top of Got Ramogi. When the Sakwa people reached Lul and Mguna (Upanda), they were clearly seen by Joyimbo. They surrounded the Sakwa people and killed all of them, except four. A group of three initially escaped and walked long distance. However, Bilo made them just go round and round, and when they saw Got Ramogi, they thought it was Got Abiero....going by the distance they had walked. They felt secure and decided to visit one of the homes and inform them about the Yimbo massacre of Josakwa. They told their story, and asked for direction to enable them reach their home. Little did they know they were asking joyimbo, just near Got Ramogi. The Mzee deliberately misdirected them towards a bush where he killed all of them. The last one, who followed personal survival instinct, was a nephew of Alego Kadenge and managed to escape through the bushes and walked upto his uncles. He later went back to Sakwa to give the bad report of all their people having been killed. At that point, the Sakwa people thought that with Joyimbo killing all their prominent warriors, they were at risk and felt very insecure. They sent emissaries, amongst them the elders to Yimbo for a peace pact. ..Jogi kara nigi bilo mager....ae giluongore mondo gidhi giket opara e kindgi. Kanyo ema nene ging'adoe guok e pap guok, kendo ema nene obedo giko mar dhau e kind Joyimbo kod Jo Sakwa.

1.9 History of the Luos (brief)

The Luo people emerged from the Semitic-speaking, Nilo-Saharan-speaking, Cushitic-speaking people. The Luo were originally a light-skinned community with the culture of Egypt (Tekidi), Kush and Meroe. They migrated to Kar Thum (Khartoum) to Wau in the Bar-el Ghazal region in South Sudan. It was here that they met a dark-skinned people who referred to them as Jur Chol (the aliens passing through the blacks).

Between 990-1125, the Luos were in Sudan and then a series of calamities, including a serious outbreak of anthrax ('opere') and population explosion whipped out the entire livestock that were owned by the tribe of the Anu which was darker, and preferred both livestock and crop production. Following this incident, the community resorted to fishing along the Aora Nalo (the River Nile) for survival and this is how the Luo earned the name Jo-Oluo-Aora (people who follow the river) which, in the course of time came to be shortened to Luwo or Luo. South Sudan is hence the first placw that the Jo-Luo were first referred as such, the subsequent birthplace of the Luo nation. This explains why most tales of the origin of the Luo nation start from South Sudan at Dog nam (the Acholi equivalent of dhowath/ dho nam which is the Dholuo for the mouth of the lake - that is, a lake shore). Whereas there is no agreement on which lake it is, most historians identify it as Lake No or River Palugo, or what the Arabs called the Sea of Gazelle (Bar-el Ghazal). The three are the same thing.

According to oral tradition, the Luo lived in Eastern Bar-el-Ghazal until the year 1300 when they dispersed because of quarrel among the three brothers: Nyikang'o, Dimo and Gilo. Feuds within the homestead triggered by a power struggle led to a split and subsequently, separate history of the three groups. It was also during this period that the Luo started separating as a nation, into different sub-groups and going different directions, while also intermarrying with the various groups they met and assimilating their culture, or being assimilated into their cultures.

The Luo-speaking peoples include the following sub-groups:

1. Shilluk/ Ochollo - South Sudan / Ethiopia

2. Anuang'/ Anywaa - Ethiopia / South Sudan

3. Maban - South Sudan / Chad

4. Thuri / Shatt - South Sudan

5. Blanda Bor - South Sudan

6. Funj - South Sudan

7. Pari - South Sudan

8. Bari - South Sudan

9. Jumjum - South Sudan

10. Joluo / Jur Chol - South Sudan

11. Acholi - Uganda / South Sudan

12. Kumam - Uganda

13. Chope - Uganda

14. Tooro - Uganda

15. Lang'i - Uganda

16. Jonam - Uganda

17. Jo-Padhola - Uganda

18. Alur - Uganda / DRC / Cameroon

19. Suba Luo - Kenya

18. Joluo - Kenya / Tanzania

The Luo-speakers alongside the Dinka (Jieng') and the Nuer (Naath) form part of the Jii-speakers. Oral traditions reveal that the Southern Luo (the Luo of Kenya and Tanzania) descended from early fishing, agricultural and herding communities from western Kenya's early pre-colonial history and dialects of their language have historic roots across the inter-lacustrine region. Besides their language has incorporated Bantu words making it different from the Ugandan Luo dialects, Dholuo is the mother tongue of the Luo community. There is only one major Luo dialect in Kenya, with minor variations of Luo language especially between the Alego / Ugenya / Gem locality, known as Trans Yala dialect by socio-linguist, and the standard Dholuo dialect which is largely spoken by the rest of the Luo people in Kenya and the neighboring Tanzania.

The Nilotic and Bantu populations now form one strong Luo community ethnic group. And despite of diverse ancestry of the Luo people, they have always remained united as one entity. The Luo ethnic group in Kenya has maintained its culture, language and sustained the political unity and prevented further separation, thus, becoming a politico-cultural bloc in Kenya. The early intrusion of the Luo in Nyanza basin was not, strictly-speaking, a conquest. Rather, it was a slow and peaceful penetration, and for a short while they lived with the original inhabitants. But when their numbers increased, friction developed between the newcomers and the aboriginals, forcing the former to use military and spiritual powers to take control of the land. Many of the indigenous people were forcefully expelled or assimilated and the Luo-speakers became the owners of a very large proportion of the land they settled.

After their last migrations, the Luo people settled on the North Eastern shores of Lake Victoria, that is Nyanza and North Mara Regions. The Luo tribe can be broken down into seven major sections based on origins. These sections are as follows:

1. Ramogi Luos (or commonly Luo proper)

2. Kawango Luos (Luo-Abasuba)

3. Kiseru Luos

4. Girango Luos

5. Sirati Luos

6. Imbo Luos

7. Other Luos

1. RAMOGI LUOS

The Luo proper are a Nilotic group of people who migrated from Bahr El - Ghazel region in South Sudan and settled in Kenya and Tanzania. According to Luo oral traditions, a warrior elder named Ramogi Ajwang' led the Luo ethnic group into present day Kenya, about 500 years ago. The Luo people migrated into Nyanza in four major waves and they first settled at what is now called Got Ramogi (Ramogi Hills) in Yimbo. They later crossed in present day South Nyanza and eventually into North Mara Region, Tanzania. The four waves include the Jo-Kajok, Jo-Kowiny Jo-Komolo and Jo-Kawango (Luo-Abasuba), with the first wave arriving sometime around AD1490.

(i) The JOKA - JOK

The Joka - Jok sub-group was the first and largest Luo wave of migration. The group is claimed to have come from Acholiland, and ultimately from Napata or Tekidi (The foot of a great stone) in Upper Egypt. They were the earliest to arrive in Kenya between AD1490 and 1550 and their history is the history of the Southern Luo migration into Kenya.

(a) Pajok Clan cluster:

-These include: Alego (Seje, Kadenge, and Kamiyawa Among the Sakwa-Kamasoga, Kamadhi, Kanyamgony and Kanyagwala); Nyakach (Kadiang'a, Kajimbo/ Kamwala, Kandaria, Kabodho, Jimo and Kasaye etc); Komwa (based in Kisumu and include Korando,Karombo,Kogon'y, Kanyulo etc); Konyango/ Kachwanya (Kochienig', Kaluoch, Kanyidwera, Kamama, Kombogo, Kabonyo and Konyango/Kanyamwa, Kabuoch Konyango and Kadem); Kagwa (Based in Madiany locality and Luo Imbo and Suba divisions of Rorya, comprising Yewe, Nyagwala, Kanyejeri, Kamsaki,and Kadigol etc); Kano (Kolwa, Kamagaga, Kochogo, Kakola, Kawamoya, Kadibo,and Usonga etc.); Ramogi (Based in Nyabondo plateau,Oyugis,Suna Migori and Rorya); Seme (Based in Seme locality comprising Kagumba and Kadipir; and Kanyinek (Based in Kanyijuok, Siaya).

(b) Migration from Alur;

These include: Kanyala/ Nyang'ori (Kasagam,Kameji, Kaugagi, Nyang'or; Kabim, Racham Gem, Katolo); Kanyikela (Inhabiting Ndhiwa and Ndori Ramba in Asembo Bay, Including Kuhaya, Kanyamudho, Katuola, Kwabambla Kongolo and Kopiyo); Karabuor (In Otwenya Maseno locality and Kagok in Kisumu); Kayadoto (Dominant in Nyarongi locality, comprises Kaganda and Kabura-Kanyakwenda and Kagola /Wapondi); Kamot (Inhabiting Kanyamkago Hills constituted by Kawere, Kajulu and Katieno); Kagan/ Kowino (Kanyiriema, Kakoko and Kachieng'); (Dominant in Bondo, Awendo, Oyugis and Luo Imbo Localities, actually a sub-clan of Nyibinya and includes Kibira and Kachiemo and Kotho, Kanyaguli, Kanyagak and Kamot/Kadera-Sakwa); Kamageta (Dominant in Girango division, Rorya and comprises Kamakwana, Kamadho, Kamgunga Kalwambe, Wamseda, Kochieng, also in Migingo Kadibo, Oyugis,,,,,,,,); Kajulu (Dominant in Kisumu and Uriri including Kamenya Koda, Rateng' and kogweno, Kadero, Kanyimony and Kamwagi etc); Omiya/ Asembo (inhabiting East Asembo Bay locality); and Komenya (Dorminant in Uranga locality, 'composed of Kowala and Kalaka).

(ii) THE JOK-OWINY

The Jok-Kowiny sub-group was the second wave of the Luo to migrate into Kenya. They are believed to be the offshoot of the Padhola community of Eastern Uganda. The Jok-Kowiny, led by Owiny Sigoma, came in the 16th century and settled around the area called Alego. They include the following:

Karuoth (Dominant in Uranga and Boro localities); Kogelo (Based in Siaya, East, Awendo, Nyando, Kendu Bay, Oyugis and Muhuru Bay localities); Kanyigoro (Inhabiting Asembo Bay, Rusinga Island and Suna in Migori County); Kanyikwaya (In Yala locality of Siaya County); Kanyakwar (Based mainly in Kisumu); Karapul (In Siaya locality).; Kakeny (Also known as Uholo, is dominant in Sigomere, Ugunja locality and is composed of Kanyambir, Uwangwe, Saga and Uwiny); Kajwodhi (Settled in the northern parts of Yala locality).; **Kowil,** Wahundha, Nyiywer,Wanyenjra, Wasenge, Wahipi, Kanyibale, Goma, **Karodi;** and **Kadimo (In Yimbo locality);** Ndere (In Ugenya locality); Kaluo (Inhabiting Nyalgunga in Siaya County and include Kachien); and Kadhola (Found in Kisumu and Ndhiwa of Homa Bay county).

(iii) THE JOK-OMOLO

Jok-Omolo was the 3rd sub-group of Luos to enter Kenya, where they arrived at the beginning of the 17th century. They originally came from Pakwach - Pawir region, via eastern Busoga. They include the following:

(a) Ragenya clan cluster: Rager (Based in Ukwala and Uranga); Boro (Inhabiting Boro and Ugunja); Kakan (Dominant in Karemo, Siaya locality); Kanyada (Kalanya, Katuma/ Koduogo, Kanyabala, Kotieno, Kanyadier, Kothidha, Kanyango; Ugenya (A broad clan of Ragenya and include Kapuny/ Masiro, Kanyamuot, Deje/ Kateg, Kanywa/ Nyang'or, Kageng' and Kanyiner); and Kanyimach (Based in Rongo South and in Kamagak Oyugis).

(b) Kakwenda clan cluster: including: Kochia (Kamenya, Kaura, Kanam, Kowili, Korayo); Gem Kowili (Kachieng', Genga and Kopole); Agoro (Based in Katito and parts of Oyugis); Sare/ Wasare (Settled in Katito and Oyugis localities); Koguta (Settled on the slopes of Nyabondo Plateau, Pala in Riana locality, Rangwe and Muhoroni); Gem-Rae (Based in Katito locality); Kadiro (Based around Simbi in Karachunyo); and Gem (Kanyiwuor/ Kawere, Kathomo and Kagilo)

2. THE JOK-KAWANGO

The Jo-Kawango or Joka-Wanga sub-group came about after interaction between the Luhyas and the Luo clans who arrived from western Kenya as the fourth wave of Luo migration to enter Nyanza. The Jo-Kawango separated from the second phase of the Jok-Kajok migration, that is, the migration from Alur and migrated to the western region where they established the Tiriki ethnic group, then to Madungu in Wanga, before enteringSiaya. The other Luos also referred to them as Joka Suba because they migrated together with the Girango people. The term Luo-Abasuba was later coined by pioneer historians who errorneouly included other ethnic groups called Rieny and Abakunta into this group of the Joka Suba.

Sakwa is the prominent clan in the Jo-Kawango sub-group and generally, the Sakwa Luos are a broad clan comprising of the Kagwa, Kamgwenya/ Waganjo, Waumi, Kanyamwanda, Kaler/ Kamageta, Kamiyawa, Kamnaria (Surwa), Kakmasia, Nyasmwa. However, these people intermarry among themselves, a clear indication that the broad clan of Sakwa is made up of descendants who cannot trace their lineage to a single ancestor.

The Kawango (Luo-Abasuba) clans are: Kamatar/ Sakwa (Comprising Nyibinya, Kanyamwanda and Nyasmwa); Kowila/ Uyoma (Dominant in Madiany locality); Kaler (Based in Nyatike locality); Waturi (Based in the areas of Luo Imbo, Rorya, is composed of Kawakswa, Kamatula, Kamresi, Kogola and Lowa, as well as Konyango, Aroya in Kano and Magoya in Ugunja); Waondo (Dominant in Gembe locality, related to the Komenya in Alego and Asumbi); Kayanja (Based in the Gembe Hills, comprisedof Waumi, Waregi and Wagi subclans and related to the Tiriki); Waumi (Excluding those who remained among the Kayanja, settled in Lambwe Valley, Rongo and Kendu Bay); Kwabai (Settled in Nyarongi locality and include Kasirime, Kadhola, Kawanga, Kamdar, and Kanyasbok sub-clans); Zanaki (Based in Musoma rural and Butiama localities, Mara region. It is composed of the Biru and Buturi).

THE JO-KALE: The Jo-Kale who migrated from Acholiland was the last and the smallest Luo migration group. They include: Kale (Dominant in West Asembo Bay, include Kakia, Kabondo, Konyango and Kochieng'); and Kamolo (Based in Madiany locality, include Kabudha and Kabweng' a).

3. THE GIRANGO

The Bagirango, was a Bantu ethnic group with their own language. They were assimilated by the Luo and adopted many aspects of the Ramogi Luo culture and language, though they have managed to maintain some aspects of Bantu and often use 'Suba' as an identifier to distinguish themselves as a separate group. The Suba or Girango people are not to be confused by the Homa Bay Luo Abasuba or Abasuba community who are Bantu of different ethnic backgrounds that reside within the borders of Suba sub-county. Moreover, their language, Ekisuba/ Ekingoe was also distinct and very different from the Olusuba (Luganda) language spoken by the Luo Abasuba, particularly the Abakunta ethnic community. The name 'Suba' is derived from Girango's father who was called Suba. So all the Girango people owed their allegiance to Sub from whose lineage they were founded. The majority of the Girango clans migrated alongside the Jo-Kawango, the fourth phase of the Luo migration into Nyanza. They came from Uganda and settled first in western Kenya at Emanyulia, where the Kawango people claim their ancestral root came from. Some of the Girango people remained behind in Western, for instance, the Bamiluha and Basuba of Tiriki, as well as the Mungoe in Bunyore. The Girango people are culturally related to the Kiseru Luos and spoke closely related dialects of the same language. A few remnants of Girango today speak Ekingoe language which has lexical similarities to the Kuria and the Kisii languages and share names with the Kuria. However, since Ekingoe is mostly spoken by few older generation members, it is critically endangered. The Girango people living in Luo Nyanza is composed of the following:

(i)The Girango Proper: The original Bantu hybrid community that is now known as Suba Girango.

- Suba (Dominant in Suna Migori locality and comprises of Kadika, Katiga, Wiga, Wanje, Wasimbele and Wasweta); Wagire (Inhabiting Girango locality in Rorya and Suna Migori, Kaksingri, Gembe and Rangwe. It comprises of the Sangia, Kakrao/ Chandwa, Nyuma and Misiru, and Karum).

(ii) Wategi/ Lang'o: These are the descendants of Muserema. Muserema was the son of Girango. Muserema gave birth to Thunya, Ongombe, Mureri, Muruga and Aderema. Muruga and his younger sister Aderema went to Lang'o (Maasai) among a clan called Alburugo. That is why sometimes today the Wategi group are called Maasai or Lang'o. Thunya, the eldest son of Muserema is the ancestral father of the present day Utegi and Kamagambo clans. They comprise: Utegi (Based in Girango division of Rorya and Suna Migori); Kamagambo/ Kimbaba (Kanyamamba, Kangeso, Kagoro, Kongudi, Kongoma, Koluoch, Kanyadieto and Kamwango); Sigiria/ Kasigiria (In Suna

Migori locality); Kakiberi (In Suna Migori locality); Kanyigombe (In the area of Rongo Central); and Kamreri (Inhabiting Gembe and Rongo localities).

(ii) Kógoro: The descendants of Ogoro, the son of Girango: Kinyenche and Ungoe.

4. KISERU LUOS

The Bakiseruwere originally a Bantu ethnic group, and outer relatives of the Abagusii community. Most of the Kiseru customs and names are very similar to those of the Gusii people. That is why many Kiseru clans have been continually referred to as Jo-Kisii by their fellow Luos and some historians, although Kiseru and Gusii were different ethnic groups. Nevertheless, the Kiseru have lost most of their cultural aspects including language. The Kiseru people today speak Dholuo and have become largely part of the Luo through intermarriage and other forms of socialization. The Kiseru people have maintained intimate cultural and political relations with the Ramogi Luos - they share clan affiliations like the Karachuonyo/ Wanjare and Konyango/ Rabala. The Kiseru remnants today speak Ekegusii (in Nyanza) or Bonchari in North Mara and their language is in danger of disappearing. Kiseru remnants in Gwasi and those in Mfang' ano island are comfortable with being lumped together with the Suba. At the same time some of the Kiseru clans like the Karachuonyo, Kowidi (Kisumo), Wanjare and Wawaria are taken to be Jo-Kajok by historians. Nevertheless, the fact that some Kiseru people have been assimilated and adopted the Abakuria and Dholuo languages do not make them non-Kiseru in origin. Those who went to Kisii highlands call themselves Bagusero or Wanchari, and moreover, some can also be traced in Kericho.

(i) The Kiseru Ajwang' this covers : Mur (Dominant in Ng' iya in Siaya, South Awendo, Kabar in Muhoroni and Kodero Bara in Rongo); Kasipul (Composed of Kowidi, Kachien,Kanyakila, Kolondo, Komala and Kodumo sub-clans); Karachuonyo (Includes Kanyajuok in Rongo).; Kowidi (Based in Maseno and Kisumu and comprises of Karateng' , Kapuonja, Karanja); Waganjo (Settled in the Gwasi Hills, Kaksingri, Hills, Suna Migori); Wanjare/ Wanchari (Dominant in Kabondo); Sidho (Inhabiting Muhoroni and Oyugis); Wang' aya (Dominant in Nyang' oma and Chemelil in Muhoroni locality); Matabori (In Oyugis locality); Watobori/ Bhatobori (Based in Awasi and Nyando); Kwera (Settled in Suna Migori).; Kalando/ Mksero (Based in Ruga); Oyengwe (Inhabit areas of Misambi, Karota and Nyamusi); Kamsagia/ Kakseru (Doninant in Nyancha locality, Rorya and include Kamseko, Kamkuru, Kakwaere, Waji); Mikiria (Settled in Oyugis and Chemelil localities, comprised of Kowidi, Miremi, Kosongo, Mikiro and Okiambe); Kamae (Settled in the area around Mawego); Soklo (Inhabit Mfang'ano Island and Kaksingri Hills); Kaguria (in Pala, Riana locality); Oongo/ Wagasi (Believed to be some of the earliest inhabitants of Gwasi Hills); Warisia (Based in the Suna Migori locality); Kakaeta (Based in Kobodo, Ndhiwa locality and are brothers to the Kakwaere clan); Kakimba/ Ramba (Mainly settled in the northern areas pf Mfang'ano Island); Wagimbe (Living in Mfang'ano Island); Wagumbe/ Wanchari (Living among the Kuria people).

(ii) The Kine: The Kine descended from Kine, the son of Kiseru. They retained the Bantu initiation ceremony and a few of them use Bunchari language, as well as the Kine (Based in Nyancha locality, Rorya district).

(iii) The Kiseru Obwere: The KiserUu Obwere refers to the Kiseru group that arrived after the other Kiseru were already established. The Kiseru Obwere (Kiseru the Elder), meaning the people of Kiseru the Elder, are also known as Kiber. Kiseru the Elder had many children from his various wives. They include: Wigi (Comprising Kubia and Kamwenda); Kanyameda/ Abagonye; Wasamo; Waoi; Wanyamongo and Kaligoe.

5. SIRATI LUOS

Originally, the Basirati spoke a different language and had different customs from the Luo, and are somehow related to the Banyore section of the Abaluhya community. They were the first to come to North Mara and Nyanza long before all the Luo clans. The few Sirati remnants today speak Olumuulu (in Nyanza) and Olusurwa (in North Mara); Surwa (Based in Nyancha locality and include the Kamsuru in Suna Migori, Kamnara among the Sakwa and Maragoli, Sanua (later corrupted to Suna) in Suna Migori and Nyore in Yimbo); Muhuru (In Muhuru Bay locality, including the Kamreme in Yimbo locality); Wakeru (In Rangwe locality); Kamgundho (Dominant in North Kanyamkago and Lambwe); Kakremba (Dominant in Rangwe).

6. IMBO LUOS

These are the people who originally inhabited the Luo dispersal point of Yimbo and all of whom now speak Dholuo, the Luo language. The Imbo were not Luo by custom. They were a minority Bantu-speaking ethnic group. They had settled in Yimbo by as early as 14th century. Some of them were displaced but those who remained in Yimbo formed 53 different groups that came to be known together as Ojwando. The clans that originated from the earlier Bantu settlers of Yimbo are as follows: Ojwando/ Imbo (In Yimbo locality); Walowa (Excluding those who spread out into North Mara. They settled in Suna Migori, Kaksingri and Mfang'ano Island); Mansawa (In Ugunja locality); Kanyalaro (In the Sihayi, Ukwala locality); Wahundha (Based in Awendo South and Yimbo localities); Bassi (In Oyugis locality and its offshoot, the Bassi of Kisii ethnic community); Kamaswa (Also known as Waswa or Umswa, settled in Awasi, Muhoroni, Yala, Ojwando in Oyugis as well as in Suna Migori); Wareje; Wayipi; Wasenge/ Ulafu; Kamhore/ Uhore (In Yala locality).

7. OTHER LUOS

The other Luos, also known as Nyokal, are generally a minority Luo adoptees. They were non-Luo clans who were both absorbed by the several streams of the infiltrating Luo. These include the following: Uregi/ Ukaya (In Maeri, North Gwasi, originally part of the Kara in Northern Tanzania); Osingo (Based in God Jope, Suna Migori locality, originally Kiroba); Kanyig'we (In Uranga, also originally Teso); Gangu (In Uranga, also called Kolunje Ja Kodera, originally Marachi); Kamrembo (From Maasai); Wasweta(Part of Basweta in Kisii, based in the areas of Oyugis and Suna Migori, from Maragoli); Waware (Found in Awendo East, originally Abakunta); Kolunje (In Otwenya settlement of Maseno locality); Osije (From Nyahera, Oyugis locality); and Wamiembe (In Kanyamkago).

REFERENCE

1. Kenya Historical Studies and Social Change in Western Kenya (2002, William Robert Ochieng')

2. Grasp the Shield Firmly: The Journey is Hard (2010, Zedekia Siso Oloo)

3. A Political and Cultural History of the Jii-Speaking Peoples of Eastern Africa (2006, Allan Bethwel Ogot)

4. The Luo Nation (2012, Ojijo)

5.2018-19 Oral interview of Mzee Ongech Ogola (diseased, Feb 2021).

CHAPTER 2: BIRTH AND EARLY CHILDHOOD EXPERIENCES

Prelude

"Giving birth and being born brings us into the essence of creation, where the human spirit is courageous and bold and the body, a miracle of wisdom" Harriette Hartigan.
"Child birth is more admirable than conquest, more amazing than self-defense, and as courageous as either one" Gloria Steinem.

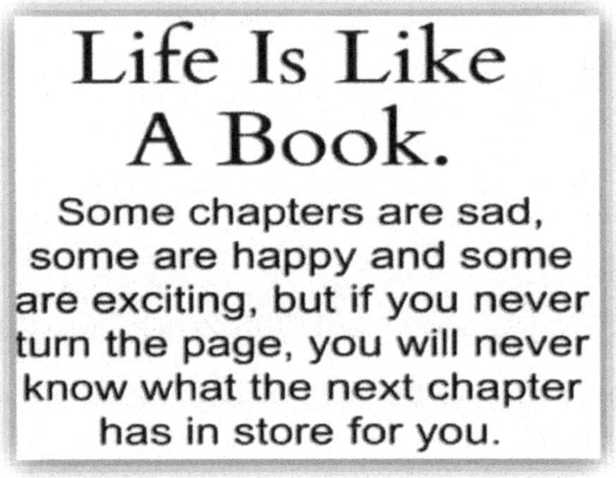
Life Is Like
A Book.
Some chapters are sad,
some are happy and some
are exciting, but if you never
turn the page, you will never
know what the next chapter
has in store for you.

2.0: About My Birth and Early Childhood

Keeping records about the exact date of birth during the time I was born was not easy. Most births were done by very experienced traditional birth attendants (TBAs). Mine was not an exception. Even with the sharp mind of my father, it was agreed that I was born 1966 at the end of the year, December. So we agreed it was 31.12.1966. There was no birth certificate issued at the time of my birth but I acquired one later on in life. My mother explained to me that she gave birth to me under a tree called Kuogo with the help of a traditional birth attendant. So I was not born in a hospital. I wonder what my Apgar score was but it must have been good for me to have made it to medical school. So I was the 5th child to Jeremiah Ong'ech Ogola and Siporah Achieng Ong'ech and the 3rd Son … sometimes I hear them say they had son called Sigar between their 1st born and second born who died very early childhood but they don't like talking about it much, so officially I will remain the 5th child and 3rd born son. I was born in Siaya County, Bondo Sub-County, Usigu Division, North Yimbo Location, Nyamonye Sub location, Ogam-Lwala village. So naming a child those days was a big thing. I was given a name at birth (which has never been disclosed to me) but I am told that I kept crying day and night, so my mother took me to his brother's wife, Patricia Ombere, who was known to have a lot of powers in prayers. She fasted and prayed for many days, then one day during her prayers she saw an image of a man that when my father was consulted, he positively identified as the late Odero Aruba from Kamhore Nyangera where my father was raised. My father instantly advised I should be called Odero Aruba. The story goes that I stopped crying immediately I was called Odero Aruba. Odero Aruba was a great man, hardworking, Energetic and played a key role in bringing forefathers of the entire Kamhore clan in Nyangera. Recollecting childhood memories can be a tall order but I will try to put down what I can remember in early child hood.

So I was born when my father was working at the WHO sponsored Yala Swamp reclamation project and was stationed at Alego Kadenge. As such, he would come home mostly during weekends but my mother was full time at home. I always looked forward to my father's weekend visits because he would come with a lot of food. My mother took good care of us, going an extra mile to make sure we don't sleep hungry. I was fond of both my grandmothers- paternal and maternal. My paternal grandmother liked me a lot. She was called Otago Nyong'iengo from Sakwa Wayendhe, Ogoya. Anytime she was taking a meal, she had to look for me so that we share. I shared with her the last supper before she died in 1971. She had a lot of knowledge on treatment of various diseases using traditional herbs. We took long walks in the forests and shambas as she tried to explain to me different plants and the diseases they treat. **No wonder when I was 11 years, my father declared to me that he had a vision that I would one day be a great Doctor. And indeed this dream of my father became a reality. The dream came to pass. I am indeed a great doctor.**

My maternal grandma, Oganga Apela Nyombere was a good friend of mine. My mother used to cook food which I would take to her. This we would eat together and talk the whole night. She would tell me a lot of stories. On the market day on Saturdays, I would assist her at her business at Nyamonye Market. We would sell groundnuts, salts and other assortments of ware. She trusted me to keep the proceeds of the sales as the day progressed, and at the end of the day I would help her to keep it in a safe place. She died in 1981 at a ripe old age of over 110. Nobody knew the exact year she was born but she was very old when she died. My grandfathers, both Maternal (Apela) and Paternal (Ogola Mtar) died before I was born, so I did not have any relationship with them.

Growing with my sibling was fun. We all worked hard during school holidays and weekends in the farm. We also did income generation activities to assist in purchasing school uniform/buying books/purchasing food to supplement/paying school fees etc. Some of the income generating activities I was involved in was cutting grass and selling to those who were building grass thatched houses (which was the most common form of housing in the community) as well as sisal fibre preparation using locally made machine (then selling) (Gowo tuoro). My brother Ochieng Ong'ech was the expert in assembling these machines. Fishing is an income activity that my father declared illegal because it was a detractor from education. Nevertheless, I would still sneak once in a while during holidays with my cousin Joseph Ombere and go fishing. Of course it was thorough corporal punishment if my father found out. Working on the family farm was not a joking matter.

We were each assigned a farm potion to work in. Before going to school in the morning I worked in my portion, as well as after school in the evening, during weekends. It was however, a full time work during the holidays. It was hard work, hard work, hard work.... when I was growing up. The school performance was scrutinized closely, led by my father and older siblings. The entire family would celebrate good performance but everyone would have one or two pieces of advice to give whoever had bad performance.

I was lucky that my performance was always good. The older siblings were always at hand to help the parents to ensure good behavior. I remember our first born Dalmas Ogola was very quiet but would administer Corporal punishment instantly to a behavior he did not like. Both my parents were strict and did not entertain a behavior they did not approve. Canning was quite common. We played a lot in the village with my peers like late Ouma Obiero, late Obange Obiero, Michael Onyango Okello, Lolwe Okello, Julia Obange Okello, Late Okoth Sipem, Joseph Ombere etc. During holidays, after I finished my portion of the farm work, I could be released to visit trusted relatives like my aunts Meresia Obwanda Apela in Nyangera, Sulmena Ochar Oyola in Sakwa Kambajo or at my Uncle Ombera Apela in Nyamonye or later when my father started working in Kisumu, I would go there for holidays.

In the village there was a lot of love for children by some special mothers like Agutu Pelesia Obiero (Nyaryamo) where we could eat freely at any time. There are 2 incidences in my early childhood when I nearly lost my life that I remember apart from the usually early childhood illness which my mother took care of very well, using traditional medicine and modern medicine. My father loved modern medicine but mother would prefer to start with traditional medicine. Around 1975, when I was around 9 years old, I almost drowned in River Yala when we were returning from the farm in Yala swamp reclaimed farmland. My brother ochieng' Ong'ech jumped into the water and saved me.

In 1977, when I was in class 4, in third term, I climbed a tall tree at home called Keyo, the branch broke and I fell down with a big force to the ground. I became unconscious for a few minutes. Luckily I did not break any bones but my chest was very painful. I was rushed to Kisumu and my father took me to the hospital. My father was working in Kisumu at that time. I recovered after treatment for almost one month. I did not do exams for term 3 class 4 but I was promoted to class 5. Interestingly, I became No. 1 in class 5 term one.

I will hand over to my childhood friend Michael Onyango Okello to say something.

2.1 John Odero Ongech childhood: From a village age mate: Michael Onyango Okelo

This is a tribute on Dr Odero's birth and early childhood from village age-mate; Michael Onyango Okelo (0722672892). We grew up with the following nicknames: Dr. John Odero Ongech – (Aruba) Michael Onyango Okelo – (Rakula).

Character Formation: This we got from the words **ORDER!! MARA MOJA!! SIT DOWN!!** These words were echoed by Mzee Jeremiah Ong'ech (Dola Jasiasa). Mzee Ongech taught us respect for older people. We enjoyed his lectures as we sat on the grass under a tree in his home. Respect to God, Parents and any old person were paramount. Mzee would always roar jokingly **(ORDER)** just to catch our attention, and the trick always worked. He would then narrate to us why childhood friendship should prosper. My father Okelo Abeyi, helped him made a home (Goyo Dolo) in Luo customary way, a bond that also kept us close. As small children we thought that for my father to do that, the blood must be very close and this made the bond much strong.

Morning and afternoon activities: Mzee taught us to live in an organized system. The day always began with homestead activities; cattle to be attended, well fed and any other work assigned. We always planned for the following day's work lest one fell on the wrong side of the order. Dr. Ong'ech was time observant. We always had sticks put on the ground to watch the shadow movement and use sun position on a cloudy day when shadows were not clear for estimating time. During our free time, we would visit each other back and forth, and the visits were endless. We escorted each other. We enjoyed eating mango and tamarind (chwa) fruits together as we prepared for football. These two fruitsis we believed were reliable energizers for the game. Failing to see each other would mean sickness or Dr. Ong'ech had gone to the uncles in Nyamonye. He loved visiting them.

Hobby: Football and Storytelling: We were members of Ogam football team in which Dr. Ong'ech was the goal keeper while I was No.5. Whenever Dr. Ong'ech wanted more goals, he insisted that 1 play no. 7 or 11. We used to continuously beat the Orom team headed by Amadi Patroba. Ragak team was also there, competing a few times. Our Ogam teammates included the late Ouma Obiero (Rangala), the late Ngesa Sipem and late Jericho Ngore. Amongst those team members Dr Ongech and I are the only survivors. The football pitch was known as Pap Kobiero. The ball we were using known as Abisidi (the kijaluo abcd) and Ajuaya (home-made mpira).

Farming: As small children our mothers gave us small Jembes knovm as Hasiri those that have been used for decades and somehow succumber to human and soil weathering. We used to trek up to our Yala Swamp shambas planting maize, whose roughest part was during harvesting. At that period, we would carry on our heads dry maize heaped in sacks, all the way to home. We rested almost a thousand times on the way. Dr. Ong'ech disliked manner-less children, feared to death people with power of the evil eye (Jasihoho), scared to death by night runner (Jajuok). We used to call ourselves children with manners. Because we couldn't eat at anybody's home apart from Dr. Ong'ech mother's food, Rakula's mother's food and Ouma Obiero's mother's food. From seventies to date our friendship have survived.

During the famous Kenyan political clashes of 2007, I lost almost every earthly belonging as well as my job. Dr. Ong'ech was so sympathetic and generously offered me both counselling and financial support. He was equally so concerned about my children education, as he sought to know how I was going to educate them. I explained to him my plans of venturing into agribusiness, a means of livelihood which I maintain to date. He was so happy how I do it that many a time he was at hand to help me find market for the produce. When the market was down he would promote me with finance. For these I am forever grateful. Dr. Og'ech loves education. When I approached him that my son wanted to become a nurse, he willingly advised me to seek for admission and let him know. During that time, getting an admission in any KMTC was not easy. I. However, I struggled and surprised him with an admission letter from the famous Thika Medical College. He was very happy for my effort to secure a chance. The admission requirements was totaling Kenya shillings 120,000 which he paid over 75 percent. Daktari en *wuoyi maonge thuol e efuke. Osiep Ma Mor Ka Nyawadgi Dhi Maber Kendo Rach Ne Ahinya Ka Osiepne Piny Ohingo*. The boy has since graduated with a diploma in community nursing. In Kenya today you can have papers but if you do not know anybody, papers cannot speak. As such, after qualifying, Dr. Ong'ech took the initiative and arranged for the boy to travel to Nairobi, organizing and paying for three months' rent just to make sure everything is in order. Dr. Ong'ech reasoned that this was his project. And indeed he really fought hard for the boy to secure a place at the famous Coptic hospital. He took the boy's papers personally, taking his time just to make sure everything worked well. The interview was done and an employment letter provided and he is now a happy nurse. He thereafter continued guiding the boy to sit professional exams which can allow him to travel and practice in USA. Daktari is a person of integrity. I have witnessed him spending money helping people no matter where they come from.

Social life: I remember him taking me to my in-laws to sweet talk the parents to give us their daughter for Marriage. Luckily we succeeded. Likewise I acompanied him to Ahero Kano with a historic 16 cows as dowry at once. It was record breaking. What a gesture! We were treated like kings. Thank you people of Kano for hosting Daktari in such a manner.

Long Live Daktari! May our good God give more wisdom, strength, knowledge and prosperity.

Michael Onyango Okello

Left: Jeremiah and Siporah Ong'ech; Right: Odero Ongech with mother Siporah and Mzee Jeremaih

Dr Ong'ech consulting my father ……………

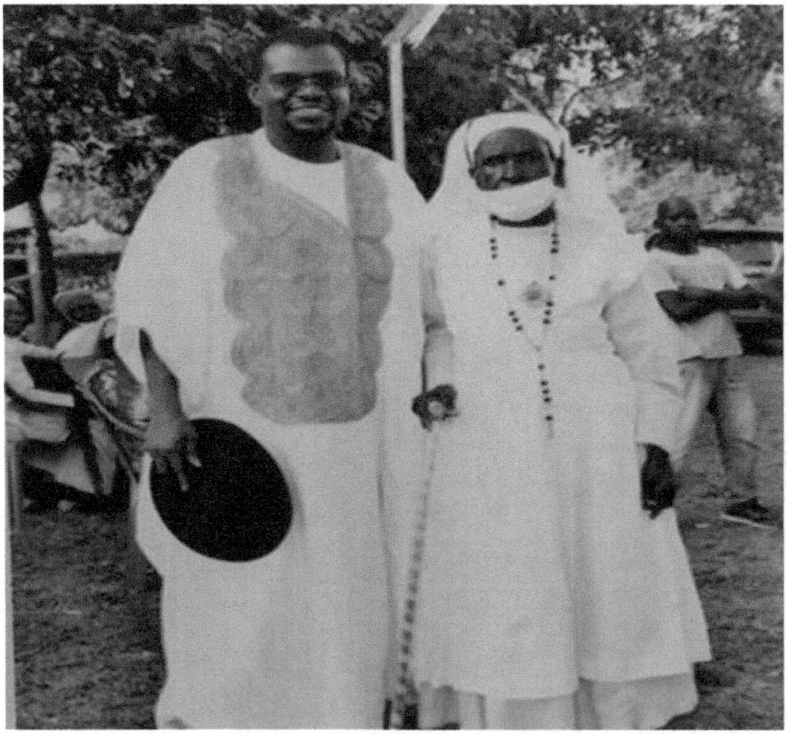

Dr Ongech with his uncle's wife, Patricia Ombere

Dr Ongech with eldest son, Jeremy

CHAPTER 3: EDUCATION: SCHOOL LIFE/COLLEGE LIFE /STUDYING IN USA

Prelude:

"Education is the passport to the future, for tomorrow belongs to those who prepare for it today"Malcolmx

"An investment in knowledge pays the best interest" Benjamin Franklin

"There are no secrets to success. It is result of preparation, hard work, and learning from failure" Colin Powell

"The roots of education are bitter but the fruit is sweet " Aristotle

"Education is the most powerful weapon which you can use to change world " Nelson Mandela

"The more that you read, the more things you will know, the more that you learn, the more places you will go" Dr. Seusi

"Live as if you were to die tomorrow. Learn as if you were to live forever"-Mahatma Gandhi

"Knowledge is power. Information is liberating, education is the premise of progress, every society, in every family".Kofi Annan

"Learning is not attained by chance, it must be sought for with ardo and attended to with diligence." Abigail Adams.

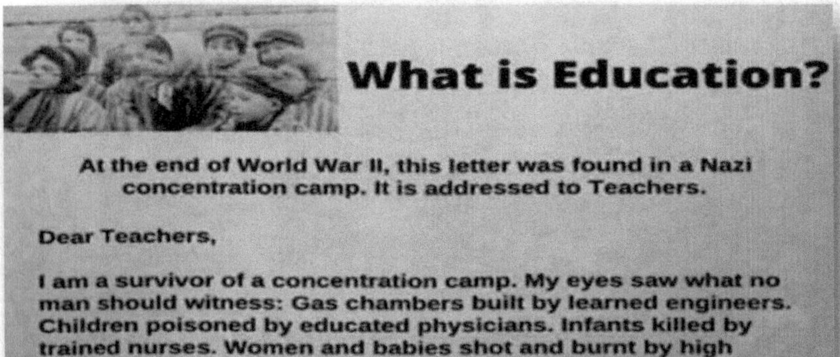

What is Education?

At the end of World War II, this letter was found in a Nazi concentration camp. It is addressed to Teachers.

Dear Teachers,

I am a survivor of a concentration camp. My eyes saw what no man should witness: Gas chambers built by learned engineers. Children poisoned by educated physicians. Infants killed by trained nurses. Women and babies shot and burnt by high school and college graduates. So, I am suspicious of education. My request is: Help your students become human. Your efforts must never produce learned monsters, skilled psychopaths, educated illiterates. Reading, writing, arithmetic are important only if they serve towards making our children more humane.

3.1 Primary schooling in Nyamonye and Majengo

I started Nursery School in 1973 at Majengo Nursery School. The Nursery School teacher was called Adera. I attended for only one term (3rd term) and passed better than those who had attended for one year. It had become compulsory that you could not be admitted to class one without a certificate from a nursery school. In 1974, I started my primary school at Nyamonye Primary School, where my elder siblings had been alumni. The school had previously a good reputation due to the order brought by Mwalimu Afulo Ogutu. It was also near my grandmother Agnes Oganga Nyombere home and Uncle Ombere Apela home. So I could go over there for lunch. There was general feeling of sense of security. Those days it was common for age mates to fight to see who is stronger at school and village with the older ones cheering. There was a lot of bullying among age mates. So I fought with a few especially from Ragak (Joshua Ondifi, Opuk Magugu etc) and won many battles but lost a few. The ones I lost, I would then team up with my uncle son, Joseph Otieno Ombere and fight fiercely to win. These fights were so many that it became survival for the fittest. During opening of the school, people would fight, closing of the school also. If you were weak, the fights would make you not even attend school. Elder siblings and relatives would come in handy for one's security. My uncle late Lucas Apela was feared as a great boxer (Nicknamed clay brother to Aluoch-'*clay owadgi Aluoch*') and therefore people would not provoke a fight with me. I performed well in class one and this also started bringing respect amongst peers and the fights got less. The Nyamonye primary school was 1.5 Km away from home and we had to walk daily. Mwalimu Afulo Ogutu had given it a bigger than life reputation as a school where children would be sure to pass, as well as have good discipline. However, in 1970, Mwalimu Afulo had left the school and by 1974 when I started schooling, the school had clearly started deteriorating in discipline and performance. My father decided I should change to

Majengo Primary School....and that is how I joined Majengo Primary School in 1975 in class two. I stayed there for the rest of my primary education till 1980 when I sat for my Certificate of Primary Education (C.P.E.). Compared to Nyamonye, Majengo was further away from home, almost 2Km. To make it worse, we had no close relatives around. So I never used to go back home for lunch in early primary school days. However, when I was stronger and had reached upper primary, from class 5 onwards, I would ran home for lunch and back. This still had its challenges, as lunch break was only one hour and one risked getting late unless one did the running.

Learning was fun in primary school because I was always doing well. There was a lot corporal punishment for those who did badly especially in mathematics and English. My closest competitors in lower primary school were Peter Ochieng Ouma Obiero (Father to Ruth Amina Ochieng) and Eric Malowa. In upper primary especially class 7, my competitors were Elisha Oluoch Kalooh and James Omondi Owiti. With the latter two, we all ended up at Usenge High School. During our primary education, the teachers very committed to teaching and the pupils were disciplined. We enjoyed the Nyayo milk-free milk offered to all primary school learners by President Daniel Arap Moi from class 5 (1978) until I left in class 7(1980). This milk was very useful to us who came from far. It used to be our lunch.

3.1.1 My early leadership

My first serious leadership was in 1979 when I was in class 6. I was appointed to be a bell ringer (position which was traditionally reserved for the most brilliant student in the school- earlier Jared Osunga Awelo did it, later George Ngeso Obara did it and Alfred Odhiambo Omenya also did it during his time). The bell ringer was also in charge of writing the late comers to school who would be punished. So the story commonly told by my sisters Mary Atieno and Margaret Auma is that we would leave home together, I would run faster than them, arrive in school in good time, ring the bell and then write down their names for punishment.

The headmaster Mr Oriaro Obalo gave me a Seiko wrist watch to use for this purpose. This is the origin for my love for Seiko watches to date. I also became a good long distance runner for 1500 meters and even represented the school during Zonal competitions. I was not so good with football like my senior brothers (Ogola and Ochieng). My long distance running used to bring trouble to the rest of the school. I used to top even though I had a small body physique. The teachers could not understand why I beat the bigger boys, and they would be canned daily. A teacher called Mr Oywer could tell them that Odero Ong'ech defeats them everywhere, in class and in the field running.

Anyway I had a good time in primary school, did certificate of primary education (CPE) in 1980 and passed well. Before CPE, we did mocks, Yimbo Zonal mocks and Siaya District mocks all of which I passed very well. Hon Dr. Gideon Ochanda, Bondo MP always reminds me of those days. He was in Jusa Primary school and he also used to do well in those exams. I also want remember my friend Luke Juma Ogono who at that time was the best student at Nyamonye primary school while I was leading at Majengo. We could set CPE prediction exams; the ones I set was done by CPE candidates at Nyamonye Primary and the ones he set was done by candidates at Majengo Primary. This helped us a lot. Luke and I ended up at Usenge High School. Another worthy competitor in class 7 was Elly Okello Rogo who joined us in class 7. We were head-on with each other in mathematics. He later joined Maranda High School (He did CPE in another school called Nyawita in Sakwa).

I cannot pen off my life in primary school without mentioning my brief stay with my brother Dalmas Ogola Ong'ech at Mageta primary school in 1976 third term in class 3. I was with him for only one term but I enjoyed my stay there. He took good care of me and my sister Margaret Auma. We were also good academically. Mwalimu Ogola Ong'ech was a good teacher, a good footballer and also disciplinarian. He would not spare me canning because I am his brother if caught breaking the school rules.

3.2: High School education in Usenge high school

So life in primary school came to an end after the CPE results of 1980 were

released. I passed well and was called to join Chianda High School while all my friends James Omondi Owiti, Elisha Oluoch Kalooh, Fanuel Ogot Anam and Luke Juma Ogono were admitted to Usenge High School. The people who were ahead of me like Jared Osunga Awelo, Edwin Otieno Okola, Vincent Ochieng Omenya, Owino Obara were all at Usenge High School. In fact there was nobody from Majengo Primary School who had ever been admitted to Chianda High School. I wondered why I was an outlier. My father came to my rescue and said he did not like Chianda High School due to indiscipline. He talked to Warom, principal of Usenge High School who was happy with my CPE marks and gave me admission at Usenge High School.

I joined form one at Usenge High School in 1981 until 1984 when I sat for my Kenya Certificate of Education (KCE) – Form 4. My dormitory was Mboya 2. The initial experience at Usenge under Warom the principal (1981-1983) was different with 1984 when left. Warom was strict disciplinarian who would cane anybody including parents at the slightest provocation. There was discipline in school. I excelled in the academics including the joint mathematics contests involving many schools.

3.2.1 The Siaya Maths contest experience

In a February 1984 siaya mathematics contest involving 8 schools, Usenge high school posted the best result beating the giants such as national schools Maranda and Ng'iya girls, and top-rated extra-county school, Ramba. Of the students who scored a pass mark of 40%, the distribution was as follows: Maranda (62); Lwak (26); Nyangoma (20); Usenge (14); Ramba (11); Ng'iya[2] (7); Nyamira (3) and Nyakongo (1). Usenge high school's John Odero Ong'ech led the pack of 145 students who registered a pass mark, with a convincing win of 89%. Three Other Usenge students followed closely with 88%, 87%, and 80%, making the 80% to a tally of 4. Other than Usenge, only Maranda registered 4 students who scored at least 80% marks. Another school which registered 80% was Lwak with 2 candidates who scored 83% and 82%. This marks the end of the top 10 students. Another 17 students scored 70's; 24 scored 60's; 32 scored 50's and 61 scored 40's.

An analysis of the contest results for the passing students scoring at least 40%

Who scored at least 40%	Usenge	Lwak	Maranda	Nyangoma	Ramba	Ng'iya	Nyamira	Nyakongo	Total
Total	14	26	62	20	11	7	3	1	144
Mean school mark (%)	66.40	53.31	59.48	50.15	50.45	50.57	44.67	40.00	56.25
Highest mark	89	83	88	76	75	61	47	40	

	Usenge	Lwak	Maranda	Nyangoma	Ramba	Ng'iya	Nyamira	Nyakongo	Total
40's	3	11	19	12	8	4	3	1	61
50's	3	8	13	5	1	2	0	0	32
60's	2	4	15	2	0	1	0	0	24
70's	2	1	11	1	2	0	0	0	17

[2] Ng'iya was a top Anglican Church centre turned school, a source of pride in which all top educated girls of Nyanza learnt from. Associating with it automatically placed one a class and name. So much so that in 1990's the late Mr Orwenjo Umidha was to openly claim he learnt in Ng'iya gal (even though Ng'iya was purely a girls' school).

80's	4	2	4	0	0	0	0	0	10
Total	14	26	62	20	11	7	3	1	144
Highest mark	**89**	**83**	**88**	**76**	**75**	**61**	**47**	**40**	
Top scorer	**Dr John Odero Ong'ech**			**Evans Oluoch Ong'ang'a**					

It is worth noting that in the Math contest, the top candidate was Dr John Ong'ech, from Yimbo, and an UHS student, while the top student from Nyangoma Secondary School (also where the editor of this book learnt) who scored 76% was Evans Oluoch Ong'ang'a [3], also hailing from Unyejra, Yimbo. It would seem Mzee Dola's soft spot for Usenge was also a blessing of a kind. In a similar exam of the previous year, the author of this book was initially scored at 92%, tying with an Usenge high School boy (Later to know he was called Omil from Uyoma), only to have 5 Section B questions reduced by 1 mark each, to make a final score of 87%. He therefore officially became overall second in this same exam in 1983 with 87% score, trailing an UHS student.

[3] Evans Oluoch, a mentee of Prof Afullo, is a Kambi alumni who hails from Usenge. He is a principal of a high school in South Nyanza.

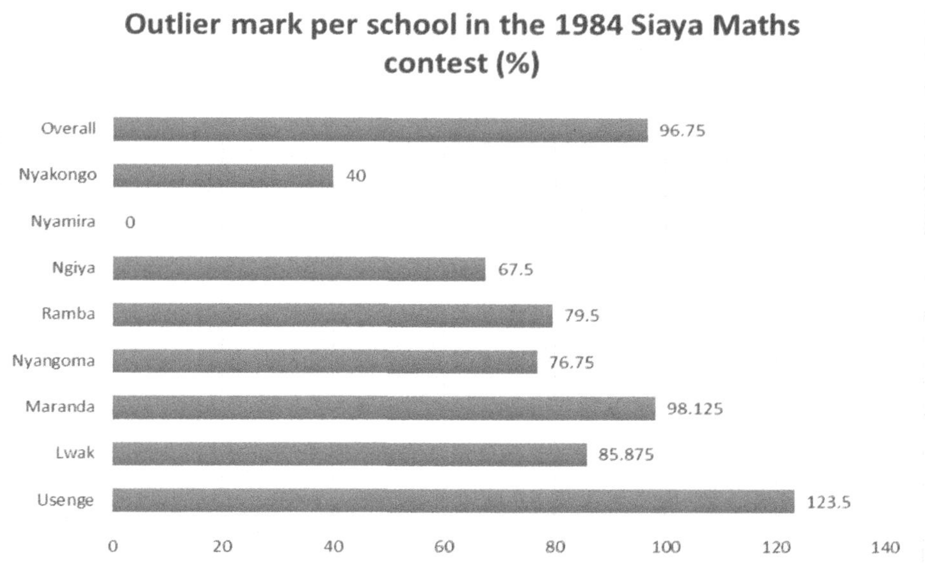

3.2.2 The hard realities of life in high school

The school did not have water so we had to go and bathe in Lake Victoria, Usenge beach. We would also bring firewood to be used in school from Mageta. School routine included waking up early, running in the field, cleaning dormitory, clearing the grass and going to class. We did not have electricity for studying at night, we used pressure lamps. At Usenge High School, Mosquitoes bites was real. The diet was mainly ugali and beans, Githeri and porridge. Meat would be served once or twice a week, in the morning we would go to class without eating anything. Porridge alone would be served at 10am. Lunch at 1pm and supper at 6pm. There were no other meals served in between. Bread and Mandazi was very precious commodity and only the privileged students would afford it. I was not among the privileged. I never used to have any pocket money. Once my school fee was paid, I would take my box to school using a bicycle then walk all the way to school, about 5km. My school fees was raised collectively by my father Mzee Ong'ech Ogola, my sister Margaret Auma (both took care of my form one) and my brother Ochieng Ong'ech (who took care of most of my form 2,3, and 4 school fees) after he finished his teachers training college in late 1981. My father Mzee Ong'ech Ogola had retired in 1981 after I joined form one. During holidays, I concentrated on studies. My bother Ochieng Ong'ech bought for me a syllabus book which used to guide me on reading relevant materials. Most students did not have a syllabus book. During holidays, we spent a lot of time comparing our study progress with my class mate Elisha Oluoch Kalooh (now late). It is only their home that I would visit during breaks from my studies. This is a culture that continued even during my form 5 and 6 studies later. We joined Kericho High School together for A-level.

I had an easy time at Usenge High School with the teachers because of the good performance. I was easily noticed. In my class, I had worthy competitors like Philemon Owino Oduor, my good friend to date, the late Chrispine Oyoo Odhiambo, late Elisha Oluoch kalooh, Oloo Kisinyo amongst others.

While at Usenge, I was not active in sports unlike in my primary life. However, I was a member of Karate club and Science club. I excelled in science club and scooped 2nd position at Nyanza Provincial science congress held at Maseno National School.

In 1984 when we sat for KCE (form 4) exams, the long serving no-nonsense principal, Mr Warom had left and the school became very chaotic. There were many indisciplined students, with fights between form 3 and form 4. Form 3 were sent home and did not learn most of 3rd term. The school main administration block was razed down by unknown people. Some students who had been expelled came at night with thugs and terrorized us by throwing stones on our dormitories.

We did not have teachers in some subjects. We relied on people like PLO Lumumba during his University vacation to teach us literature in English and English language. By the time we were sitting form 4 KCE exams, the teachers had given up on us. However, a clique of us kept reading even harder amidst the crisis. When the results for KCE, came out, we posted very good results, despite the storm the school was going through. Being focused paid.

3.2.3 The 1984 Usenge high school KCE results

KCE 1984 results at Usenge High School was special. When we compared notes, we found that the best results in Nyanza Province was as follows: First division of 10 Points (2 people - Philemon Owino Oduor of Usenge High and Uhuru Ogola of Mbita High School); followed by 1st Division of 11 points (Aroko of Homabay High School); followed 1st Division of 12 points -which was me..John Odero Ongech. It was history made: Usenge High School recorded Division 1 of 10 points for the first time in the history of its 7.4.2.3 system.

3.2.3.1 The detailed analysis of the 1984 Usenge high school KCE results

Usenge High best O level record in 7.4.2.3 system is held by Dr Philemon Owino Oduor of KNH, Dr Odero Ong'ech's classmate who scored a Division one of 10 points followed by 4 people in a tie with Division one of 12 points. These are: James Ratiri Kowade in 1976, Omil Abonyo in 1983, Odero Ong'ech in 1984 and Opeya in 1987. As such, Dr John Ong'ech stands tall as one of the top record holders of Usenge since inception.

Ten points division 1 means as follows: Of the 6 contributing subjects, a student scores on average 4 distinction two's and two distinction ones. Alternatively, since Usenge was best in Science in general, the best first division students scored distinction 1's in all three sciences offered as Biology, Physical Science and Mathematics. As such, if the candidate scored distinction 1 in each of these 3 subjects, they scored another distinction 2 in two other subjects, and most likely a credit 3 in a last subject: I.e. it could be either (a) 1(2) 2(4) or (which was most likely) 1(3)2(2)3(1)). This means the candidate literally scored more than 75% in each of the 6 rated subjects. For a division 1 [4]of 12 points[5], this is the meaning: scoring a distinction 2 in each of the 6 considered subjects, ie, 2(6). In 1983 Form 4, there was a very sharp Guy at Usenge High called Erastus Omil Abonyo. He scored a Division 1 of 12 points (Math 1, Physical Science 1, and Biology 1), went to Mangu High, was best there with 17points MPC, went to UoN, got 1st class honors in Architecture, went to Britain for Masters and PhD. He is now teaching at UoN architecture department. He is from Uyoma. This is just but an introduction.

3.2.3.2: Dr John Ong'ech sterling record in Usenge, 1984

On 13th July, 2021, at 18:45 hrs, Dr Ong'ech O J shared a very inspiring record of his Kenya Certificate of Education (KCE) results for his class 1984. In these results, the following are revealed in the 1984 KCE Results for Usenge high school 1984 KCE hereby presented. In a class of almost 100 candidates, Dr Ong'ech with 12 points (4,3,1,3,2,3,2), following Philemon Oduor who got 10 points (4,2,3,2,1,2,2) being English, Literature, CRE, Geography, Math, Additional Math, Physical Science (covers both C and Biology. In the Siaya Math contest, Philemon had scored 87%, just 2 marks below Dr Ong'ech. However, they both scored a distinction in the final albeit with Oduor getting a 1 while Dr Odero scores a 2. Either way, these were excellent grades. The first 2 were exceptional.

---

[4] The KCE was a form 4 exam done under the 7-6-3 system, the predecessor of the 8-4-4. The subject grading ranged from the best: Distinction grades 1 and 2; credit grades 3-6; pass grades 7-8, and a fail grade 9.

[5] The KCE grading was based on 'Divisions': 1st Division 1 had points 6-23; 2nd Division had points 24-33; Division 3 had points 34-48; 4th Division had points 49-54. .division 1 of 6 points meant one scored distinction 1 in all considered subjects, with a pass in both Math and a language (English or Kiswahili).

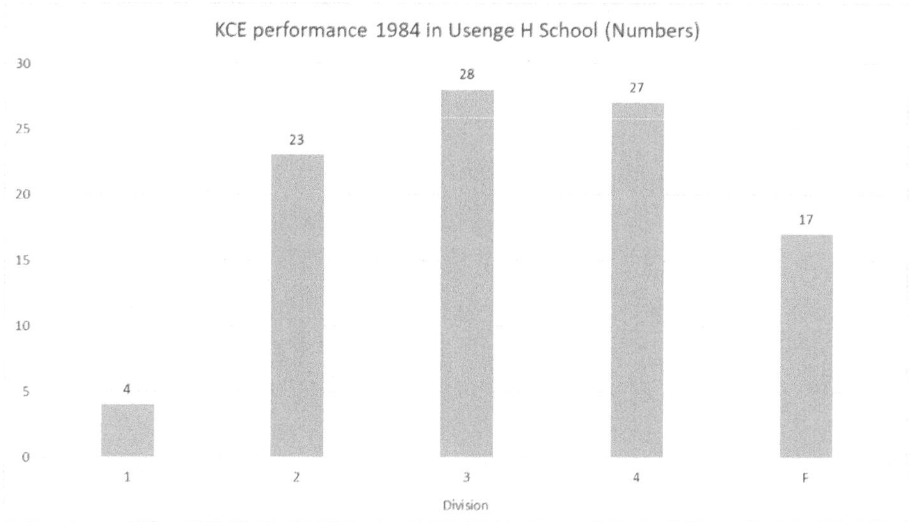

The difference between number 1 and 2 best student grades were statistically insignificant. Whereas Dr John beat Philemon in CRE, the two scored distinctions in Math, additional Math[6] and Biology, while also scoring the same credit 4 in English. The English performance was the best, qualifying them to get 1st division…a condition that affected at least 6 students who because of poor performance in Math or English, could not get a division 1 even though they got points for the same. They scored 16, 18, 19, 20, 21 and 23 points, all within the division 1 range, but unfortunately fell into division 2. This is because of imbalance pass. Whereas Christopher's grade 9 in Math pushed him to division 2, the remaining 5 (Chrispine Odhiambo, Elisha Oluoch Olooh, Peter Oloo Kisinyo [7] (now a professor and dean, Rongo University); Moses Omondi and Pius Otieno Oduol all scored a pass 7-8 in English, disqualifying them from placement in division 1. The KCE studies required intelligence and tact to get the best; not working smart could push

[6] Additional Math was an extension of the normal Math subject, offered in schools (and students) which generally had a good numerical literacy grounding. Its syllabus was largely introductory material to the Form 5 and 6 Math syllabus.

[7] Pater Oloo Kisinyo, now a professor and Dean in Soil Science in Rongo University (Migori), was later to become a classmate of Prof Augustine Afullo in Kabete Campus of the University of Nairobi in 1987-1990 double intake class.

one very far. Its Dr Ong'ech and Philemon Oduor who scored the best aggregate points, 12 and 10 respectively, beating their number 3 (who scored 19 points though still in division 1) by 7 points. Across the board, the two worked smart, getting a clear advantage over the rest by capitalizing on Math, additional Math and Biology. Philemon only escaped at the top through a slight edge in Literature, geography and Physical science. No doubt the two remain the top performers in the school in the entire KCE life. It's no surprise that each excelled in respective fields, with Philemon becoming a top Orthopedic Surgeon at KNH., while John Odero became a top medical specialist in Gynaecology and Obstetrics at KNH and a respected medic Nationally, to the point of being appointed the Chief Executive Officer (CEO) of the top referral and teaching hospital in the whole East and Central Africa.

On the whole, the 4 division 1's scored 10, 12, 19 and 21 points; 23 division 2's got 16, 18, 19, 20, 21, 23, 25, 26 (2), 27 (2), 28 (2), 29, 30(2), 31(2) and 32 points; the division 3's scored 33, 34 (5), 35 (4), 36 (2), 37, 39, 40 (2), 41 (4), 42, 43 92) and 44 (3) points. 27 candidates had division 4, while 17 scored an X (ungraded due to various reason, the most common reason being lack of a grade in key / mandatory subject). It was indeed a class to reckon with.

Table: Academic performance among the top 60 candidates on page 1 of the KCE 1984 results for Usenge high school.

	Distinction 1-2	Credit 3-4	Credit 5-6	Pass 7-8
Eng	0	3	14	27
Lit	3	3	15	20
CRE	5	31	11	4
Hist	6	21	13	3
Geo	2	7	25	11
Math	5	6	7	16
Add Math	3	3	3	2
Phys Sc	1	5	6	6
Bio	5	11	20	15

It is these results that earned Dr Ong'ech a form 5 and 6 chance in Kericho High school in 1985-6, scoring highly and qualifying for admission into the University of Nairobi's faculty of medicine. The performance was: Math A,

Chemistry B, Biology C and a credit 5 pass in general paper- totaling 16 points in KACE. This excellent pass was not an accident; it had a history and was actually coming.

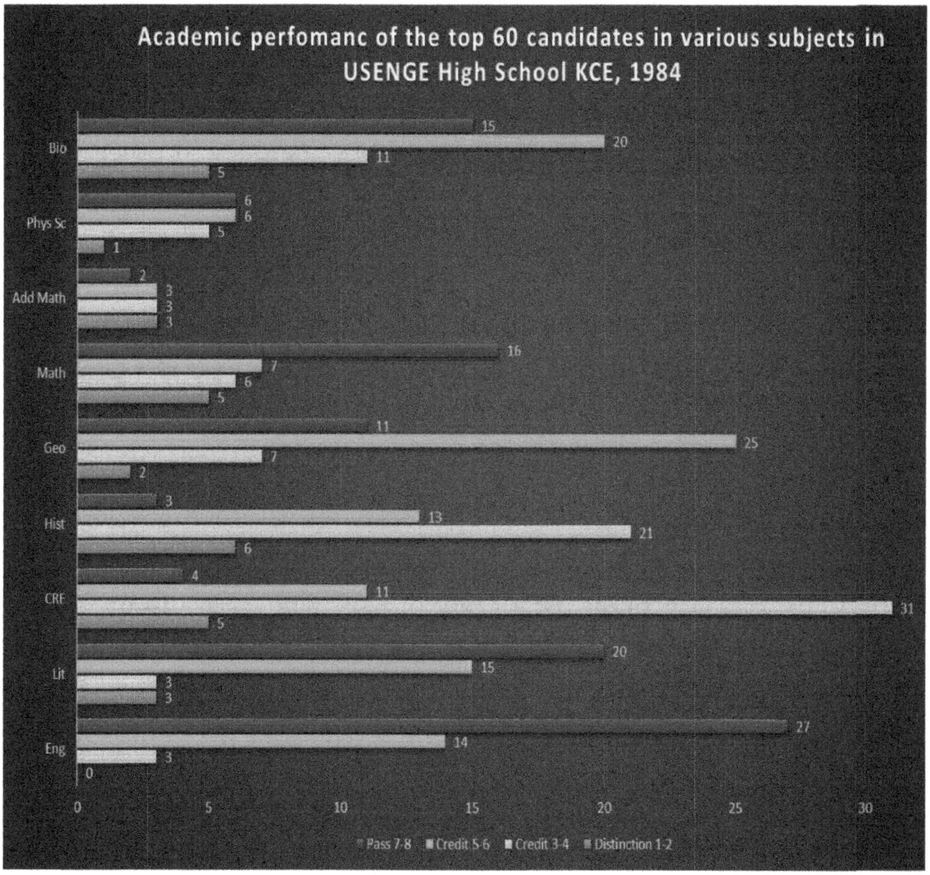

3.3: Advanced level Education in Kericho High School

Any way we moved on to Advanced level (A' Level), then in Kenya coveted forms 5 and 6. While I qualified to join any school including Alliance High School which was Prestigious at that time, I chose to join Kericho High School. Those days a candidate's school choices were followed strictly. In my case, two factors influenced my choice of Kericho High School. First, Alex Kirui, who was ahead of me at Usenge High, had joined there the previous year and was full of praises for the school. The second factor was that schools in the then Rift Valley Province during President Moi era were performing well in exams.

So I joined Kericho High School for my form 5 in 1985 and left in 1986 after completing form 6. My form 5 school fees was paid by Brother Ogola Ong'ech while form 6 school fees was paid by my brother Ochieng Ong'ech. I must comment here that my school fees from form 1 to 6 was always paid promptly and I was never sent home for school fees. The commitment of my father, sisters (Margaret and Mary) and my brothers Ochieng Ong'ech and Ogola Ong'ech was commendable. Mwalimu Ochieng Ong'ech provided overall leadership in this and had the lions share.

So when I joined Kericho High School, I quickly realized that the school had good learning atmosphere. There was good infrastructure, many teachers, good discipline and a well-balanced diet. Food was available even though in small portions. I was top of the list for the students who were admitted there for A -level and everyone wanted to associate with me from O-level to A-level. I enjoyed the popularity. Alexander Kirui (Usenge High School Alumni) oriented me well and supported me. The weather was very cold most of the time, making us shower irregularly. But we had water, good toilets, electricity and good dormitories. My dormitory, Tengecha 2, was the newest.

I met good friends there like Moris Omollo Makobong'o, Vincent Okoth Ong'ore, Benson Ochieng Singa, Sylus Chuchu and worthy competitors Benard Odhiambo Odoyo and Wyclife Owino. From Usenge High School, I was with my village mate Elisha Oluoch Kalooh. Life in Kericho High school was very orderly. It was mostly academics. I excelled in science congress, scooped 1st position for "A" Level Biology exhibition in Rift Valley Province in 1985 (while in form 5) and in 1986 (while in form 6). In both case I represented Rift Valley Province in Nairobi at the National Science Congress held at Kenya Science College. This was the first time I ever stepped into Nairobi. We were always with my buddy Elisha Oluoch Kalooh (late). I later realized that my friend, age-mate and editor of this book, Prof Augustine Afullo who was then doing his A-Level in St Pauls' Amukura (Western Province), same MCB Combination, had also been at the 1985 national science congress, presenting an A' Level Maths talk-Linear programming. He emerged position 2 and was awarded a present and a certificate. Back to Life in Kericho.

3.3.1 An exceptional performance in Kericho high school

In class I excelled well and the competition between Benard Odhiambo Odoyo (who emerged the best in KACE with 18 points), Wyclife Owino (emerged No. 2 in KACE with 17points) and myself (No. 3 in KACE with 16 points) was real. Maximum points one could get in KACE was 19points. The best results in Kenya for the subjects I was doing (Maths, Chemistry, Biology) in KACE in 1986 was 18 points. At the end of the day our school did well and we were No. 11 Nationally with over 110 students qualifying for the university. Generally, my form 6 performance (KACE) in 1986 was excellent and I ranked in the top 100 nationally. Six of us from Kericho High School joined the medical school namely: Benard Odhiambo Odoyo, Wycliffe Owino, John Odero Ong'ech, Elisha Kalooh, Benson Ochieng Singa, Obangi. Wycliffe Owino studied Pharmacy and the 5 of us Bachelor of Medicine and Surgery. This was a record as the previous class, only one student joined medical school from Kericho High School. Those days, there was only one medical school, The University of Nairobi.

1986: Kericho high school, form 6

3.4 Admission to the Medical School, University of Nairobi

It was prestigious to be admitted to the only Medical School in Kenya at the University of Nairobi (UoN) during my time. So when my name appeared in all the national newspapers that I was among the 90 students admitted to study Bachelor of medicine and Bachelor of surgery at the UoN in 1987, it was all excitement and celebrations. My family, friends and relatives were excited. The names appeared in the newspaper in order of merit, and clearly I was among the top 20. I had been among the top 100 nationally in A' Level performance, covering both Arts and Science combinations. Among the science candidates, I could easily have been among the top 30 nationally.

So in June 1987, I reported to the medical school at the University of Nairobi (UoN). As I mentioned earlier, we were 5 from Kericho High school. Here at Medical school, all the academic giants met from all the top performing schools in Kenya. The Highest number was from Alliance Boys High school with 17, followed by Mangu High school with 14. At the medical school reading was hard. Human Anatomy with Cadavers was something else. I remember we were housed in Chiromo Campus and the top KACE performers who scored 16 points and above were all housed one in Block A 3rd floor. I belonged to this group. Guys here were too serious with books with no social life. Anyway I quickly adjusted and settled down to focus and read. I had to cut links with my friends in other faculties who were always partying. Many people could not withstand the pressure and they either changed faculty or drooped off. My own good friend from Majengo primary school, Usenge High School and Kericho High (longest school mate in my life) late Elisha Oluoch Kalooh was among the first causalities to change faculty. This shock did not discriminate which school one came from, for some of the top students who came from top schools like Alliance, Mangu etc. were not spared either; they also either dropped off or changed faculty. I pulled through and passed first year. This gave me confidence and psychological momentum which helped me in the subsequent years. People used to read the whole night, putting cold water in their foot. At the medical school, all one wanted was to get 50% mark in all subjects offered and proceed to the next year of study. It was a most challenging task achieving this since any question with wrong answers one was given negative marks…meaning if you gain 2 marks in a question and miss another of 2 marks, these would balance to a net mark of zero. In second year, during the end year exams I read Biochemistry the whole night, I almost missed the exams when I dosed off in the morning (some people actually missed the exams due to this) but a friend knocked my door and saved me.

At the end of our first semester in 1st year, we were required to go to Gilgil for a Pre-University National Youth Service (NYS,) program. As a pre-university program, people used to go before they were admitted to the university. However, things changed a little in our year. My 1986 A' Level class having been a double intake class with the 1985 A' Level cohort, the latter joined the NYS in February - May 1987 before our A' Level results came out. Come June 1987, our Form 6 results had come out and both cohorts joined the University, giving the 1986 class no time to attend the NYS program. Since it was a mandatory national pre-university program, all had to go, except under special circumstances. In my case, Dr. Hayanga GT saved me from this by writing for me an exemption letter. This was recognized as it was a professional letter written by a competent authority. Going by what we had heard from our predecessors, Life at the National Youth Service was tough, with a lot of horror stories on how people were treated.

Back to the medical school. Medical school life was tough, required disciplined, focus and hard work. Yet it was also a place to make new friends and network, and I met many friends who are still my close buddies to date. As I said earlier, we reconnected there with my Usenge High School classmate and Competitor, Dr. Philemon Owino Oduor and we became best friends to date. People like Dr. Edwin Otieno the surgeon have remained true friends to date. It was a tough, tough tortuous life in medical school and something had to keep one going. For me, I was **following the dreams of my father**....and i could not afford to let the ball fall. This spirit made me keep my eyes on the ball throughout.

1987: 20 year old UoN Medical student; 1st year

1987: 20 year old first year, UoN Medical; school

3.5 Behold, a new doctor and gynaecologist is born!

However long the night is, the day is sure to come…the saying goes. I successfully finished my medical school training in 1993 and was posted for Internship at new Nyanza provincial hospital in Kisumu. I worked there in 1994 and 1995. I soon relocated back to Nairobi and joined Kenyatta National Hospital (KNH). I went back for my post graduate studies in 1999 at the University of Nairobi Sponsored by KNH. I finished my Masters in Medicine, obstetrics and Gynaecology in 2003. I enjoyed my postgraduate studies better than my undergraduate. I even excelled well and was on top of my class. Two people influenced my decision to study masters in Gynaecology & Obstetrics. First it was my first mentor, +Dr Hayanga GT who I used to stay with during my holidays at Machakos when I was in medical school. He exposed to me to the practice of Obstetrics & Gynaecology right from 1st year. I would assist him during his surgeries. The second person was Dr. Badia Willis. He was a seasoned Gynaecologist who had a lot of confidence in me. When I was in 4th year Medical School during elective term, he assigned me his Hospital called Mt. Sinai Hospital in Bondo to be in charge. It was a nursing home but dealing mostly with obstetrics & Gynaecology cases.

3.6 The Hubert Humphreys grant and the Tulane University studies

In between my master's program I got full bright Scholarship to study Public Health (International Health) at Tulane University in USA. Mr Odinge Odera (late) was the one who introduced me to the USA Embassy. I went through a competitive selection process for the full bright (Hubert Humphrey Fellowship) program. An oral interview and a detailed concept write up. The final selection was done in Washington DC, USA by the Institute of International Education. We were only 2 Kenyans who got the Scholarship in 2001. So in June 2001, I left for my studies in Tulane University, New Orleans, Louisiana State, USA. This was a prestigious scholarship and everything was well organized. There was a program Co-coordinator called Penny Jessop that organized everything for us. We were from Different countries (from all over the World), with diverse culture and interest. Pick up from the airport was well organized and the accommodation well arranged. I was accommodated in the campus in a 2-bedroom apartment that we shared with Logan Ndahiro from Rwanda. The next day, we were taken to the bank, opened accounts and our allowances deposited immediately. It was enough for upkeep and buying books. Our program coordinator gave us enough orientation and support. This ranged from food, culture, social life, education etc.

I settled very quickly and started participating in the program. It involved taking academic course in Public Health (International Health) at the university besides professional networking. I enjoyed the academic work especially Biostatistics, Epidemiology, Monitoring and evaluation courses. I was actually on top of my class in Biostatistics with many American Students coming for help. Compared with Kenya, I learnt that American Education is very practical. The Education involved a lot of group work, assignments and research. It was not just end of year exams centred like was at UoN. The continuous assessments, group work and assignments constituted 70% of the total marks. The final exams was only 30%. There was no pressure during end of semester/year exams like UoN. At the end of the training I really felt properly educated. The way I was taught monitoring and evaluation, was so good that up to date I do not need to refresh it in mind, it is part of me. Most lectures used books they had authored to teach and research papers they had published to teach research. They were true authorities in what they taught us. Lecturers had to write research grants to pay their salaries with university only giving 30% retainer. Lecturers teaching contracts depended on students' evaluation. One or two lecturers lost their jobs because of poor students' evaluation. I truly appreciate the American system of education especially at the post graduate level. I enjoyed professional networking which were organized by program coordinator Penny Jessop and the assistant Megan. We also had a lot of cultural exchange activities amongst the Hubert Humphrey Fellows and also with the American people. It was truly fulfilling. I did my attachment in Washington DC with Family Health International (FHI) who offered me a job but I decide to come back to Kenya. Some people remained in the USA to work. But this was also against the program rules which required us to come back to our home country for at least two years before going back to USA.

An outstanding achievement for me during my study in USA was being the First Kenyan to win Hubert Humphrey Fellowship Alumni impact award grant. We submitted competitive proposal on what we wanted to do when we come back home. I was among the best 4 that received the funding from Institute of International Education (IIE). This was a global competition. The USA embassy in Kenya later monitored my work when I was back in Kenya and awarded me alumni of the month recognition (see USA embassy Publication on Alumni of the month featuring me).

As I pen off on my experience in studying in the USA, I must say that I missed home and family dearly. I experienced some culture shock and there were some things like Lesbian and Gays clubs which were official in the campus that truly shocked me beyond any imaginations. The activities of madigras & beads in New Orleans interesting though. The Jazz Festival was of course fun. Halloween parties were confusing. Thanks giving holiday was great with a lot of Turkey eating. Some silent racism was also shocking. So this education in America changed my world. It created research opportunities and collaborations with the American Universities/ American people that I still enjoy to date. Upon my return, the American embassy which had received good intelligence report about me during my stay in the USA, invited me to be participating in the interviews for scholarships for Hubert Humphrey Fellowship. They also invite me to celebrate Americans important holidays like the Independence Day etc. at the Ambassador's residence. These recognitions has made my family also get USA Visas easily to travel to USA.

I have also recommended many people to the USA embassy that have been awarded scholarships or exchange program grants like Prof. Augustine Afulo, (Author of my Auto biography), Elly Gordon Ogutu from Yimbo Nyamonye who attended Emory University, Prof. Omondi Oyoo (Tulane University), Dr. Violet Okech (Johns Hopkins University), Dr. Ndege (Johns Hopkins University), Dr. Ndirangu (Emory University) etc.

Long live the American tax payers that funded my study in USA and opened the world to me for Global recognition

3.7 Life in Primary School (Majengo)-Tributes

3.7.1 Fanuel Ogot Anam: My life and times with Dr. Ongech

It is a fine Friday afternoon as I sit on my editing bench to finalize a video documentary that I had been working on for the past two weeks. The afternoon sun steaks across the room bringing with it the joy of sunlight that

I rarely get in our tiny office based at the far end of the corridor in a building along Kenyatta Avenue in Nairobi.

As I pull the office chair towards the window to enjoy the sunlight and get a bit of vitamin D, it hits me that I have another pending story to work on, but this time round on reproductive health. I need to get a few facts right from the expert so I reach for my phone and strike a conversation with Dr. Ong'ech, my friend since childhood. After exchanging a few pleasantries, we go straight to the point and discuss the matter. It is then that we go back down memory lane.

"I want my autobiography done titled IN THE DREAMS OF MY FATHER" said Dr. Ong'ech. At this point, I'm getting a bit over-excited. 'There is no way your autobiography can be done without me sharing our childhood experience", I said.

Majengo primary school is located along Bondo-Usenge road. It is blessed with a good playing pitch, so most of the surrounding schools' sporting activities used to be hosted here. This is the school that Dr. Ong'ech and I attended. The children of those days were literally made of steel. I find it hard to classify the financial standing of the surrounding villages and its occupants then but I may not be wrong to say that we were from a poor background. You will agree with me if I said the children of the then years were made of steel because of the following reasons:

i. It was not uncommon to find one walking for a distance of five kilometers or more before they could get to the nearest school.
ii. The same distance would be travelled on foot to get to the lake, the only source of clean water otherwise you would be forced to drink muddy waters from the nearby ponds, especially during those rainy days, never to mind the tadpoles or mosquito larvae that were frequent residents of such waters.

iii. Most pupils, especially the females, used to double as parents as they were the ones to fetch water and firewood after school, grind millet mixed with dried cassava to make flour for dinner(only legends will understand what I'm talking about). This was so because the parents were always out there trying to secure food for their families in any small way they could, either by selling small wares at the market place, offering menial labour in peoples' farms for a small payment, mostly in terms of commodities like maize, millet, beans and the likes. The boys were tasked majorly with taking care of the livestock after school. Girl child education was unheard of in this part of the world and so it was okay for them to double both as children and caretakers of the rest of the family in times of need.

As children growing up in the village, we went through good times and bad times in equal measure. We had a lot of time to play in the dusty fields within the school compound and outside as long as you were not caught by an elderly person who would administer instant disciplinary measures on you for playing when you are supposed to be doing something more meaningful. School uniform was just a pair of shorts and a single shirt which was to be washed over the weekends and sometimes you would go to school on Mondays while they were still wet and you would put it on for the rest of the week. The case was the same with girls as well.

Wearing shoes was such a big luxury and would be such an offence, in most cases attracting a punishment for the wearer. This means every pupil was to go to school barefooted exposing learners to dangers like jiggers, being pricked by thorns, wounding your feet by accidentally hitting a stone or any hard objects. This is the kind of environment that Dr. John Odero Ong'ech and I studied during our primary school days. Daktari (as we fondly call him) also had his fair share of ups and downs. He was one of those pupils who was coming from the farthest point from school, over 3 kilometers. He was the smallest person in body size in our class. In Majengo primary school, it was then a tradition that a bell ringer is picked from a suitable pupil in class six. Despite his small body size and distance from home, the school administration and in particular the headmaster, one Mr. George Oriaro Obalo saw it wise to appoint him as the bell ringer. The school used to own a clock which was always in custody of the bell ringer but some cheeky boys would wind the clock to suit their sinister schemes in the absence of the custodian so the clock used to be faulty in most instances. At some point the clock could not function so the headmaster offered the bell ringer his wrist watch to use for time keeping purposes. This was to become a big challenge as the size of bell ringer's hand was tiny and could not fit in the watch. This made Daktari to always raise his hand up in a manner that the current generation would call swag otherwise it wasn't going to hold in his hand.

To say that children of then were made of steel may be an understatement. I still vividly remember one of those sunny afternoons when we were returning to school from lunch and it was just a few minutes to 2.00pm. On this day, Daktari was almost late so he came running very fast. As he was crossing the fence to jump into the compound to ring the bell, he was pricked by an acacia thorn that pierced through the middle of one of his toes and got stuck midway. It was such a terrifying experience and for a moment, we didn't know what to do under the prevailing circumstances. We then gained courage and pulled out the thorn from his toe, took a piece of cloth and tied the wound to stop bleeding. Perhaps this experience made him think about pursuing a medical course, not sure about that.

Class Work

Daktari was a top brain and always topped our class, a feat he kept repeating for almost the entire period of our primary and secondary education. He used to top in almost all the subjects and this made him a darling to many teachers. As much as we were friends, there were times when I felt he contributed to the number of strokes I used to get especially during Mathematics lessons. Sometimes we could have double lessons of mathematics running to break time at 10.00am and then followed by physical education (PE) and as fate would have it, Mr. Paul Awino Abonyo was in charge of both Mathematics and PE. Anybody who was taught Mathematics by this teacher and managed to attend his combined double lessons without faking illness and going to the dispensary is a hero of our times. Mr. Awino would combine the double lessons plus the time for break and finally with the PE time, a mathematics marathon. He would write a sum on the black board and give people two minutes to calculate and get the answer after which everybody stopped and stood up, then he would go around marking and the only people who got a tick would sit down. The rest would remain standing waiting for the stroke to be administered.

Alternatively, he would instruct the first person to finish to command everyone to stop writing, put pens down and stand up. For this reason, I sometimes thought Daktari was willingly contributing to the suffering for the not so fast majority.He was very quick with sums and before you even started figuring out the formula, he would have finished his calculations and would shout the infamous word 'stop'. The danger here was that for every sum failed, you would receive two strokes of cane on the back of your trunk, not forgetting we never used to wear vests. As much as I and a few other pupils were good in mathematics, we used to get more than our fair share of the strokes for we were always stopped before reaching the final answer, courtesy of Dr. Ongech. It is during this subject that pupils used to look for lame excuses to absent themselves from class especially during the double lessons.

As friends, we used to share a desk. There were occasions when we used to share some pleasantries oblivious of what transpired around us. Sometimes we even forgot that the teacher was in class and a lesson was in progress. It was one of such moments when we got engrossed in a deep chat during a Geography lesson. The teacher, Mr. Otieno Ogutu, noticed what was going on. Those teachers were not very kind to disobedient pupils and he immediately descended on us with all manner of weapons within his reach. It was an experience that even Daktari himself is not likely to forget in the near future.

In the year 1980 as we were preparing for our CPE on a mid-Saturday morning, an old lorry with a cage like truck drove into the school compound. The sight of that truck could make children in the village scamper for safety for mistaking it to belong to the fiery 'Kachinja'. Myths had it that these were highly dangerous people who could sack your blood dry and leave you for dead. As the truck roared to a stop in the middle of the football pitch, we saw students in games kits jumping superciliously from the truck and moving randomly around the school compound, some of them heading towards classrooms especially class seven which was the only one with pupils as it was on a weekend and the rest of the pupils were at home.

This was Maranda high school boys' truck and the occupants were the school football team. They were on a mission to play football with their arch rival Usenge high school. Because of the rivalry, a middle ground for playing this match was none other than Majengo primary owing to its good quality football pitch and the fact that it was a neutral ground. As the senior boys moved randomly around the compound, some walked straight into the classroom where our studies were ongoing. As Daktari was the smallest in body size, they started making mockery comments by asking why a child of his age was in class seven and if he would ever go to form one. Though they were a bit boisterous, they became more accommodative when they realized how serious we were.

Usenge boys' football team arrived around 3.00 p.m. The match started after a brief standoff as there was a disagreement on which team to start on which side of the pitch. By the time the final whistle was blown after 90 minutes of play plus injury time, the score line was 7-0 in favour of Maranda high school. A few months after this encounter, we were in an examination room sitting for our CPE The following year, both of us would be heading to Usenge high school to join form one.

Secondary Education in the eyes of a classmate

The year 1981 was a year like no other in our education journey as it is the year we joined form one at Usenge high school. We got introduced to a no nonsense principal in the name of Paul Warom Owele aka Owadgi Leah. Both of us plus a few more pupils from Majengo were admitted at the school. Bullying by senior students was a very common occurrence. At the mention of form one, it made one shiver and sweat under the armpits. Fortunately enough for us, we joined when the entire school had been sent home for engaging in a strike so all of us were new to the school and nobody had an upper hand over the other. By the time the rest of the school were called back from strike, we had already gained some confidence and apart from that, Owadgi Leah had issued a strong warning to the senior students never to lay a hand on form ones and anybody who defied such an order would meet the full wrath of the principal, so nobody dared to transgress.

Learning then started on a serious note and by the end of the term, John Odero Ong'ech went ahead to prove to all who cared that he was an academic giant and was to be ignored at one's own peril. He became a force to reckon with especially in science subjects, mathematics included. He actually became a favorite student for physics teacher, one Mr. Vincent Odhiambo aka Stingo. When time came for Annual National Science Congress, held in Maseno high school, John and I would come together with a project on electricity generation which would look into the possibility of using the power from a generator to run the same generator instead of fossil fuel. At this point, we were in form two and had wild ideas running in our heads.

When we joined form one, it is like the person charged with allocating the rooms knew how close we were and we were allocated the same dormitory, Mboya II. Once in a while, fruits would be served after lunch and on this particular day, it was brought in the absence of the house captain so the students who were around the table on their way out for afternoon studies saw the opportunity and tried to grab as much as they could. A scuffle then ensued and the entire place was in a total mess. As this was happening, the commotion attracted the attention of the deputy principal, Mr. Ndolo. He rushed fuming into the dormitory and found a few students still inside, amongst them the dorm captain. At this point, the rest of the students disappeared as the he demanded to know who did the mess. Sensing danger, the captain looked around and the only two people remaining were John and I. He conveniently pointed at us and we were both summoned to the office to have an encounter with 'Nyanam', a special whip used for disciplining students. 'Nyanam' was only meant to be used by Owadgi Leah but in his absence, the deputy would also steal it and imitate the principal. As innocent as we were, we received our share of the stroke and life continued.

The story of Dr. John Oder Ongech needs a lot of time and space to be told and this forum may not offer enough opportunity. The work of an editor is to cut the long story short so I would like to conclude by saying that Dr. Ongech right from school was a top performer and still is, in his professional practice. He is man of stature, unquestionable integrity, international recognition, kind and considerate, giving back to the society in many ways. One only needs to see his contribution to Usenge high school as the patron of alumni association to understand the magnitude of his inputs.

May his flag keep flying high, his light shining bright for those in darkness to see.

Long live Ajuoga!

By Fanuel Anam

3.7.2: Secondary School life in Usenge from the eyes of classmate Omondi Owiti: Only One Mission at Majengo and Usenge Schools

About our lives at Majengo primary and Usenge Boys High school, I wish to be as crisp and brief as possible. John, I know you know like you do the back of your hand that in telling this story, saying something about life in our families is inescapable. For our success in the two schools was certainly a result of the inspiration we got from it. With meagre incomes, our families had similar financial limitations that manifested in a number of ways. Parents and children, alike, had to do something to have some food on the table, buy school uniforms, fountain pens, ink and any other necessary things. Children went to school in the same uniforms, unwashed, for five days a week, and barefoot. Brother Mary, do you still remember that afternoon when, rushing back to school, you stepped on a thorn that pierced through one of your toes? One could repeat a class or even drop out of a secondary school for other siblings to carry on with their education. A host of other such limitations beset our families and, naturally, one would think that children from such families would rarely make it from primary to secondary schools.

We went to Majengo primary school which, in all respects of a school, would not be a good school for the children of the rich and, therefore, existed merely because the poor were the majority. Here, one was not only a learner but a laborer as well. In addition to the home chores such as digging in the family farm or fetching water very early in the morning, and going to school without taking even a small calabash of uji, one had to work on the school fence, sweep the classroom, wash the toilet, slash the grass, work in the school farm and, if one was a girl, fetch water for teachers resident in the school compound.

We were already inured to hardships and the ones at Majengo did not, in the least discourage us. Besides, on the other side of the coin, this school had a number of strengths worth exploiting. Let me mention just a few of them. The classrooms had roofs. There were books. There were good teachers, among them being Mr. George Solomon Obalo, our last headteacher there. With our purpose, being able, someday, to improve the living conditions in our families, and inspiration from our poor family backgrounds, our preoccupation, from this early, was with passing the national examinations from primary through secondary and high schools to university. And doing so by dint of diligence in our studies. We passed the Certificate of Primary Education Examinations in 1980. The following year, 1981, we were admitted in Form One West, a government stream, at Usenge Boys High School. From the foregoing, there is no gainsaying that we were long-term strategists and, therefore, at Usenge ours was business as usual. After all, with our home and Majengo backgrounds, we were now even more inured to hardships than ever before. There, we had no time to see the little and badly cooked ugali or beans or kales or cabbages or uji or 'nyoyo'. Instead, we had time to see the advantages of boarding there, and the availability of books, good teachers and a smart head teacher, the late Mr. Warom Owele. We grabbed this opportunity and studied harder than ever before, passed the Kenya Certificate of Education Examinations in 1984 and were admitted in High schools in 1985. This is how we have come to be a far cry from what we were initially. And from the whole experience, allow me to make the following conclusions.

One, a hunter who tracks, locates and then gives the quarry a serious chase will certainly bring it down.

Two, the bee is wiser than the fly. Both visit the filthy latrine but only the former comes out with something good.

Three, we must forever be grateful to our parents, dead or still alive.

Finally, we must forever be grateful to God, the GIVER of everything good.

James Omondi Owiti.

3.7.3: Usenge and University of Nairobi life in the eyes of a classmate: Dr Philemon Oduor

Dr John Odero Ong'ech: Chief Medical Specialist, Obstetrician/ Gynaecologist, reproductive health and research specialist based in Nairobi, Kenya.

Usenge High School (U.H.S): I met Dr. Odero Ong'ech in the year 1981, when we both got enrolled in form one and placed in the same stream, Form one west, after successfully completing Primary Education in different schools, where we both achieved very high grades and could have as well been admitted to any high school, had we applied for the same. I later learnt from him that he, and his parents, just like in my case, selected the school prior to sitting for the Certificate of Primary Education (C.P.E) after considering the cost implication of secondary education, and the then fair school performance at Usenge High School (U.H.S) then. We immediately became close friends, shared a lot of common experiences in our earlier lives, studied together, did chores together though we stayed in different dormitories. This school contributed a lot to the education trajectory that Dr. J.O Ong'ech took.

As a routine by the then head teacher/principal Mr. Warom (owad gi Leah), he personally participated in induction of all form one students. The first week in the school was dedicated to introduction to the U.H.S rules and regulations. I can remember us sitting in a class with Mr. Warom pacing up and down carrying the tools of discipline on his hands and stressing that they were always ready for use. The first tool was Nyanam, a hippo hide whip whose indications he stated clearly. The second was Nyar-Ngiya, a huge wooden club with a rounded head (rungu) which he explained is used in serious cases of discipline. He stressed that we would see the practicality of discipline when the higher classes we reported while away due to indiscipline cases report back, to see for ourselves how not to behave in his school.

The second session involved what he called practical learning. He clearly stated that there are good reasons why a school, or any institution of learning should not have all amenities and food. It was to make students always be reminded that life is about hard work and to always wish they had more. The third thing he stressed is that at U.H.S, we are not coached to pass exams but to be successful in our future lives, and hence the balance between reading, resting, sleep and work must be observed stringently. In his school, no reading will be allowed during games time and beyond 9.00 pm, in line with these rules. We settled and started the routines:

1. Wake up time- 6.00 am
2. Classes start at 7.00am
3. Classes end at 1.30 pm
4. From 2.30pm – 4.00pm- Self-studies by students
5. 4pm to 5pm games time
6. 5pm to 6pm- students go for bathing and water collection from the lake, came back carrying water for use in the morning and pieces of firewood for the kitchen.
7. 7.00 pm- 9.15- student prep-self studies
8. 9.30 pm- all lights must be off and each student on bed in respective dormitories.

Mr. Warom would personally supervise the above, and once in a while even cross the fence to the primary school section to check for defaulters to the rule.

U.H.S Incident to Remember: One evening, being thirsty to get more study time, Dr. Ong'ech, two other students and I decided to have a group discussion past 9.30pm and knowing that the U.H.S compound was unsafe for such an adventure, we crossed over to the primary section, just across a porous fence, light some kerosene candle and started our studies and discussion. Few minutes later, a loud knock on the door and a roar of "open this door, I can see you all "split across the classroom. We all froze. It was the disciplinarian Mr. Warom who spotted light through the roof vents from across and talked after peeping through the spaces on the door. Our first discipline with Nyanam was delivered there and then and we were warned never to try again.

Mr. Warom sat us down after the corporal punishment and told us it's a good thing we are starting a study group early in form one, but we are doing it at the wrong time and hence a form of indiscipline. He advised we continue but at designated time. He stressed we got a lesser "discipline" measure just because of that observation. The four of us, under the devotion and discipline from Dr. Ong'ech continued with this group discussion to the end of our four year stay at U.H.S. During this period, the class of 1984 at U.H.S outperformed all the schools in the District and most of the schools in the former Nyanza Province. Our Kenya certificate of Education (K.C.E) results were a masterpiece, and from the same class stream i.e. four west, three of us proceeded to be admitted to the University of Nairobi School of medicine to study Bachelors of Medicine and Surgery, out of a class of 90 students nationwide.

Advanced Level Education: After passing our form four (KCE) examinations in the year 1984, we were admitted in 1985 to different A-Level schools. Dr.

Ong'ech to Kericho High School, and I to Njiri School. We continued exchanging learning materials from different institutions, especially past papers as we took same subject combinations i.e. Mathematics, Chemistry and Biology. We both passed with all distinctions in the 1986, Kenya Advanced Certificate of Education (K.A.C.E) exams and reconverged in medical school to pursue the bachelors degree in Medicine and Surgery.

University Of Nairobi: We found ourselves together again; Dr. Ong'ech, the late Elisha Oluoch and myself from Usenge High School in the same first year class at Chiromo campus. Introduction to the rules at the school of medicine was done by the head of anatomy at the time, and we realized the work a head was a different piece of cake. We were taken into the anatomy laboratory, allocated tables with chairs and asked to sit down, each group of student like a round table arrangement. Each table had a white plastic cover with an obvious object underneath. The inductor, the head of anatomy gave a brief talk, said for two years that will be our office, the most important "persons" in the whole lab and throughout the years will be the covered specimens and that they must be treated with utmost respect and confidentiality, and that the same will apply in our practice of medicine throughout our lives.

The plastic covers were then removed, and we were amazed they were human cadavers, and we wondered where they are from. Some students fainted. After a lull, he gave us a talk that these are important people, without whom there would be no modern medicine, that they willingly gave away their bodies and signed legal documents before their passing, to make the basis of medicine and surgery, Human Anatomy possible. A number of students changed courses after this, but those who remained greatly benefited from the two years of dissection, pre-clinical years. In addition to Anatomy, the first 2 years in Chiromo involved study of biochemistry, physiology and Psychiatry. Dr. Ong'ech, myself and a group of other students formed knowledge sharing and discussion group and our pre-clinical years was a success.

The clinical years started in third year of Medical School, when we moved to the Kenyatta National Hospital, school of medicine hostels and we did all the required rotations in Pharmacology and Therapeutics, Medicine, Paediatrics, Surgery and Orthopaedics, Obstetrics and Gynaecology, Community/public health, accident and emergency. Our sound footing in the discipline of life balance, importance of study group etc. that we started from U.H.S made it easy to go through this as a team. We graduated with bachelors degrees in medicine and surgery in the year 1993.

Internship: After completion of the bachelors degree we were posted to the Nyanza Provincial General Hospital, currently Jaramogi Oginga Odinga teaching and referral Hospital, where we worked together for one year for practical independent assessment in hands on medical practice prior to registration to practice as doctors. We completed this attachment together successfully.

General Medical Practice: We had a short stint of general medical practice in Kisumu together with Dr. Ong'ech before we temporarily went to different stations. Dr. Ong'ech to Kenyatta National Hospital and myself to Kisumu District Hospital before reconverging again at KNH in the year 1997, when Dr. Ong'ech facilitated my transfer to the said institution to join him, and as he explained it was better for professional development. Since he was already established in Nairobi, Dr. Ong'ech was very instrumental in ensuring my easy of integration into the practice at Kenayatta National Hospital and in getting part time jobs in private institutions to boost my income. We worked together in Kenyatta National Hospital accident and emergency department, comprehensive medical services, Canaan Medical Centre etc.

Post Graduate and Specialization: As we worked in the above named places, it became clear to me that Dr. Ong'ech heart was in research and reproductive health. This is an area he enjoyed and excelled in even during the general medical practice. It is no wonder then that he opted to pursue a course in reproductive health at the University of Nairobi and followed with a research based subspecialisation abroad and other many aligned courses that has propelled him to be a leading specialist in this line of practice.

Administration/ Practice in Speciality: Dr. Ong'ech has been an astute administrator with strict financial discipline in public expenditure. This potential has been adequately tapped and has benefited the Kenyatta National Hospital as in all the areas he has been given the mandate to lead, people have realized positive change. He worked as the head of department of reproductive health (Obstetrics & Gynaecology), head of surgical services division and was then earmarked to be the CEO of Kenyatta National Hospital, which he politely declined in principle. He decided to take early retirement thereafter and he is running a very successful private practice. Indeed, the doctrine of discipline and balance has been vindicated.

Social and Family Life: Since our time at Usenge High School, we have remained very good and close friends out of work. While we were still studying and staying in the village, we could make turns visiting one another in our parents' village homes, cycling a distance of sixty kilometres with easy and we could spend days either way together, socializing with respective families and discussing. Our two extended parental families became like one big family. When it came to marriage, each one of us played the role of first man/Grooms man for the other in turns. In Dr. Ong'ech, I found a trusted friend who I can always lean on for advice and help.

Dr. Philemon Amos Owino Oduor
Senior Consultant, Orthopaedic Surgeon/ Upper limb Specialist
Kenyatta National Hospital

3.7.4: Kericho HS and UoN life in the eyes of a classmate:

Dr Benard Odoyo Odhiambo

My name is Dr Benard Odoyo Odhiambo, from Awendo Sub County in Migori County. I knew Dr John Odero Ongech in 1985 February when we joined Kericho High school in Form five. Dr Ongech had come from Usenge High school in Siaya County where he had completed his form Four and passed his O-level exams well with a strong Division one. I was joining the same school from Ringa secondary school in former south nyanza, but currently Homa Bay County where I had also passed my O-level exams. Since we were both admitted in the same class stream doing Maths ,Chemistry and Biology (MCB class) , we interacted literally every day in most places of the school except in the dormitory where Dr Ongech was domiciled in Tengecha while I was in Boyles.

Dr Ongech struck me from the time we met instantly as a very intelligent witty young boy (of course we were all young boys then). He was very outgoing, sociable and thorough in all our combination subjects especially Mathematics. In fact when we started learning, dr Ongech used to teach us the form five Mathematics which was then modelled in books called KAMPS (Kenya advanced math's Projects) 1, 2 and 3. The A-level foundation in Maths was very hard to some of us and its dr Ongech who used to give us encouragement. Later I learnt that Dr Ongech"s love for Maths and sciences had started way back in his secondary school where he had done very well in these subjects and even performed in science congress up to national level. He did the same in Kericho High school. Dr Ongech had done the additional

Maths in his O-level syllabus and this was an indication of his love for this subject

Dr Ongech was equally a good orator and debater. He could convincingly win in any arguments intelligently. He used to have intelligent quotes like" monkey Tricks" during conversations that I used find very interesting and stimulating. I would say Dr. Ong'ech was a complete man so to say and this continued throughout his life and because of this completeness we used to call him Mak'Ongech system, a name he has maintained among his close friends up to now. I developed friendship with Dr Ongech during our early days in Kericho high school and this progressed and has been maintained up to now when am writing this manuscript. We were friends discussing academics initially in Kericho and later we became very close such that in form six when we were choosing our University career courses, we ended up choosing Medicine at the University of Nairobi. I remember some of classmates in Kericho during the time were like the late Oluoch Kaloo who had come with Ongech from Usenge high school, Dr. Ong'ore, Dr. Benson Singa, Prof Makobong'o, Mr Okeyo Ogal, Mr Riaga Kennedy who is my village mate and friend up to now, Mr Andrew Buop, and many others.

Luckily enough, we both did our A-level exams in 1986 and passed well and we were admitted to do medicine at the University of Nairobi in 1987 July. Again we were in the same class for the next five years until we qualified as young intern doctors and got posted for internship. Dr Ongech went to Kisumu's New Nyanza provincial General Hospital (currently Jaramogi Oginga Odinga Teaching and Referral Hospital) while I went to Kakamega Provincial General Hospital (currently Kakamega County Referral Hospital) for internship. I remember most of our classmates in Kericho High school including above mentioned did very well and were admitted to different universities to do very good courses including medicine, education, agriculture etc.

During our undergraduate medical school days, life was very good as young men in our formative years and the medical course kept us busy. We were well taken care of by the Government. We were getting " **Boom**[8]", free hostel, food including all the good meals you can imagine. I remember how we used to go to town to do shopping together after getting our boom. It was a life I remember with nostalgia. I recall one time in our second year after getting our boom and passing one of the many CATs we used to do, Dr Ongech, Dr Oduor, Dr Okuthe and I went on a shopping spree and each one of us bought a number of new things plus eye glasses from the streets just to look tough academically. It was a life full of fun. We used to have academic discussion groups where we had new friends including Dr Philemon Oduor, Dr Juma Onyalo, Dr Amoth, Dr Ochiel, Dr Otieno Akula, Dr. Otieno Walter and many more. We grew up and became men while at the medical school and this made us to be who we are now.

Dr Oduor Philemon from Alego happens to have been Dr Ongech's classmate at Usenge High school in O-level, he went to Njiris for his A-level then we met at the Medical school. Since he was Ongech friend, he also became a good friend of mine up to now. This friendship has continued because dr Ongech is a very honest man, very trustworthy, very straight forward and above all very friendly too. And am confident that Daktari and me will be friends the rest of our lives despite us working and living in different towns or locations in Kenya.

I pray that Almighty God to continue giving us and our families good life, Health, blessings and keep us together. Amen.

Dr. Benard Odoyo Odhiambo

[8] Boom was the University students allowance issued per term / semester for Kenyan Public University student upkeep. It was part of a loan automatically offered to students for tution, meals, medical and accommodation, and payable after graduation and getting employment.

Chief Orthopaedic Surgeon, Mombasa County

to Rutgers with experience in teaching English and working with non-profit youth leadership programs in New Jersey, as a project coordinator and long-time volunteer.

TULANE UNIVERSITY

It was a great year! But then we probably say that every year. And we mean it. We were fully engaged in bringing the best possible program to this year's Fellows—and we had fun at the same time. The Fellows were offered unique programs of coursework and professional activities in health care policy and planning, health economics and finance, mental health programs, implementation, monitoring and evaluating health programs, family planning and reproductive health. Fellows also engaged in a full program of "Experience America" activities, which included participation in fund-raising charity walks for HIV/AIDS prevention (where one of our Fellows won a medal, and some of them were just happy to finish the walk!). We also had a year-end retreat in Cajun country, watching swamp creatures and then eating them the next night, dancing to the local music, and learning how refugees lived and prospered over 100 years ago. It is rewarding for us to see the goals and objectives of the HHH program put into action.

Because of continued funding for reproductive health and family planning we were able to offer fellowships allowing two Fellows to complete the MPH. The fellowships were another example of the university's strong commitment to the participants in the Humphrey Program.

Tulane University Fellows

UNIVERSITY OF WASHINGTON

This year's Fellows came to Seattle at a time of global turmoil, when the university and the nation were searching for meaning in the aftermath of the events of September 11th. Our Fellows reached out to the university, to the greater Seattle community, and to each other, building friendships and shared understandings that transcended national borders.

... lectures and speaking events throughout the year. Topics ranged from discussing ... to the business climate in Yemen and

Alumni of the Month

March 2009

A publication of the U. S. Embassy Nairobi

DR. JOHN ONG'ECH

Many of us may not know Dr. John Ong'ech; and even if we do, we may not know him as an alumnus of a U.S. government sponsored program. He's humble, as a visit to his office demonstrates. It's a little office amongst others within the precincts of Kenyatta National Hospital, which would easily go unnoticed. However humble, Dr. John Ong'ech is proud of his exchange program experience. When I ask the doc; "What it was like as a Hubert H. Humphrey (HHH) Fellow in the U. S.?" he instantly has a glow on his face.

"Thanks for uplifting my spirit this morning," quips Dr. Ong'ech, "That was one of my favorite experiences in life… Not only did I have a wonderful time in the U.S., but I was also the first Kenyan recipient of the Hubert H. Humphrey Alumni Impact Award after my program." The award, which provides funding for projects that

Ogam dispensary

will impact an alumnus's country, enabled Dr. Ong'ech to build a dispensary in his home village. "It was for me a way of saying thank you to the community that brought me up and also showing the HHH program that my experience was the entire community's gain." The dispensary has since been taken over by the government and gazetted as a community health center.

A 2001 HHH fellow, Dr. Ong'ech is economical with words about himself, and it takes two visits to his office for me to realize just how active he

Children having their meal on the feeding program

is in the community. An Obstetrician/Gynecologist, Dr. Ong'ech is the head of HIV training and research at Kenyatta National Hospital. With two masters degrees, he is also an honorary lecturer at the University of Nairobi's Obs-Gyn department where he is also the Prevention of Mother to Child Transmission (PMTCT) technical advisor.

The list of Dr. Ong'ech's publications is endless. He has published numerous books and papers on his research findings. A winner of the 2007 Elizabeth Glaser Pediatric Aids Foundation (EGPAF) award, Dr. Ong'ech is also the principal investigator in the Perinatal HIV transmission studies funded by the Bill Gates and EGPAF foundations. He is a member of several professional associations, including the Kenya Country Team, which implements reproductive health best practices in Africa, a WHO initiative. Due to his rare expertise, Dr. Ong'ech is in demand from several local and international organizations. He is currently a consultant with EGPAF (USAID funding), Intra-health (USAID-CDC funding), IPAS, HLFSP (UNICEF funding), AB2000 (US department of state funding) in the area of HIV/AIDS and reproductive health project design, implementation, monitoring and evaluations.

Back in his community, he has initiated various projects for poverty alleviation and HIV/AIDS widows and orphans support. His organization AB2000 provides pediatric care, psychosocial support and counseling for the community through ***Kahoch Widows and Orphans Group***. It also supports an outreach VCT program, provides supplies for early childhood education, and

One of the dairy goats bought for the women's group

bought water tanks for the widows with which they harvest water and sell as an income generating activity. As a food security measure, AB2000 has trained the widows in farming skills and bought them dairy goats.

The orphans have benefited from an AB2000 run feeding program, while the widows have also received bicycles, which the community health workers use for home visits for people living with HIV/AIDS

A community health worker ferries a sick child to hospital using a bicycle provided by AB2000

and taking the sick to hospital. "I do these projects because it makes me happy to help my community," says Ong'ech. "I am glad that my area MP recently saw the benefit and installed electricity at the health center through the rural electrification program." Dr. Ong'ech continues to say that one of his challenges is lack of funding to help this program. "I always have to pump in my own money. For every consultancy payment I get, I spend about 30% on the community projects."

Dr. Ong'ech's is yet another success story from Kenyan state alumni. More on his work with AB2000 is on the net. http://www.ab-2000.org

state alumni

https://www.alumni.state.gov

DR. JOHN ODERO ONG'ECH AUGUST VERSION 2021
Nairobi Reproductive Health Services
Prof Nelson Awori Centre
Next to Nairobi Hospital
Ralph Bunch Road, 3rd Floor Suite,
PO BOX 26617-00504, Nairobi
Office: 0723737315/0706069808; *Cell: 0722282449*
Email: ongechjohn@gmail.com
Website; www.nairobireproductivehealth.org,

BACKGROUND EDUCATION

2005: Masters of Public Health (International Health)
Tulane University, New Orleans, Louisiana USA
2003: Master of Medicine in Obstetrics/ Gynecology
University of Nairobi, ~enya
1993: Bachelor of Medicine and Surgery
University of Nairobi, Kenya
1986: Kenya Advance Certificate of Education
Kericho High School
1984: Kenya Certificate of Education
Usenge High School
1980: Certificate of Primary Education
Majengo Primary School

OTHER TRAININGS

2008: Certificate, management and leadership
University of California Los Angeles, USA
2008: Certificate, International Grants Management, CDC, Atlanta, USA
2011: Certificate, Principles of Research, University of Washington/NIH, USA
2012: Certificate, Responsible conduct of Research, University of Nairobi/University of Washington.

Certificate, Leadership Development Program (LDP), MSH

Tulane University Health Sciences Center
SCHOOL OF PUBLIC HEALTH & TROPICAL MEDICINE
Department of International Health and Development
1440 Canal Street, Suite 2200
New Orleans, Louisiana 70112-2737 USA
(504) 584-3655 (504) 584-3653 Fax

Thursday, May 23, 2002

re: recommendation for John Odero Ong'ech

To Whom It May Concern:

John Odero Ong'ech, citizen of Kenya, was enrolled at Tulane University, School of Public Health and Tropical Medicine, as a Hubert H. Humphrey Fellow during the academic year 2001-02. The fellowship is a non-degree program designed to enhance leadership potential and increase managerial skills. John completed academic courses for credit in our Masters degree program. The fellows are encouraged to seek out opportunities to broaden perspectives and to establish international professional contacts for the ultimate benefit of their respective countries. The program includes a combination of course work, independent projects, consultation with U.S. faculty and off campus experts, field trips, special seminars, and the professional affiliation/internship.

John had a wide range of experiences in his professional field at the national, state and community level before the fellowship year. He was highly competent academically and articulate in English. He was a fine representative of his country and profession. He was a pleasure to work with and technically very capable.

John was a hard working student who had great success in his courses and professional development activities. He took full advantage of his time here at Tulane University. We feel sure that he and his country will benefit from these experiences. John has our highest recommendation. If you need any further information about this fine individual please feel free to contact me.

Sincerely,

Penny Jessop, MPH
Sr. Program Coordinator

The following is pictorial story of my Stay in the USA -2001-2002

Inside my apartment; The Madigra beads

Receiving Hubert Humphrey fellowship certificate

Touring America

Visiting New York City Right: **Our (me and my roommate Logan Ndahiro from Rwanda) American Host family in New Orleans, Louisiana - A Pedetrician and his wife**

Tulane University Hubert Humphrey Fellows 2001-2002

CHAPTER 4: MARRIAGE LIFE:

Prelude:

"A good marriage is one where each partner secretly suspects they got a better deal"- "by unknown"

"The greatest marriages are built on teamwork.........mutual respect, a healthy dose of admiration and a never ending portion of love and grace"- Fawn Weaver.

4.0 Marriage in My own words:

My first marriage partner was Deborah Adhiambo Okumu. She was introduced to me by a mutual friend when were in the medical school in 1993. I was in my final year pursuing Bachelor of medicine and surgery and she was in her third year pursuing Bachelor of Dental Surgery. We got married on 1.5.1998 in a church wedding. We had 3 children; Jeremy Ong'ech Odero, born 25.3.1999; Grace Obuya Odero, born 1.6.2000; and Humphrey Dave Odero born 16.6.2006.

One thing that we agreed on was to raise disciplined children with moral values. This we did collectively together and gave the children firm foundation that has contributed to their success to date. On our personal relationship, we had many differences and this resulted on dissolution of our marriage in a court of law due to irreconcilable differences in 2015. The dissolution of our marriage was very civilized without the usual court dramas many couples go through. The children decided to stay with me but continued with their relationship with their mother, visiting her whenever they can. Personally I encourage them to do so. We did not involve the courts on the children issue and the arrangement worked just well for us to date.

Generally, since our marriage was dissolved by court of law and my parents gave me approval to remarry, we have not gone through the dramas that the most couples go through in such circumstance. There is mutual respect between us and our families. I thank God for this and it has helped the children grow in a good environment without worrying too much. However most of the responsibilities on parenting and all the financial support on the children has been done by me but God has given me the strength and resources to do it. I have given it my best and all the 3 children have been given a chance to have quality education and life.

My second marriage partner, the love of my life is Beatrice Adongo Odero. She was introduced to me on 12.7.2016 by a mutual friend. Traumatized by my first marriage, I had decided to stay single and raise my children. But when I met her, it was love at first sight and a strong voice kept whispering in my head that she is the one. Interestingly, I had rejected introductions to many prospective marriage partners by relatives and I was very hostile on the subject of re-marrying even to my parents, brothers and sisters. I gave in to the voices and set a meeting to discuss my intentions to her. I told her we could have serious dating for 2 years and then get married.

She listened to my story and said she will accept my proposal but I should never hurt her feelings. Interestingly she said she was also tired of dating and was ripe for marriage. So here we were, 2 single adults falling in love at first sight and ripe for marriage. Things actually moved pretty fast and we never dated for 2 years as was initially envisaged. Now that we had agreed with Beatrice on the nature of our relationship and the road map, my next step was to consult my children; Jeremy, Grace and Humphrey.

I had stayed with them alone now for sometimes, doubling the role of father and mother. I had sacrificed a lot to take care of them and they were aware of it. They could also see how lonely I was at times. I had committed all my life to them and they had never seen me with any woman as I had decided that I only wanted to concentrate on their upbringing. So we had a meeting and they unanimously agreed that I need to move on and get married. They said I need a helper and companionship. This gave me a lot of encouragements. I introduced them to Beatrice whom they liked instantly. We all enjoyed going out together for lunches and dinners. They made a comment that for once we are now complete family. It was a dream come true.

We then travelled to Yimbo with Beatrice to meet my parents, brothers, sisters and relatives. She got instant approval from my folks. We then went with my brothers and sisters to meet her parents and relatives in Ahero, Kano in Kisumu County. We made our intentions loud and clear. After some thorough questioning especially on my past, we got an approval. Beatrice's mum, Mrs Joyce Owaga, remained my greatest supporter until her untimely demise in August 2019. She became a great friend to my mum and they visited each other. My brothers in-laws George Owaga and Philip Oswago became my best friends. So the Luo traditional customary marriage process was undertaken and dowry paid. On 10.12.2016 we finalized the dowry payments in Kano and she was officially released to me and we travelled to Yimbo as husband and wife. In Kano we had the ACK Reverend bless our marriage even though our marriage was conducted under Luo Customary rites. It is blending Christianity and traditions.

There was a lot of celebrations involving Yimbo & Kano relatives on 11/12/2016 and 12/12/2016. The Anglican Church of Kenya (AC) K Reverend in Yimbo also came and blessed the marriage. On 14.2.2019 we upgraded our marriage from a Luo customary marriage to a civil marriage as per the civil marriage act of 2014 in a ceremony at the registrar of marriages in Nairobi witnessed by close relatives from Yimbo and Kano. This by a law is a monogamous marriage just like a church wedding marriage. Customary marriages are by law polygamous.

When we got married in 2016, my father, now late Mzee Jeremiah Ong'ech Ogola who died in Feb 2021, predicted that our first born child shall be a boy and we must name him. This was his dream which we vowed to honour, as much as Dola's naming business surprised me because my first born son from my first marriage had been named after him, Jeremy Ong'ech. Anyway his prediction came to pass, and our son was born on 30.6.2017 and we named him Jerry Ong'ech...honouring his dreams. But this was not the last of Mzee Jeremiah Ongech's dreams on my family: he also predicted that our second born shall be a girl and directed we must name my mother. Interestingly, there were 35 grandchildren and none of my siblings had named my mother. My father predictions also came to pass and on 16/11/2018 a pretty girl was born.... as light skinned as my mother ...and we named her after my mother, Zippy (for Zipporah) Achieng. We honored Mzee's wish and dream. I must say that my parents have always given me wise counselling. A dream of a kind. And in the dreams I vow to live. Am happy my family is helping me live the big dreams.

When I built my rural home in 2010 and my former wife refused to step in, my father told me not to worry, they will pray for me so that one day I will get good wife who will stay with me there. He guided me well through what is acceptable culturally and within the Christianity context. Many detractors talked negatively but he told me not to listen. So when I married Beatrice in 2016, yet another of his dreams and wishes for me became true. Upon Beatrice's arrival home, the parents, together with the church blessed us in our rural home and my father informed Beatrice that from that point onwards, the home was officially hers. We have enjoyed staying in our rural home together with my loving wife Beatrice. We travel there as many times as possible. Beatrice designed a new face lift and it is very nice and homely. Upon Mzee's advice, we also built for his namesake, Jeremy, a magnificent Simba in my home. This we ensured was in use by the boys before his burial.

My father really loved my darling wife Beatrice until his death on 6.2.2021. My mother loved Beatrice from day one to date. My soulmate Beatrice has not disappointed. She has had an excellent relationship with my parents, brothers, sisters and all my relatives. My soulmate Beatrice has stepped in and help raise her stepchildren perfectly well. She is very supportive in all the things I do including my work. She is my fan number one.

Our relationship from the time we met to date has been awesome. In the beginning there were many detractors but she told me, she will never listen to them, she will only listen to me. She said my parents had told her all she wanted to know from a third party about me and she is satisfied to be married to me. She said we shall have the last laugh and indeed we have it. We have built our marriage on good communication, consultations, open dialogue, forgiveness, love, trust and prayers. We are soulmates and best of friends. We share many beliefs, visions and values. I consider Beatrice the best gift God gave me when in need. We have travelled for vacations to many places like USA, United Kingdom, Spain, Italy, France, Dubai, Abudabi, Mombasa, Game parks etc. Canada is loading, Visas ready.... Lots of these are expressed pictorially at the end of this chapter.

She has been fun to be with. During the family vacations, she organizes everything to detail and at the end of the vacations, everyone is happy. She is great Organizer. She is a great worker in the house, a great cook and great with kids. Beatrice just loves peace around her. I can't do without her around me. I have actually told her that I will not agree for her to take up any employment that will make us stay apart as long as I shall live. Beatrice is great with finances. She has made me have a better understanding of financial management and investments options. The best part is that she is very trustable with money, it doesn't matter the amount. She manages the house budgets and expenses per excellence. She is also a firm believer in saving for the rainy day. She is a family person. Enjoys spending time with the family. She is giving the children the best. I am very happy with my marriage to Mrs Beatrice Odero and I pray to God to give us more years together to help shape our legacy.

Now let me give my soulmate Beatrice a chance to say her part.......

4.1: In the words of Beatrice Adongo Odero

Breaking news: Marriage as God intended

The first time I came in contact with Dr John Ong'ech when he visited my workplace in 2013 as a wellness doctor conducting routine medical clinic that was organized by the bank. I met him again mid 2016 through a mutual friend and it was love at first sight. I remember in the early days of our meeting he requested me to meet him at Java in Upper Hill. When I checked in that evening I found him sitting at a corner patiently waiting for me. That evening was the culmination of a defining moment of my life, our marriage. That was the evening that I got the opportunity to be introduced to my father in-law the late Jeremiah Ong'ech.

Mzee spoke with me through the phone for a few minutes and invited me to Yimbo officially to meet the family. This idea was actualized two weeks later. Prior to meeting the love of my life, I had given up on dating or otherwise marriage, As I woman, society can be judgmental at times especially when you attain a certain age without proper arrangement of settling down or having kids. I had never introduced a suitor to my family with any intension of marriage, and dating was proving hard. Whereas these bothered me at times, I vowed never to settle down just for the sake of pleasing a few individuals, society or even my mother. I was at peace with myself as a spinster.

I experienced a paradigm shift in my view of life and marriage in totality after meeting John. When you meet your soulmate, you're undeniably joined in every facets of your body, and you speak the same language.... you are on the same page....this is our story. After the blessings of our first three children, parents and family, our union was and is still a blessed one. John is a rare human being in all spheres of life. He has taught me and I still continue to learn from him. He is very kind, humble and so loving. He loves travelling and having fun with his family. In addition, he is very strict and a disciplinarian.

Not all men are of the idea of educating their women to seek higher education. Right from the onset John was keen that I do my post graduate degree (PGD). He has supported my dreams in education, and I not only achieved the PGD dream, but did it in the best institution in the country and East Africa as a whole. This journey was the most challenging one, as juggling between school, work and raising toddlers, was not a walk in the park. Many a time, I would cry in the evening from work to school and was on the verge of giving up or quitting altogether, but he held my hand and encouraged me throughout the journey. He was so involved and not once did he stay late with me just to keep me company as I finished school work which was immense. He even employed three domestic workers to assist at home as I studied. I am forever indebted to you for this kind of sacrifice that you wholeheartedly endured just to see me through this phase of life.

Our older children have been given the best support system ever. Noticeably, kids who are raised well and portray highest level of mannerisms are a reflection of good parenting. This is evident in their characters and general wellbeing. We have blended so well and our home environment is full of love and happiness. I thank God for this rare and peaceful coexistence; it is only by His grace.

John is so passionate about supporting both our families. He truly lives by the bible quote of 'my people shall be your people and my God shall be your God'. Sometimes I tend to think that God placed both of us in this union to bring sanity and hope that marriage is indeed ordained by God...and we live it every single day of our lives as God intended. He has become very close with my brothers and sisters, my cousins as well as my extended family. He has supported them whenever he is in a position to. In addition, he gives his wise counsel and advise whenever called upon.

My lovely husband has entrusted me with his finances. Before I digress further let me give a bit of my background in this matter and why I believe it is a very important point to note. I work in a financial sector where I have seen and experienced different scenarios in matters financial management especially between couples. Some of these are extremely ugly and most of them do not end well. Money matters in a family if not handled in a transparent and truthful way can be a deal breaker….where there is no truth and everyone keeps their monies in a way that the other party is not privy to it at all cost. I have seen couples fight and say unprintable words because of money. I have to admit that in our house this is very different. We are very transparent about our finances, we both budget together and plan for our future and that of the kids together. We are making our hay while the sun is still shinning... for the rainy days. This is our mantra in matters finances.

For the love of holidays and vacationing, one day we were having a nice evening just relaxing and enjoying each other's company when John casually enquired if I have ever travelled out of the country and if I ever owned a passport. I told him I had a passport and that I had travelled out of the country once. When he asked which country I did not hesitate to respond that I had been to Arusha Tanzania. As much I was proud of the fact that I had travelled out of the country, he felt really sad and sorry for me but did not show it .His next plan was to organize for a serious trip out of Africa. Since then, I have travelled with him and the kids to major cities and continents in the world, with a lot more in the pipeline. In all the trips, he ensures that we get the best that can be offered. We once visited Paris, France during our Euro tour and checked in into this beautiful hotel right in the middle of the city. Personally I liked the hotel since it was a five star located right in the middle of the city, the location was superb. But even with all that he still went ahead and booked a presidential suit, for the first time in my life I was attended to by white waiters and waitresses literally running on their toes just to deliver their services. You see, it feels great and it humbles you! John loves class yet he does not show it. You can only feel it.

My husband is a high achiever and success follows him. I have witnessed his life predictions come to fulfillment. His thought process and decision making skills is very prolific. He is disciplined both in his personal life and career. I believe being a medical doctor is a calling and not for the faint hearted. There's no single night that John has slept for six hours uninterrupted… he must be woken up by phone call after phone call, and amazingly he picks all of them and responds accordingly. He treats emergencies with utmost caution and attention it deserves. My husband values and protects the sanctity of human life.

John has proven that no man is never too busy to attend to his woman if he truly loves and cares for her. A classic example was during his employment at Kenyatta hospital as chief medical specialist and deputy director; running his private practice; handling a heap of dissertations and research papers; attending to early morning meetings and classes as a lecturer at the university of Nairobi medical school; and attending to patients all over city hospitals. There's no single time I have called him and he missed picking my calls. He would and still picks my calls amid his busy schedules even when he's in operating room albeit shortly. He would alert me of every single move that he makes, a practice we have both inculcated in our lives as a routine.

One of the things that women look for in their partners is the relationship their partners have with their parents. I fell in love more with my husband because of the way he loves his parents / loved his late dad. From taking care of every single need to constantly getting in touch through phone calls, to home visits and consulting them constantly has given him a score that I believe not all are able to do. He is simply an adorable son and family oriented. My husband loves spending time quietly in the house with our children. Whenever he is free, especially evenings and Sundays, he loves listening to Rhumba and Luo music. He is passionate about our children's education progress and is fully involved in their lives. Jerry and Zippy calls him super daddy.

I know God has a lot in store for us in the coming years, and as we continue to embrace and inspire each other in this journey, it is my prayer that we remain as strong as ever and that the bond we have shall inspire our future generations. Whenever I am counting my blessing's I count you several times, because that is simple who you are, a blessing. My family loves you so much and to my late mother you were much more than a son in law. My husband is a provider. We have never lacked in our house. We live a very fulfilling life. I am forever indebted to you my love. Stay blessed.

From Mrs Beatrice Odero

Pictorial expresion of our marriage:

2016, the week of our first meeting

Left: Light moments; Right: 2016: initial weeks of our meeting

2016: Our first visit to Betratice parents home in Kano

Arrival for marriage negotiations and dowry payment as paer Luo customary rites

Arriving for marriage negotiation and dowry payment as per Luo Customary rites

Luo customary marriage negotiations ongoing at Beatrice's parents home in Kano

Luo customary marriage negotiations over, Beatrice's parents have just handed her over to me as my wife

Congratulations from Mwalimu Ochieng on completion of marriage negotiations

Celebrations in Yimbo after completion of the Luo customary marriage rites

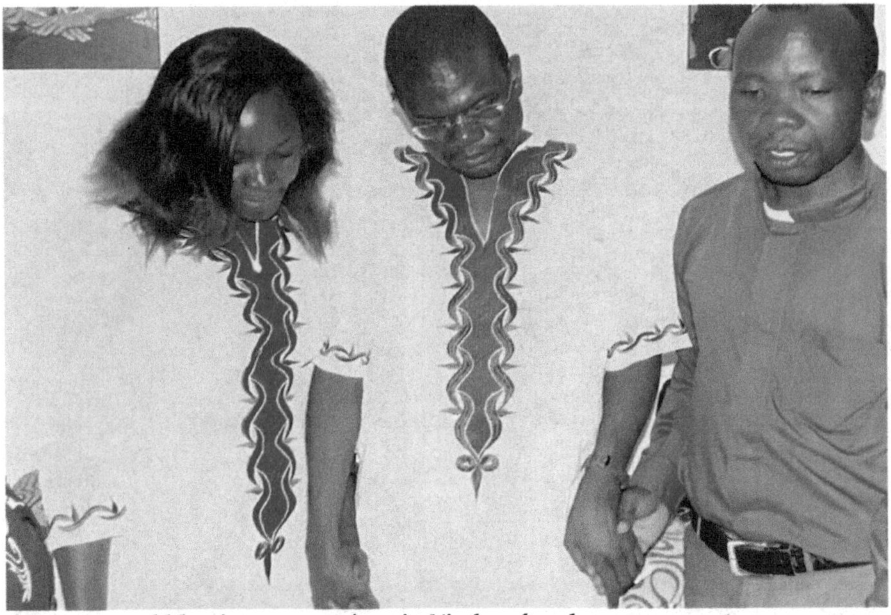

ACK reverend blessing our marriage in Yimbo after dowry payment

Civil marriage registration ceremony as per the Kenya Laws

Civil marriage registration ceremony as per the Kenya Laws

Happily married as per the Luo customary rites, civil registration as per the Kenya Laws and blessings from the Church (ACK)
Right: Visiting the first Anglican cathedaral in London, UK

2016 holiday in Mombasa Diani south coast

Left: Holiday in Italy, Rome, Vatican City   Right: Holiday in Italy, Rome

Holiday in Italy, Rome at Vatican City

Chicago, the windy city (USA) tour

Left: Holiday in Mombasa, private beach house; Right: Holiday in UAE, Dubai

Holiday in UAE, Dubai.

Holiday in United Arab Emirated, AbuDhabi

Holiday in Bacelona, Spain

Light moments at Usenge high school during Dr Ongech Alumni patron day

Light moments in our house in Yimbo

Light moments in our house in Nairobi, Lavington

Left: Holiday in Paris, France **Right: Celebrating Jeremy's graduation**

Odero Ongech Special family photo gallery

Dr Odero Ongech family poses in a relaxed environment

The senior children's poses of the year with Dad

The Dr Odero Boys and Girls pausing for family photos

CHAPTER 5: CHILDREN AND PARENTING EXPERIENCE

5.0: Prelude

"When you become a parent remember: Don't allow anything in your life that you don't want reproduced in your children" Unknown.

"The sign of great parenting is not the child's behavior. The sign of truly great parenting is the parent's behavior". Andy Smithson

"Children have never been very good at listening to their elders, but they have never failed to imitate them" James Baldwin

"At the end of the day, the most overwhelming key to child's success is the positive involvement of the parents". Jane D.Hull

"Encourage and support your kids because children are apt to live up to what you believe of them". Lady Bird Johnson

"Good parenting does not mean giving him a perfect life. It means teaching him how to lead a good and happy life in our imperfect world". Family share.com

"Parents can only give good advice or put them on the paths, but the final forming of a person's character lies in their own hands". Anne Frank

"If you have never been hated by your child, you have never been a parent"- Bette Davis

"When a man dies, if he can pass enthusiasm along to his children, he has left them an estate of incalculable value". Thomas Edison

"Children are apt to live up to what you believe of them". Lady Bird Johnson

"Most things are good, and they are the strongest things; but there are evil things too, and you are not doing a child a favor by trying to shield him from reality. The important thing is to teach a child that good can always triumph over evil". Walt Disney.

5.1 Jeremy Odero

Jeremy Ong'ech Odero is my first born. He was born on 25.3.1999 at Kenyatta National Hospital Private Wing (Ward 1C). He was delivered by Caesarian Section after prolong labour due to Malposition (Persistent Occipito Posterior-POPP). This would subsequently influence the birth of Grace Odero and Humphrey Odero that was also through Caeserian Section (CS).

During the antenatal period, the radiologist gave a misdiagnosis on sex and so we were not prepared for a baby boy. I was in the operating room when a bouncing baby boy weighing 3900gm was born at 8pm on 25.3.1999. I was very excited as my dream to have a son to name after my father was here. So I changed Jeremiah to Jeremy and the name Jeremy Ong'ech Odero became official. His birth brought a lot of joy to everyone around us. In the 3 months of his life, Jeremy cried every night, only sleeping during the day. This reminded me of the story I was told about my first 3 months of life. It was a replica.

But at the end of 3 months, he calmed down and became a quite baby. Jeremy mother and me were very strict parents. We both agreed on good parenting. The early childhood up bring of Jeremy involved around Christianity (church children's clubs teachings), children story books reading, storytelling, visiting children playgrounds and many other outdoor activities.

Jeremy from early childhood was a very social person and a crowd puller. Many of his age mates would always be knocking our door requesting to see him or asking for permission for him to join them to play. He had a fulfilling childhood life and during his primary school at Riara, he was a confident child, well behaved and hard working. In his early childhood, he was always calling me a superman.

I went to study in the USA for one year when he was about 2 1/2 years old. He had seen me off to the airport, and subsequently for the whole year, all the planes passing would according to him be carrying me. Anyway I had fulfilling relationship with him. I was very keen on his success and so I would supervise his homework closely and sometimes put a lot of pressure on him. His threshold for pressure was high and this kept us going. I liked showering him with presents during my many trips abroad and he was always looking forward to my return trips. At the airport he would run very fast pass the security to the restricted arrival area to give me a welcome back hug (Grace joined him later in this act). He would leave the security Personnel speechless and laughing.

So when Jeremy sat his KCPE in 2012 (End of Primary Education), he passed his exams. He never gave me any pressure about specific high schools that he preferred. He was very open minded. Interestingly, he hinted about joining the rural schools in Nyanza that could offer him form one admission. We took a trip to see some of the Nyanza schools namely: Maseno School, St. Mary's Yala School, Maranda High School and My former High School, Usenge High School. We left his results to those schools except Usenge High School which at the time I was not keen as the standards had gone down. We came back to the city and also put in application at Sunshine Secondary School- finally he got admission at Sunshine Secondary School in Nairobi County and Ramba Secondary School in Siaya county.

The pressure the parents go through to get form one chance was not a joke. The system was not like during our time. The students were being admitted to funny schools they never chose. Jeremy was open to joining any school that I felt was good. I decided that he joins Sunshine Secondary School in Nairobi County after doing thorough background checks. So we reported to the school in 2013 march. He found almost 10 other students from his former school, Riara, also joined the school. He started the high school life on a positive note. I was immediately elected a PTA member, representing his class. He became a focus of his classmates and teachers. He had to conform to a very high standard. He did not disappoint, he was even elected a prefect. He worked hard, consulting various teachers to support him on areas of weakness (with my support and Guidance) and this made him improve a lot. I participated in all school functions, all official school visits (taking him a lot of food), All academic discussion visits etc. I also made motivational presentations to all the students in his school upon invitation by the principal. I purposively had become close with his school administration and Teachers. This really helped alot in shaping him. In 2016, he sat for his KCSE (End of Form 4) exams- The 1st Matiangi Exams where there was no cheating that witnessed massive failure in KCSE. Jeremy posted impressive results with an A in Mathematics and good performance in other subjects as well. He was admitted to a public university (JKUAT) to study Business and IT.

He had wanted to study law but he didn't mind switching to It. We agreed that Strathmore University offered a better quality Education. So in 2017, he immediately after KCSE results he joined Strathmore University to study Business Information Technology. He successfully completed the course in 2021 and joined Minet Insurance company where is at the time of writing this book. He turned down my offer to fund his further studies in USA. He is interested in professional courses and Entrepreneurship. I have facilitated most of the proposal he has brought to my attention though some we have discussed and agreed are not practical. Jeremy is very interested in trading in shares at the stock exchange and I have supported him on this venture. I have entrusted him to trade on my behalf at Nairobi stock exchange with positive results. Jeremy likes to chat his path in his own way. He doesn't like comparisons. He believes he is unique in his own way. He likes to learn but not to replicate. These are his characters that identified as a parent and decided to leverage on.

Jeremy is a social person, a crowd puller and doesn't like to hurt other people. He is very friendly. Parenting him has been an exciting journey with normal expected ups and downs. He takes corrective measures positively. During early childhood he went through strict parenting including canning. His desire to be always a better person makes parenting him nice. He avoids repeating same mistake once corrected, he listens very attentively to advice. He doesn't hesitate to seek audience with me for guidance or to clarify issues. He is never quite on issues, a virtue that I instilled on him from childhood.

This has made parenting him easy. Sometimes I am a very tough parent, on such occasions he prefers to forward to me a written document on what is in his mind. We sometimes hold structured meetings.

We have good father-son relationship and both of us respect our boundaries. Being the firstborn, my expectations on him have been quite high. He is aware of this. He tries to be gently to his younger siblings, providing help, support and guidance whenever called upon. He was the first grandson to be named after my great father Mzee Jeremiah Ong'ech, I pray that he lives long to fit in his great shoes. I have ensured that he has a very good house in his ancestral land and a nicely landscaped piece of ancestral land with many trees planted to allow him continue the legacy of his roots in Yimbo-Ogam – Lwala.

Long live Jeremy. God bless. So let me allow him to say his part of the story:

In Jeremy's own words:

From First born son Jeremiah Ong'ech the second. My father has been a role model for me, he showed me that should I want to succeed then I have to do so with my own knowledge and with my own capabilities. He has never been the person to shield me from the realities of the world, but at the same time he helps me to understand what is happening and how these world problems could potentially affect me. He was the one to show me that life will continue to happen whether or not I was prepared to do so. My father conveyed to me the importance of searching for opportunities instead of letting them come to me because life does not work that way. Life is not just going to provide me with help if I do not give an honest attempt to produce results myself. A main reason that I had for looking up to my father was due to his strong commitment to go heritage and culture, always finding an opportunity to pass on to me what was taught to him by his father. My Journey with the great man that I proudly call my father began on March 25 1999. The day on which I officially knew him as dad and I to him as his first-born son named in loving memory of the late Jeremiah Ong'ech, my grandfather. Thus, we begun the 22-year journey called life, which is still ongoing. He is a person whom I revere a lot. His hard working personality and tranquil nature have immersed my mind. He goes to work early in the morning and returns back late at night. He still works over-time for managing the fiscal needs of our family. No matter how much he is tired after the work, he always takes good care of the entire family. Whatever kind of person I am now and whatever I will grow to be in the future rivets his encouragement and support, shaping me to be a sincere, devoted and an honest person. There are situations that things go wrong, and I feel bad. My father can always find right words and give good advice. These moments are important for me because I feel the support, I know that I am not alone, and it gives me confidence. It is important to mention that the way he moves and acts reflects his personality a lot. He prefers a fast-paced walking style as opposed to a calm slow one. It means that he wants to do everything he has planned in a timely manner. My dad does not waste his precious time in vain; after all, time and tide wait for no man therefore one must neither procrastinate nor delay. He enjoys every part of his wonderful life. Even when he eats you can get jealous of him, as he will eat the simplest dish with such a delight as if it is the most expensive and delicious food in the world. He is happy and thankful for every piece of meal he gets, and he enjoys it. Obviously, my father is a very smart man. He likes to share his experience as well as learn from the experiences of the people surrounding him. You can always find out some new information, learn something and share your experience with him. I can always rely on my father and I am confident that his opinion is objective. His opinions and advice always come sincerely. On the other hand, he knows how to choose the best time for it; he waits for the time when I am calm and relaxed so that I can easily perceive the information. While I was younger, my childhood superhero was wolverine but knowing what I know now, he is the true hero from my childhood. Times may have changed but the things I have learned from him are both ageless and priceless. I am forever grateful that I get to call him dad and look forward to more experiences on the life journey.

Jeremy Ong'ech Odero-Son

Left to Right: 1 and 2: 16 year old jeremy at sunshine secondary school; Jeremy 16 year old; Jeremy 5 years old, and 14 years old respectively;

Left: Jeremy 4 years old and grace 3 years old (2003); Right: 15 year old Jeremy

2019: Jeremy in USA, California

Left: Jeremy internship at police sacco in 2019 Right: 2017: Jeremy joins Strathmore University

Left and centre: light moments; Right: jeremy receiving blessings from his grandfather and namesake the late Jeremiah Ongech

17 year old jeremy , Form 4 at Sunshine secondary school

2018: Jeremy Enjoying summer holidaysin London, UK

Left: Celebrating Grace's 18th Birthday Right: jeremy hanging out at Nairobiclub with Hon Raila Odinga

2015: Dinner at Oleshereni Hotel; Right: Jeremy enjoying holidays in Mombasa Diani Beach

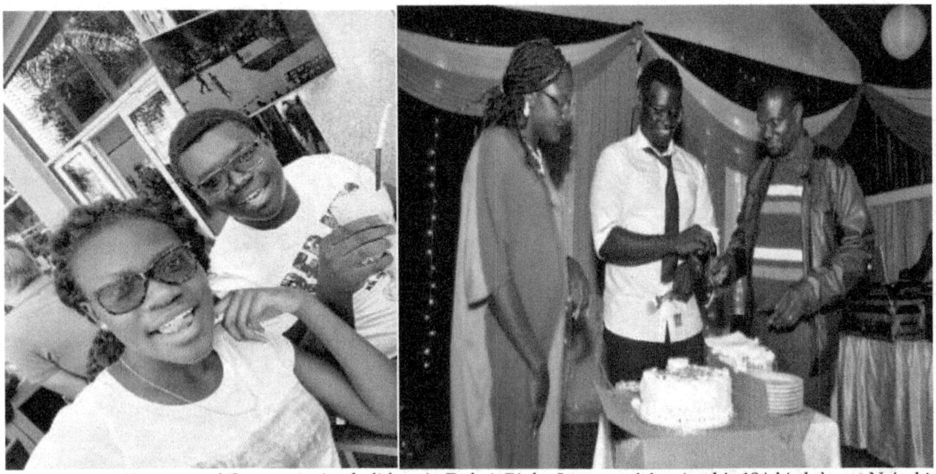

Left: 31.12.2016 Jeremy and Grace enjoying holidays in Dubai; Right: Jeremy celebrating his 18th birthday at Nairobi club

Jeremy 15 year old Left: Right: Jeremy graduation at strathmore University, 2021

Jeremy graduates at Strathmore University with a Bachelor of Business Information technology degree

2021: Jeremy personal manager for David Owino ochieng, sign 4 year contract rto allow David to play in Gor Mahiafootball club

5.2: Grace Odero:

Grace Obuya Odero is my second born. She was born by elective Caesarian Section (CS) on 1.6.2000, 3pm at Kenyatta National Hospital Private Wing (Ward 1C) and weighed 3800gm at birth. It was an elective CS because his elder brother Jeremy had been born by C/S. During the antenatal care, we did not do an ultrasound for sex determination because of the Misdiagnosis earlier during Jeremy's case. Those days' ultrasound was not accurate as compared to these days that you can do 3D/4D ultrasound with almost 100% accuracy.

Grace was named after her maternal grandmother, Mrs Grace Obuya Okumu. She came pretty soon after Jeremy birth, age difference between them is 1year 3months 5 days. So their upbringing exposure was similar, very strict parenting with caning for any disobedience. Church attendance, singing in church, church club activities attendance, reading story books and children fun fare outdoor activities were part of her upbringing. I used to like spending time with her and Jeremy whenever I could, including the famous Lollipop days. Grace was a very calm child at birth. In her early childhood she was more of an indoor person with very selected friends. She was always very structured, a personality she has maintained to date. She feared being canned and would take such an incident very personal.

She always behaved well and was generally a quite child and very observant on things around her. I remember when we applied to take her to Riara Nursery school, the teacher said the class was full and by looking at her, she didn't think she would cope in the nursery school. She gave her an exam which she did not think Grace would pass. She was shocked. Grace score 100% in all the exams she was given. The teacher quickly changed her attitude, became friendly and gave her an admission letter. She did not disappoint for the rest of her school life in Riara. She had a fulfilling early childhood life getting a lot of awards in academic excellence which she celebrated quietly with modesty. She did not have any disciplinary issue in Riara. I participated actively in all her school functions. In class 7 and 8, I was their PTA Motisha Chairman. She made my work easier because she was always excelling and receiving awards. She sat her KCPE in 2013 and passed very well. She was admitted at Machakos Girl High School which she openly told me she did not want. In her class, almost 20 of them were heading Moi High School Kabarak. So categorically she told me that the school she wants to join is MHSK. During Grace Primary school days, she rarely would speak her mind so openly like she did on this occasion. Getting Moi High School Kabarak (MHSK) was not easy. The school had just become number one in KCSE 2013 in the whole country. Everybody was heading there. I went there, formally applied. The school principal had switched off his phone and there was no one to talk to. I must confess it was a tough moment for me with sleepless nights. I called everyone I knew in this country with no help. Then the name Richard Lesyampe came into my mind. He had been my boss at KNH as the CEO and recently had just been promoted to be a principal secretary. He was also chairman of the board of Sunshine, sister school to MHSK. I called him, he directed I drop Grace documents to his office and the next day I got a call from Moi High School, Kabarak to pick Grace Admission letter. Meanwhile Grace had been so down, hardly eating any meals. Every evening I came home, she would come from her room to enquire if I had any news. This was very depressing for me as I did not want to disappoint her. Finally armed with the admission letter, I knocked on her door loudly, and told her to go through the documents I had brought home that evening. She was very excited. Eventually she reported to MHSK and I must say that she did not disappoint. She turned the tables on those who defeated her in KCPE and started excelling from day one. She went to that school with one agenda- to excel. She did excel beyond my expectations, sometimes becoming number one out of 350 students. I was elected PTA representative of her class for all the four years she was at MHSK. As per my parenting tradition, I became very close with the teachers and the school administration. Due to Grace exemplary performances, I was invited to represent all parents as a guest speaker to the entire Kabarak School community from primary to high school in 2017, just before Grace sat for KCSE. I was very happy and a proud parent on this occasion. Grace had kept her career choice secret from me. She wanted to give me a surprise. As per my tradition in parenting, I let the children choose what they want to study. But when consulted, I give my advice generously based on what I know. So the bombshell came in third term before KCSE that she wants to pursue a career in medicine. Wow, Ok, I did not ask questions, I said proceed and choose. My only advice was she should perform well in the sciences and be aware she will be dissecting dead people during Human Anatomy in 1st year of the study of medicine. Of course inside me I was very happy and proud that at least one of my children will follow in my footsteps. For me, my father was not a doctor but I fulfilled his dreams. Despite the challenges that comes with the career in medicine, I had all along told my children the positive things in this field. I have learnt that if you always tell your children negative things about your career/ what you do, they will automatically hate it and despite those with the potential, none will follow in your footsteps.

Grace passed KCSE 2017 with many "A" s and was among the best 100 female students in Kenya. She was keen in the USA system of training, so I took her to Philippines which was more affordable than in the USA soil. She did pre medicine degree at South Western University, Cebu, graduated on top of her class with Bachelor of Science, Biology degree that earned her admission to the best medical school in that country, Cebu Institute of Medicine. Of course, she fainted on her first day of her anatomy class, dissecting dead bodies is never an easy thing even during my days. She has maintained good performance and by the time of writing this book she has less than 2 years remaining to finish. She is also planning to start sitting the United States Medical licensing exams (USMLE) that will automatically open for her opportunities in USA, if she chooses to go there. At the moment she seems keen to go that route. Grace always wants to be the top student which is tough in medical school and this sometimes take a toll on her. During her vacations we have operated together and she is very good in theatre as an assistant. We have also reviewed patients together in the wards and she is very keen and good. I continue praying for her and wish her a successful career in medicine in the footsteps of her father and mother too who is also a doctor. I hope one day she will write her memoirs, in the footsteps of my father.

Parenting Grace requires a different style from Jeremy. In early childhood, she would talk less about things disturbing her so I had to probe her all the time. This has changed and as she grows up, she is more open to seeking guidance on number of issues. We at the moment hold healthy discussions on any topic that she needs guidance on. This ranges from her health, academics career, life issue etc. she sometimes holds her opinions very strongly but with factual pursuance, she becomes flexible. She is a very indoor person and interacts with selected clique of friends which she makes sure are introduced to the family fully and in details. Most of them are pursuing excellence in career and life. She is a very much aware that I don't approve mediocre. She is very structured and open about her movements, always sending a pin location on her whereabouts. She doesn't like partying.

She knows that I am very proud of her and ready to give her my best anytime.

I pray she lives long to fulfil all her dreams in life. May God bless her abundantly.

I will now give her a chance to say her side of the story.

In Grace's own words:

As I sit down to write my tribute, a million memories of my dad and I flood through my mind. It is now, at 21 years old, that I really see how much of me is made from what I have learned, and continue to learn from him. One of my most favorite memories with my father and elder brother, Jeremy, is a tradition the three of us would call 'Lollipop Day.' Basically, every Sunday when we were younger, Jeremy and I would wake up at the crack of dawn to go wake up our father. Thereafter, my brother and I would ride our bikes to the main gate of our estate as our dad walked beside us. He would hand us about 30 shillings each to buy sweets and biscuits at the kiosk near our estate and he would buy his newspapers. We would then go back home and eat a lovely breakfast together. This happened every single Sunday like clockwork until I guess my brother and I decided that we're too old for a 'Lollipop Day.' This is just one of the memories I have that are an example of how my father has consistently shown up for me in ways that mean the world to me. Every school event, he would be there. He was the PTA chairman of my class both in class eight and form four and constantly reminded me of how proud he was of me. From this, my father taught me the importance of showing up for the people who matter to you and this is a lesson I hold very dear to my heart and actively apply it in my life.

As I've grown older, my relationship with my father has evolved as expected. As I have grown older, I have also begun to form my own opinions about the world and life in general. I am growing into my own person and in this period, I have continued to value his ability to step back and see things from my point of view. This has also taught me to learn to step back and see where he is coming from as well. He has tried his best not to hide me from the harsh realities of life, but in the same breath, remind me that as long as it is within his capabilities, he will always be there for me no matter what life throws at me. Living life knowing that when push comes to shove, my father will always have my back has always been a source of comfort and peace for me.

My father has been my role model all my life. His hardworking personality is a source of motivation for me as I continue to pursue my medical degree. I keep reminding myself that 'if daddy is doing it, I can do it too!' I remember the first time I observed my father perform surgery (August 2020) I was in awe. His composure, the meticulous way he performed a simple cesarean section and even the way he interacted with the rest of the operating team. I remember thinking that I want to be a doctor exactly like my father. With the same mannerisms, with the same dedication and with the same love for what I do. I am always going to be grateful for my father for being someone I can look up to.

He has continued to advise me and share his life experiences as I continue on this journey of figuring out who I am. His words of advice are so instrumental in key moments of my life when I need encouragement, support or just the confidence to tackle whatever life throws at me. I once got him a mug for Father's day that was written " you are the luckiest father in the world to have an amazing daughter like me" but it is in fact I, who has been blessed with an amazing father like him.

GRACE ODERO

Life pictorial story for Grace Obuya Odero

Grace and Jeremy in Early life

Grace, Jeremy and Dad in early life

Grace and Jeremy in early life

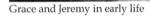

Right: 3-year old grace

Left: : 13 year old grace, class 8 Riara, receiving Motisha award from the chairman, Dad Dr John Ongech
Right: 14 year old Grace reports to Moi High School Kabarak to start form 1 (2014)

14 year old grace (2014);

left: 17 year old grace;   right2016-Grace at MGHS Kabarak Form 4;

Left: Grace in Form 4 at MHSK (2017); Right: Grace has just scooped position 1 out of 350 Form 4 students at Moi H S Kabarak (2017)

Left: 17 year old Grace in Dubai (2016) ; Right 17 year old Grace

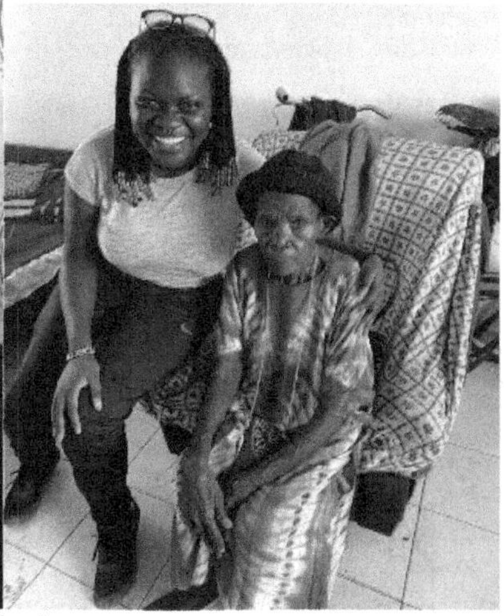

Grace bonding with her grandparents and receiving their blessings

2018: Grace has just passed her KCSE exams with disctintion, among the best 100 feamles in the country, and overall number 145 nationwide. She has received admision to studt her dream career, medicine in the philipines
Right: Grace enjoying summer holidays in London (2017)

Grace celebrating 18th birthday

Grace enjoying summer holidays in London

Grace with her brother Jerry (2018); Right: 19 year old Grace

19 year old Grace enjoying nature in the philipines (2019)
Right: 2020, 20 years old Grace at JKIA , coming back for holidays during the Covid pandemic

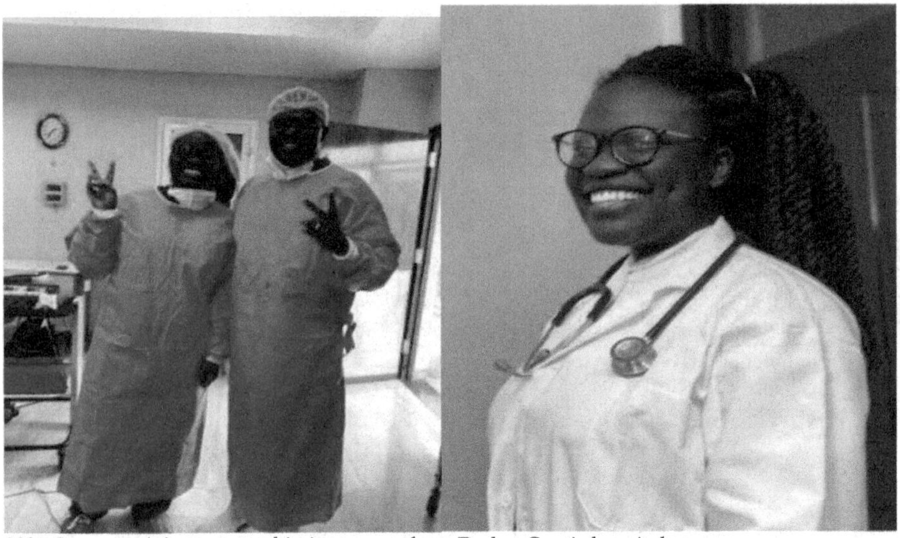

2021 Grace receiving mentorship in surgery from Dad at Coptic hospital

2020 in Mombasa for holidays

2021- 21 years old Grace with Sister Zippy; Right: 2021: Grace celebrating in Nairobi, her Bachelor of Science, Biology degree from South Western University, Philippines which she got in 2020

2021- 21 years old Grace

5.3: Humphrey Odero

Humphrey Dave Odero is my 3rd born. He was born on 16.6.2006 through a Ceaserian Section at Nairobi Hospital. His birth was a bit dramatic. The doctors discovered in the morning of the surgery that the mothers Total Blood Count (Heamoglobin and Platelets specifically) had suddenly dropped to a very low level. This was unusual as there was no explanation. This was a threat to a successful Caesarian section delivery. The mother would die easily during the surgery. This was corrected but still it was not easy to control the bleeding during the surgery. It took almost 3hours instead of the usual 45 minutes. At 9pm, 16.6.2006, a bouncing baby boy weighing 3750gm was born. The mother's condition was not so good immediately after birth, she almost got admitted to ICU but she pulled through by the grace of the Lord. I provided the necessary support. Even after discharged, she developed unexplained fevers for a long time. Finally,

2 months later, the doctors diagnosed a lupus disease and put her on lifelong treatment. Meanwhile at birth I decided to name the bouncing baby boy Humphrey Dave Odero. The name Humphrey was derived from my prestigious Scholarship program that saw me study in the USA. His African name was Odero, my name, that was in summary naming myself, Odero Junior.

Humphrey was a calm child from birth through early childhood. He was very brilliant and appeared very gifted. He skipped a class in Kindergarten. I took him in third term to go and play so that he could start proper school the following year but wow, I was told at the end of the term he was the best they have and so he just had to move to the next class. It reminded me of my time when I was in nursery school for only one term. He went to Riara from Kindergarten until class 8. He did KCPE 2019.

I had very special bond with Humphrey from birth. Unlike my previous parenting style, I never canned him when things were not right. He went through early childhood parenting at a challenging time. I however sacrificed a lot to make sure he gets the best. I remember cancelling a trip to Canada which was fully sponsored to attend FIGO Conference so that I could be with him and provide him with the necessary support. He also had a school trip to Italy later which I went out of my way to support to make him happy. He has travelled to many other countries at a younger age including United Kingdom, UAE Dubai, Abu Dhabi etc.

At the tender age of 9years, in 2015, in class 4, I took over his care alone. This was critical stage in his development, so I put up robust support system for him. All went well, he progressed well in school and in character. Jeremy and Grace were at hand to provide him support. His cousins like Walter Okeyo and nieces like Jackline Onuko and Lavenda Ochieng did an amazing job.

I was made the PTA Motisha Chairman for his class 7 and 8. This gave me an opportunity to be close with the teachers and the school administration. The school provided a very conducive environment that helped shape up his character and academic performance. He performed extremely well in KCPE 2019, scoring all ''A''s. He was admitted to a national school, Chavakali High school. We took a trip to the school. The school has very good infrastructure in terms of laboratories, classes, libraries but the congestion in the dormitories was a mess. I decided this will not work for him. I applied to Moi High school, Kabarak, he got instant admission. This time there was no struggle. Grace had set a good record and I was also remembered as a good PTA class representative. Humphrey had also passed very highly.

Before joining MHSK, he had his own ideas of joining Light academy. I am not familiar with the school and I have not met giants in life produced by the school, so I declined. I have seen many schools that post good results at KSCE after drilling students but when they proceed to the university, the story is different. The students fail miserably. I have seen many successful Alumnis produced by MHSK. The school has a tradition and culture. So we have had several discussions with Humphrey that MHSK is the best for him. He is doing very well at MHSK and I pray he continues to do so. By the time of writing this book, he is one of the best mathematician in form 2 at MHSK. He posts results that reminds me of my time.

Parenting Humphrey is different from Jeremy and Grace. He has does not tolerate too much pressure. He works best if you give him his own space. Once in a while, he requires polite reminders to be on track. He is very much indoor person. He has extremely very few trustable friends. They seem to adore him. He is a very quiet person. He prefers quiet factual discussions during parenting sessions. He is extremely very independent. He will rarely talk about what is bothering him. He prefers sometimes to write a brief note and put it strategically where I will see it. He does not like to inconvenience other people or hurt them. As a parent, I always have to reach out to him.

I was recently elected PTA representative for his class at MHSK. This has worked for me in the past parenting. I there intend to take full advantage of it to help him go through MHSK.

I pray that he goes through his education and life successfully to achieve his dreams. May God bless him. I will allow him to say his side of the story.

In Humphrey's own words:

Having daddy as a father has been an inspirational journey. From the moment I was born, he has always supported me in all I needed to do to achieve my best. He has taken care of me for 15 years. He took me to the best primary and High schools in Kenya and ensured I got the best of the best in terms of holistic education. On top of that, he has been a fun father; taking me on trips abroad, funding my birthday parties with my friends and even taking me out. He has been critical in my development up to this point. I would not have achieved all I have, had it not been for his influence. I love him and appreciate his impact on my life. He was very active in my primarily education especially in class 7 & 8 being the PTA representative for my class and the Chairman of the whole of the Riara class of 2019 motisha. He has had an impact not only on me but also on other people in my life. I could not ask for a better father and mentor. So to daddy, thank you for the past 15 years and I can't wait for the many more we'll have.

Loving Son, Humphrey Dave Odero

Humphrey Dave pictorial milestones

Left and Middle: Jeremy and Grace teaching their little brother Humphrey on how to work
Right: Humphrey in his younger days

Left": Humphrey in his younger days; Middle: Humphrey visiting Dad at his KNH office
Right: Young Humphrey is from School 2015

Left: Light moment for Humphrey and Jeremy 2015; Middle: Humphrey 8 years old arrives at JKIA from Italy (school trip); Right: Humphrey at Riara primary, making a presentation to parents;

Left: Humphrey at Riara primary School receiving an excellence performance award from Motisha PTA chairman Dr Ong'ech (Dad); Right: Humphrey Light moment with Dad

10 year old Humphrey

Left: Humphrey reporting to Form 1, MHSKabarak; Right: Humphrey catching up with his friends from Alliance and light academy during their early days in Form 1

Left: Humphrey at JKIA heding to Dubai, UAE Right: **Humphrey in holidays in UAE, Abudhabi**

Left: Humphrey in Abu Dhabi; Right: Humphrey in Dubai

Left and Right: Humphrey celebrating Jeremy's 18th Borthday

Left: [redacted] **2017- Humphrey celebrating Jeremy's 18th birthday**

Right: Humphrey taking care of His young brother Jerry

Left and Right: Humphrey in holidays in London, United Kingdom.

Humphrey light moments

Humphrey light moments; Humphrey light moments; Humphrey light moments

Humphrey light moments; Hupmrey light moments

Left: 2019: Humphrey just finished his KCPE Exams in Riara;
Right: Humphrey being congratulated by Bondo MP Hon Ochanda for excellent KCPE 2019 performance

Humphrey in 2021-15 years old, Form 2, Moi High School Kabarak , posted best Mathematics results (99%) in Form 2 -No 1 out of 419 students

2018- Humphrey celebrating Grace 18th Birthday;

5.4: Jerry Ong'ech Odero

Jerry Ong'ech Odero is my fourth born. Was born by Caeserian section on 1.6.2017 at Aghakan University Hospital Nairobi.

My father predicted even before conception that Beatrice will give birth to a boy and we shall name the boy after him. This came to pass and he was named Jerry Ong'ech Odero. So I am in record in my family and community to have a named my father twice. In the first 3 months of life Jerry could really cry at night. He was never calm. He reminded of my story when I was born and also Jeremy my first born.

After 3 months, he became relatively calm. He celebrated his 1st birthday in United Kingdom - London. But again he was very restless at this time like all other children. The terrible two stage was a piece of work. Jerry after that settled and became a calm nice boy. He very intelligent could say ABCD……Z and identify all the colours before formal schooling.

The Kenya Education system has changed to what they call Competency Based Curriculum (CBC) which I have no idea what it is all about. I asked my brother Ochieng Ong'ech who was a head teacher before he retired, he appeared also not clear about this new system. I therefore decided that my next 2 children Jerry and Zippy will not go through this experimental education system.

So Jerry is now doing the International system of Education (British Curriculum) at Braeside School and he is doing well. My parenting style has changed over time. I am still keen on jerry respecting authority, some grounding and some pinching when he is on the wrong. But I employ more negotiation approach. I noticed that the fear of failure of the 1st child makes a parent go over drive but with time and successive children, the parent relaxes. Jerry is growing up as a promising scholar, I wish him all the best and may God grant him his wishes. May he live long to fulfil his dreams and one day write a book either **in the dreams of my father** or in the footsteps of my father.

In Jerry's own words:
Although I am only four years old, I have every quality of my father, I have great desire for science and nature, my dad has enrolled me for young engineers club at Braeside school where I am currently in foundation stage two, in this club I get to understand how to build and operate machines which is a lot of fun and very interesting. At home, my dad is my hero and I call him super daddy, he loves me and I love him too. My first birthday was celebrated in London, Mummy keeps on showing me videos and pictures and this makes me happy. May God continue blessing you daddy.
Master Jerry Ongech pictorial story

Master Jerry Ongech pictorial story

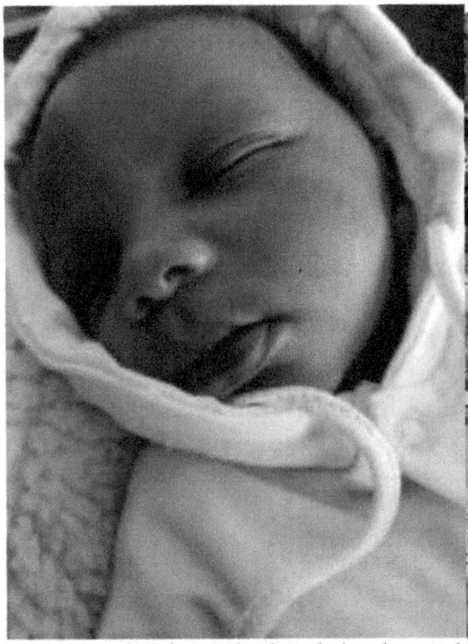
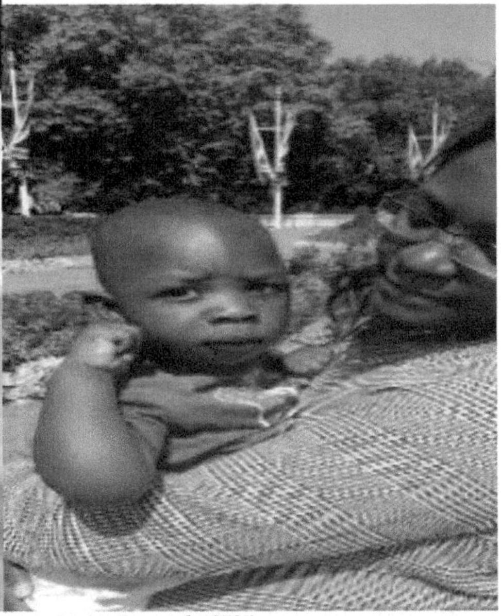

Jerry Ong'ech Odero at birth Aghakan hospital Nairobi; birth weight 3525gm;
Right: 30.6.2018 - Jerry celebrating his fist birthday in London

Extreme Leftt: Jerry, 1 year old;
Right: April 2019: Jerry receiving blessings from his late grandpa and namesake, Mzee Jeremiah Ong'ech;

Left: 2020-Jerry 2 years old

Right: Middle: 2020-Jerry 3 years old

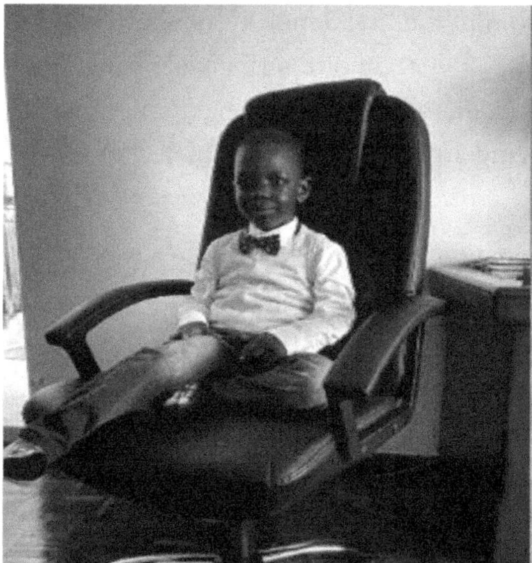

Left and Right: 2021-Jerry at 4 years;

5.5: Zippy Achieng Odero.

Dr Odero Ongech's words:

Zippy Achieng Odero is my fifth and last born, thus the name "chogo" as I don't intend to have more children. She was born by Caeserian Section delivery at Aghakan University Hospital, Nairobi on 16/11/2018. Just like Jerry, my father predicted we shall have a baby girl, and we name her after my mother, Siporah Achieng. So we gave her the name Zippy Achieng Odero. This is the first time my mother was named despite the fact that she has 40 grandchildren and 36 great grandchildren. Zippy became very special instantly at birth and subsequently everyone loves her too much to date. This is something at the moment she seems very much aware of. Zippy was relatively a calm baby from birth apart from the normal colicky abdominal pains children suffer from in the first 3 months of age. The age difference between jerry and Zippy is 1 year 5months 15 days. So just like Jeremy and grace, Zippy and Jerry has the usual sibling rivalry. Each fighting for attention. Their growing up resembles that of Jeremy and Grace.

Zippy is a nice little girl, full of love. She likes to help. She doesn't like to hurt people. She is always saying sorry, If she feels she has wronged someone. Whenever I have had a tough day, she looks at my face and tells me "Daddy be Happy". Since I don't understand the Kenya new education system CBC, I have taken her to Braeside School where she is doing international Education System (British Curriculum). She is doing very well in school and the teachers are happy with her.

My parenting style has changed overtime, so with Zippy we are doing more talking and negotiation. But I am still keen on her respecting authority thus grounding and some pinching is still part and parcel of her upbringing. Zippy and Jerry are growing up with a lot of love, lots of outdoor activities, storytelling and watching relevant children cartoons and movies. Their church attendance was disrupted by Covid 19 pandemic but that will resume soon. Zippy is coming up as a promising child in life and I wish her all the best. May God grant her blessing to achieve all her dreams.

As I conclude this section, I wish to thank beloved wife Mrs Beatrice Odero for a helping hand in parenting all the children. It is important for parents to speak one language when it comes to parenting. Through these children, the Odero Ong'ech legacy will prosper for my many years to come. May God bless all of them to either walk in **my dreams or my footsteps.**

In Zippy's own words:
My daddy is my friend, I love him so much, and you named me after your mother, my grandmother. You continually teach us the values of honesty and integrity and we have moments of joy and playfulness which are my most cherished times with my daddy. I remember when you came to pick me up from school amid your busy schedule, we had just came back from our school trip, I run up to you and shouted your name and hugged you very much to the amusement of my teachers. This is a moment I will forever remember, I am lucky to be your last born child and daughter.

Zippy Achieng Odero Pictorial story

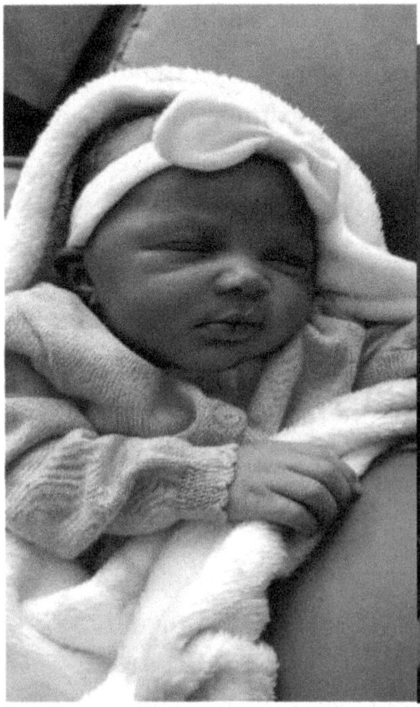

Left: 16.11.2018: zippy Achieng Odero at birth, 3580g, CS at Aga Khan Hospital, Nairobi
Right: Zippy one month old

Left: Zippy 2 years old; Right: **Zippy at 3 months old Jerry 18months old**

Zippy at 3 months old Jerry 18months old

Zippy at 6 months old, receiving blessings from namesake, Mama Zipporah Achieng and the late grandfather, Mzee Ong'ech Ogola

Zippy at 3 years old

Left: 2019- Zippy one year old; Right: 2020-Zippy at 2 years

CHAPTER 6: THE GREAT MZEE ONG'ECH OGOLA FAMILY:

6.1: introduction:

My father is called Jaduong' Jeremiah, who married Mama Sipora Ong'ech from Nyamonye Kowil (Yimbo). Sipora is the daughter of Apela Ombere and Agnes Oganga of Kowil, Nyamonye, Yimbo. The Ombere's family offered land for the current location of the Nyamonye Catholic Church, after the initial Kowil families who had been earlier approached declined, claiming the Mzungu wanted to take their land. This made Fr Auderaa (locally known as Odera) to go to establish the first ever parish in the district in Nyang'oma (Sakwa) instead. Later, when fresh plans were made to now establish a catholic parish in Yimbo, Mago offered land instead (the Othieno Family, led by the strongly Catholic Mama Monica- the mother of the late Owala and Osuri Okwayo[9]- who also has her roots from Kasau). The Omberes thought this was not right, and offered land where the main Yimbo Catholic Church was built. Mzee therefore married from a very progressive

[9] Osuri Okwayo remains one of the few surviving elders of Kanyathuon (Nyaugagi of Mago). He is aged 82.

and visionary family. Apela Omberes, Mzee's fathers in Law, have a prominent home at the Barkanyango Nyamonye Junction, just over looking St Augustine Nyamonye Girls Secondary School. The family therefore remains blessed, with the ladies from the Apela family managing a prominent fish business at the same junction just next to the road, on the side facing their home.

Mzee's marriage to Sipora started in 1949. Mzee had just come back from the 2nd world war (ended 1945). His Jayo[10] was his friend, Ogalo Kopol, with Mama Sipora being kidnapped in 1950. Dima and Onjiko, renounced musicians, were the singers to welcome the bride home. A total of 17 heads of cattle were paid as dowry. Mgele Odiang'a (Ja Kanyathuon ma Kadongo) was the Mzee's friend who took him for dowry payment, and gave him a suit to use. All the required marriage processes appropriately took place between 1950 and 1952, when Sipora was now officially married to then young and energetic Ong'ech Dola. Mzee's marriage therefore followed strictly the Luo cultural marriage process.

Mzee and Siporah Ong'ech [11]had many children, the first born being retired Japuonj Dalmas Ogola, who was born in 1953 in Nairobi. He was followed by retired Japuonj Joseph Ochieng Ong'ech born 1958 in Bondo, then Mary Atieno born 1962 in Uganda, followed by Margaret Auma born in 1964 in Kenya, then John Odero (Dr) in 1966 in Yimbo, Ogam (under a tree), followed by Benta Aluoch in 1969 in Yimbo, and lastly Grace Akoth in 1972 in Yimbo. Due to high child mortality rate, a number of children also died, but 7 children (3 sons and 4 daughters) survived to adulthood, of whom 6 are living. These have in turn given birth to 40 (up from 39 in 2018) children (Mzee's grandchildren, comprising 17 boys and 23 girls), 36 (up from 27 in

[10] Jayo is a Luo Go-between for the two families in marriage

[11] Sipora Ongech is a Nyakowil from Nyamonye. Her family remains one of the most prominent, the top being Councilor Obera Ombere. They have dominated the Omena business in the Nyamonye- Barkanyango/ Got Ramogi junction for decades.

2018) grandchildren (Mzee's great grandchildren, comprising 15 boys and 12 girls). The entire Mzee family therefore comprises at least 83 people, including Mama Sipora and her 6 surviving children. The youngest record holder is Zippy Odero.The breakdown is as shown in the table below, with details of each Mzee child given in more details in a later section.

An aerial view of Dola's home in February 2021

6.2: Ong'ech II's Family:

The late Jaduong Jeremiah Ong'ech gave forth 3 sons: Dalmas Ogola, Joseph Ochieng and John Odero, who in turn have among them 23 children (nyikwa

Mzee), comprising 9 boys and 14 girls. The Mzee also has four married daughters namely: Mary Atieno, Margaret Auma, Benta Aluoch and the late Grace Akoth, who have given forth 17 children comprising 8 okepe and 9 nyikepe. The details of these, as well as the entire lineup up to ndhukluhunda (Great grandchildren) and tukluhunda (great great grandchildren) are given as well. Overall, between 2018 when his autobiography book was being written and 2021, the year of Dola's demise, the family had approximately 76, comprising both parents (now I parent left), 6 children (remains same), 39 grandchildren (now 40), 27 great grandchildren (now 36), and 2 great great grandchildren (now at least 5). It means some marginal changes has occurred between 2018 and 2021, now comprising 84 (83 alive). Other than Dr John Odero, all Dola children now have grandchildren as well. The Dola children's family details are given below in a comparative summary table with detailed account of each of the children, their children, and their children's children.

6.21: Current size and structure in the great K'Ong'ech Ogam home

Currently (i.e., as at December 2021), resident at the Dola's Ogam home are at least 51 people comprising Mama Siporah, three sons, four daughters in law, 9 grandsons, 14 granddaughters, 10 great grandsons and 10 great granddaughters. Here the great great grandchildren are not included, thereby contributing to the + sign attached to the totals listed. From the daughters' side (all married) come in the rest of the family members with okepe[12] and nyikepe as follows: three daughters (surviving), 8 okepe, 9 nyikepe, 7 Okepe II and 9 Nyikepe II. This gives a total of daughters, okepe and nyikepe Ka Dola as 36+. The + accounts for the great great grandchildren from the daughters' side.

---

[12] Okepe are boy children born by daughters; the mothers' brothers call the sisters' children okepe; the daughters of the girls are called Nyikepe by the girl's brothers. Eg Dr Odero and Ochieng call Mercy Achieng Okoyo and Eunice Atieno as Nyikepe, but they call Felix Odhiambo as Okewo (Plural Okepe).

	2021							
	PARENTS & SPOUSE	CHILDREN			GRANDCHILDREN			
		BOYS	GIRLS	SUBTOT	BOYS	GIRLS	S/TOT	GRAND
PARENTS	**1**							**1**
DALMAS	**2**	1	2	**3**	5	4	**9**	**14**
JOSEPH	**3**	5	10	**15**	5	6	**11**	**29**
JOHN ODERO	**2**	3	2	**5**	0	0	**0**	**7**
SUBTOTAL	**8**	**9**	**14**	**23**	**10**	**10**	**20**	**51+**
DAUGHTERS	**3**	8	9	**17**	7	9	**16**	**36+**
TOTAL	**11**	17	23	**40**	17	19	**36**	**87+**

6.22 Detailed breakdown by Dola child

1. **Dalmas Ogola**: with his spouse Carren Ogola (Nyar Kano), Dalmas has three children and ten grandchildren (Dola's great grandchildren as follows: The **Children are**: Dalmas Ogola Ong'ech's children are: Kennedy Ogola, Dr. Roselyne Ogola Mwangale and Faith Ogola; **Grandchildren**: Lenny Ogola, Consulate Ogola, Emmanuel Ogola, Leah Ogola, Zawadi Mwangale, Amani Mwangale, Yohanna Mwangale, King David Heri Mwangale, and Princess Leah Imani Mwangale.

	2021							
	PARENTS & SPOUSE	CHILDREN			GRANDCHILDREN and great grandchildren			
		BOYS	GIRLS	SUBTOTAL	BOYS	GIRLS	S/TOTAL	G/TOTAL
PARENTS	1							1
SONS	8	9	14	23	10	10	20	51+
DAUGHTERS	6	8	9	17	7	9	16	39+
TOTAL	14	17	23	40	17	19	36	87+

2. **Joseph Ochieng** with his three spouses, Nyagem, Nyalego and Nyagoma- have fifteen children and eleven grandchildren (Dola's great grandchildren as follows: The **Children are:** Vincent Onyango, Christine Juma, Joshua Odhiambo, Seline Atieno, Irene Akinyi, Lavender Awuor, David Owino, Rhoda Awuor, Zipporah Adhiambo, Peggy Auma, Eunice Awino, Jeremiah Ong'ech, Vallary Achieng', Leaky Ogolla and Grace

Anyango. **The grandchildren**: Evan Jacobs Onyango, Leticia Akinyi Onyango, Divockmilla Ochieng, Bruce Nollan Ouma, Precious Victory, Dotry Herly Odhiambo, Liam Allan Opiyo, Ashley Talia, Ainsley Zawadi, Kyler Roze and James Junior.

3. **Mary Atieno Ong'ech** has 4 children and 7 grandchildren. **The children are**: Christine, Joshua Odhiambo, Walter Omollo and Emmanuel Okeyo. **Grandchildren** (Dola's great grandchildren) are: Eugine Ochieng, Agatha Amandi, Abraham Omondi, Sharon Odhiambo, Mary Atieno and Anne Odhiambo.

4. **Margret Auma Ong'ech:** has 3 children and 5 grandchildren as follows: The **Children are**: James Omondi, Millicent Anyango and Jackline Akinyi. **Grandchildren** (Dola's great grandchildren) are: Graffin Andrew, Ian Goga, Lashawn Tavin, Tamara Aquila, and Catherine James.

5. **John Odero Ong'ech:** has five children comprising 2 daughters and 3 sons. **The Children are**: Jeremy Ong'ech Odero, Grace Obuya Odero, Humphrey Dave Odero, Jerry Odero and Zippy Achieng' Odero.

6. **Benter Aluoch Ong'ech:** has 7 children comprising 4 daughters and 3 sons, as well as 3 grandchildren. The **Children are**: Lucas Onyango, Teresa Awiti, John Ochieng, Everline Achieng, Michael Dache, Susan Akinyi [13]and Roseline. In addition, Benter has three grandchildren (Dola's

---

[13] Susan Akinyi is a granddaughter of the late Dola, and Nyakew Dr Odero, Ochieng; She was fondly called ASU by the grandfather who she took care of till his demise. Asu was Mzee's trusted home bank. He ordered his family to ensure ASU joined Nyamonye Girls Secondary school, which she did join in August 2020, a month after Dola's demise. Mzee Nolamone Nyamonye kod Nursing.

great grandchildren) namely: Fidel Castro, Maxwell Onyango and Henry Donel. Susan Akinyi is Dola's darling granddaughter who used to take care of him in his office (Duol), while she was learning in Kasau primary school. Jaduong' used to call her..ASU…she was his most trusted caretaker, including taking care of his accounts. In his final days, Mzee had no sense of sight. As such he relied on ASU's word…whatever she told him was the truth. And she did not disappoint. Asu did her class 8 exams the term Dola passed away. He told the family to ensure ASU is admitted in Nyamonye girls..another school Mzee had a soft spot for, and supported in his own special way…where a number of his granddaughters had previously learnt. This they ensured happened. Immediately after the KCPE results came out, Japuonj Ochieng communicated this to the author of this book, a former chair of the BOM of the school. This he connected to the Current BOM chair, Charles Obiero Afulo and the principal, Sr Agatha, who gave her admission. To sustain Mzee's passion for education, Dr John Ong'ech ensured that ASU becomes one of the founding beneficiaries of the Mzee Ong'ech educational scholarship, by giving a full 4-year scholarship to Susan. This is an excellent gesture sure to sustain the good that Dola stood for. Well done the Dola family, especially Dr John Ong'ech and Mwalimu Joseph Ochieng' who ensures all the documentation and records are kept up to date.

7. **Grace Akoth Ong'ech's** children are Mercy Achieng, Eunice Atieno and Felix Oduor. In addition, she has one grandchildren (Dola's great grandchildren) named Shania Grace[14].

---

[14] **Shania is Mzee Dola's Ndukluhunda**

Left: Mzee Ongech grandchildren; Right: Right: Jeremy Odero, Mzee grabdchild, graduates

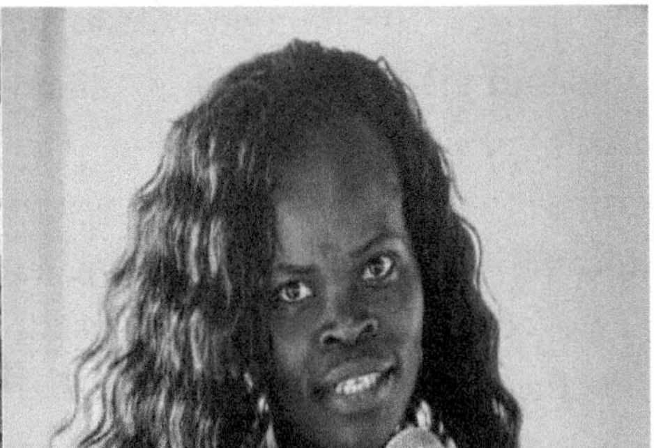

Left: Mzee children (Sons and daughters) Right: mercy okoyo, Mzee grandchild

Walter okeyo, mzee gandchild and wife

Mzee Ong'ech family celebrating graduation of grandchiold, Jeremy Odero

Mzee Ong'ech sons Ochieng' and Odero Ong'ech

Mzee Ong'ech daughters Mary, Benta and Margaret

Mzee's zeal and determination to ensure that all got education... the very thing he missed in Usenge due to school fees... was not in doubt. This he pushed at family level and beyond. This is **a dream** that all his people are out to pursue. **And in it I dare to dream.** First, the thirst for education then quenchable only at Usenge sector in his days left him with a debt: his own children must drink from the same cup of that he missed- Usenge. He thus ensured that what he did not read at Usenge, he sent his two sons, the eldest and the youngest to accomplish. He therefore ensured that right from family level, this long standing pressure (a debt of some sort) gave him the much needed momentum which helped push his family to vey advanced educational level. This had a long beginning, starting with his own schooling experience hitherto detailed earlier, but summarized here.

Mzee's schooling dream.

Mzee Dola had **a dream**. **A dream** of education. He missed it, dropping out in class 3, but still **maintained the dream** that he shall concur at the right time. He **had dreamt** that the Usenge where he dropped in Class 3 is would give foundation and lifeline to his children. What he missed they must get…from Usenge. **We dare to live in his dream**. Mzee Dola, with his meagre income, struggled and ensured his elder sons, Ogola and Ochieng went through high school and college. When need arose, he would sell his livestock, bicycles, clothes etc. to supplement. He was also supported by the hard working mama Sipora through farming. Mr Warom[15], the then prominent Head teacher of Usenge high school, would collect sacks of maize from home as part of school fees for Dalmas Ogola, and later John Odero. Mzee was unable to support the daughters to compete high school even though they were brilliant. However, he ensured Auma got employed and Atieno settled in business. Auma employment by the government came in handy for the family later. In addition, close friends came in very handy at times. A key pillar in this front was the late mama Doreena Okelo Abei who was Mzee's greatest supporter for family education.

The understanding of Mzee's financial position and his willingness to pay full school fees given time (**He had a dream**…, much the same as he did with Mwalimu Ochieng and Ogola enrolled in Nyamonye under Japuonj Afulo, who never sent the children home for fee….and **had a dream** that the two were great performers and would one day save the family and community. Dola believed in this, and kept his side of the bargain following an agreement with his friend Afulo) and alternative options by Mr Warom made Mzee have a special liking for Usenge. According to Mzee, when

---

[15] Mr Warom was a long service no-nonsense headmaster of Usenge high school in the 1970's to mid-1980's. He hailed from Gem Sub county in Siaya and was instrumental in getting Dola a Form 1 admission letter for Dr John Odero. Warom was a strict disciplinarian who shaped Usenge and gave it shape and performance spirit and tradition. He hailed from Gem, and his people are believed to have been a long distant relative of the Kamhore clan. . At retire, he was the founding headmaster of Kawere secondary school in 1985, the same school where Prof Augustine taught as a volunteer teacher after his form 6.

Odero passed class 7 CPE exams, he got a form 1 admission to Chianda High School in Rarieda Sub county. But Mzee didn't like Chianda. According to him, children there were spoilt, and Mzee wanted Odero to learn in Usenge secondary, a school he was sure of, where even Odero's brother Ogola learnt. He talked to the late senior principal, Warom who gave Odero an automatic admission. At that time, Only Ogola had finished college studies in Kisii, but Ochieng was till in college. Knowing fee would still be a challenge, Mzee needed a place close enough, with someone whom he could easily approach and bank on his support and understanding to sort school fees issues. Warom offered this support'. Due to Mzee's good record at work, he was appreciated by the government by being offered an opportunity to nominate a family member for government employment. Mzee nominated Auma. She was therefore empowered and was able to partly support the family. This came to be handy when Odero was joining secondary school, and Auma contributed in the payment of the first high school fee.

According to Mzee, he encouraged Auma to use half of her salary (Kshs 300), while he also took salary advance to add to his salary to enable Odero go to school. For school uniform, Mzee used part of his arrears to take care. Therefore the first fee was paid, and school requirements purchased, with school uniform, and Odero went to school. Through the rest of his schooling in Usenge, Mr Ochieng took charge. However, whenever the full payment was not possible, Mzee would sell livestock to pay the fees. He ensured Odero did not remain at home due to lack of school fees. At University, Odero got full government scholarship, and used to use part of the allowance to support the family. The latter imparted early sense of responsibility in Odero, who has to date maintained the same in offering family support wherever it is needed.

6.4: Educational And Professional Profile of Mzee's Children and Their Families

6.41: *Dalmas Ogolla -1st Born*

Dalmas Ogola Ong'ech is the first born in Mzee's family. He is retired teacher who taught in many schools in Yimbo and Kano. He was an intelligent pupil in Nyamonye primary school, a quality that made Japuonj Afulo want to keep him even without paying school fee. However, Dola had a dream and a plan how to ensure his eledest child got the education that eluded him very early in life: he agreed with Japuonj Afulo on how to pay the school fee in instalments. This paid off, and Mwalimu Ogola was able to pay fee for Ochieng, who in turn paid fee for Odero (Dr Ongech). The peak of Mzee dream was fully realized through Dr Ongech who became and remains the key family, Kamhore and Yimbo pillar. To fulfil the last of Mzee's wishes and dream of having his eldest son Ogola having a well-established home, Dr Ongech alongside Dr. Roseline Mwangale have made a mark by honoring this dream: The Mwalimu Ogola Ongech home stands magnificently overlooking Mzee's home, a dream realized post Mzee burial. It's called living the **dreams of Mzee Jeremiah Ongech Ogola**.

6.42: *Joseph Ochieng -2nd Born*

Japuonj Joseph Ochieng, locally known as '*Mo*[16]*r*', is the second born of Mzee. He learnt in Nyamonye, alongside Ogola his brother. They were never sent home for school fees, because Dola had a dream of educating them despite meagre salary. An agreement with Japuonj Afulo, the founding head teacher of Nyamonye, paid off. Dola paid the fee in bits to the last coin. Through this, Mwalimu ochieng trained to become a teacher, head-teacher, and retired gracefully in Barkanyango. During his time of service as a

[16] Mor is the village / pet name for Dola's second born son, Japuonj Joseph Ochieng Ong'ech

teacher, he taught in many schools in Yimbo, starting with Majengo as an untrained teacher, and then Mago for 8 years immediately after his training. In all these cases, Mwalimu gave his all, ending up in an exceptional and exemplary service and teaching career spanning 37 years as he retire in 2018. He was a head teacher for many years, and has been in Bondo Teachers Sacco leadership for 2 decades.

At home level, Japuonj has contributed significantly to the education of Mzee's family, as a mentor, and as a parent. While teaching in Majengo, with the likes of the late Otieno Ogutu, Mr Solomon Oriaro Obalo (As head teacher), he helped push the academic standards of Majengo, to the extent Majengo led the region for many years. Japuonj Mor is a gifted footballer number 8 and was a football captain in high school and college. He is a great mathematician who posted the best math results in his class in Maliera secondary school.

At family level, he partly mentored Odero (Dr John Ong'ech) while studying in Majengo, and later Usenge High School. He also contributed significantly in paying Odero's school fees (Dr Odero has mentioned this elsewhere). These all contributed to make Mzee's home shine academically and intellectually. Mwalimu has a fast growing family comprising 15 children and at least 10 grandchildren. The Degree holders and ongoing professional, degree programmes and College programs and qualifications in his family include: (i) Vincent Onyango Ochieng-BSc Computer Science; and a Masters in health informatics (Jaramogi Oginga Odinga University Of Science & Technology (JOOUST, Ongoing) ; (ii) Seline Ochieng- B.Com (Finance); (iii) Lavender Ochieng – Bachelor of medicine and Surgery (Ongoing); (iv) Irene Ochieng- Bachelor of Education (Ongoing); (v) Joshua Odhiambo-Electrician; and (vi) Christine Juma – Trained Teacher. Currently, Mwalimu Ochieng Mor plays general home duties, especially family guidance and counselling, wearing the huge Mzee shoes (Dalmas is largely in South

Nyanza), and other roles. Below is a sample of the government appointment and gazzetement as a member of the health management committee of the then new Ogam dispensary.

THE KENYA GAZETTE

Published by Authority of the Republic of Kenya
(Registered as a Newspaper at the G.P.O.)
Vol. CXII - No. 98, **NAIROBI, 01 October, 2010; Price Sh.**

CONTENTS

Page: 3585

Gazette Notice No. 11897

THE GOVERNMENT FINANCIAL MANAGEMENT ACT

(*No.* 5 *of* 2004)

THE GOVERNMENT FINANCIAL MANAGEMENT (HEALTH SECTOR SERVICES FUND) REGULATIONS, 2007

(*L.N.* 401 *of* 2007)

APPOINTMENT OF HEALTH CENTRE AND DISPENSARY MANAGEMENT COMMITTEE MEMBERS

IN EXERCISE of the powers conferred by Regulation 5 (1) of the Government Financial Management (Health Sector Services Fund) Regulations, 2007, the Minister for Public Health and Sanitation appoints:

Under paragraph 2 (1) (e) of the Schedule

NYANZA
PROVINCE
BONDO DISTRICT

Anyuongi Dispensary
(1) James Abidha Rabet
(2) Nelly Guga
(3) Florence Oguda
(4) Margaret Magambo
(5) John Omungi

Gobei Dispensary
(1) Maurine Odhiambo Olwa
(2) George Atieno Bonyo
(3) Annastacia Augo
(4) Doris Omolo
(5) Amos Ochieng Aloo

Got Matar Dispensary
(1) Mrs Lorna Agina
(2) Millicent Ajuma
(3) Celline Ogutu
(4) Tobias Ouma
(5) William Okal

Kambajo Dispensary
(1) Boaz Aketch
(2) Charles Achieng Apol
(3) Emelda A ongowo
(4) Joyce Okuku Mware
(5) Grace Atieno Omollo

Kapiyo Dispensary
(1) Gordon Onyango
(2) Anna Jura
(3) Irene Onywero
(4) Joyce Oketch Ouma
(5) John Odhiambo Onywero

Mabinju Dispensary
(1) Aloyce Oketch
(2) Gladys Auma
(3) Sara Auma Okumu
(4) Hubert Onyango
(5) Lydia Ogolla

Mageta Island Dispensary
(1) Joel Ogwire
(2) Millicent Odhiambo
(3) Lydia Atieno Sidho
(4) Gladys Atieno Sumba
(5) Geoffrey S.O Ogutu

Mawere Dispensary
(1) Wilfred Ogada Oyaya
(2) Rose Ondiko
(3) Samuel O. Honge
(4) Grace Atieno Otieno
(5) Maurice O. Angira

Ndeda Island Dispensary
(1) Daniel Ajwang
(2) James Gumba
(3) Pamela Lumumba Orieba
(4) Christine Achieng Ominde
(5) Millicent Atieno Japalla

Ogam Dispensary[17]
(1) Joseph Ochieng Ong'ech
(2) Ann Caroline Anam
(1) Philip Okelo
(2) Conslata A. Ochola
(3) Judith C. Odwar

Ouya Dispensary
(1) Joseph Owegi Ojoro
(2) Stephen Ominde
(3) Tarcicias Okumu
(4) Risper Lwala
(5) Josephine Abala

Oyamo Island Dispensary
(1) Philip Ochola
(2) Maurice Ogonji
(3) Judith Ogutu
(4) Lilian Omondi
(5) Lillian Ochieng

Radier Dispensary
(1) Wilfred Asingo
(2) Joyce Oyoyo
(3) Otieno Agutu
(4) Selestine Owino
(5) Patrick Opiyo

Serawango Dispensary
(1) Leonard Auko Milla
(2) Kennedy Rabuku
(3) Irene Wasonga

[17] Ogam Health Centre is the brain child of Dr Odero Ongech. The chairman of the health committee at its initiation was Dola. Mwalimu Ochieng Ongech was later to be gazette as a member of the health committee.

(4) Ann Helida Odoyo
(5) Dominic Ogot

Ulungo Dispensary
(1) Wilson Nyangayo Abuya
(2) Macbain Odongo Ongombe
(3) Olga Achieng Juma
(4) Lydia F.A. Ochola
(5) Sarah Achieng Ooko

Usenge Dispensary
(1) Samson Okome More
(2) Juliet A. Ochieng
(3) Jane A. Were
(4) Margaret A Ngesa
(5) Pastor Philip Owawa

Usigu Dispensary
(1) Walter Winja
(2) Mary Odhiambo
(3) Sospeter Obumba
(4) Domnic Owigo
(5) Consolata Onyango

Uyawi Dispensary
(1) Peter Otieno
(2) Damaris Ajuong
(3) Hanington Lai Onditi
(4) Joanes Ayieko
(5) Jane Okuku

Appointed to be members of the Health Centre and Dispensary Management Committees for a period of three years.

Dated the 18th August, 2010. **BETH MUGO,**
Minister for Public Health and Sanitation.

PRINTED AND PUBLISHED BY THE GOVERNMENT PRINTER, NAIROBI

6.43: Mary Atieno -3rd Born:

Mary Atieno is the third born of Mzee, and is a business Lady.

6.44: Margaret Auma -4th Born:

Margaret Auma, a retired civil Servant, and currently a Business lady, is Mzee's fourth born.

6.45: Dr. John Odero Ong'ech- 5th Born:

Dr John Odero is the fifth born to Mzee. According to Mzee, Odero has *snatched* him a name (Odero *omaye nying*[18]...on a jovial and light note). Odero is now a practicing health practitioner in Nairobi, and retired formerly a renowned Chief Medical Specialist- Gynecology and Obstetrics, with a Bachelor of Medicine and surgery, a Masters degree in International health, (Tulane, USA); and a Master degree of Medicine in Obstetrics and Gynaecology. In 2018, he was appointed as the chief executive officer (CEO) of Kenyatta National Hospital (KNH), the national Teaching and referral hospital in Kenya and the region. However, upon consultation, he declined the offer largely on grounds of the potential to interfere with his professional practice and growth. The degree holders in his family are:

i. Jeremy Ong'ech Odero- Bachelor of business information Technology - Strathmore University;
ii. Grace Odero- Bachelor of Science (Biology)-South Western University, The Philippines.

The ongoing degree programs in Dr John Odero's family are:

i. Grace Odero – Bachelor of Medicine and Bachelor of Surgery at Cebu Institute of Medicine, The Philipines.

[18] Omaye nying- has taken the father's name and now more known with the name than the father himself

9/26/21, 7:19 AM - Dr Ongech O J: We had graduation party yesterday, for Jeremy Ong'ech Odero, my first born son. He graduated from Strathmore University with degree of Bachelor of Business Information Technology; 9/26/21, 7:22 AM - Dr Ongech O J: Grace Odero late last year had received Bachelor of Science degree in Biology (Pre-Medicine degree) which we had not celebrated, so we celebrated both degrees

6.46: *Benter Aluoch Ong'ech-6th Born:*

Benta Aluoch is the sixth born to Mzee. She is a business lady.

6.47: *Grace Akoth (Late) Was 7th Born- Last Born:*

Grace Akoth (deceased) was a business lady. The college graduate in her family is Mercy Achieng Okoyo with a Diploma in Nursing and Midwifery.

6.5: Dr Odero Children education:

Names	Son/Daughter	Education	Institution	Completion status
Dr. John Ong'ech	Jeremy Ong'ech Odero	Bachelor Of Business Information Technology (BBIT)	Strathmore University	Completed
	Grace Odero	Bachelor of Science (Biology, premedical)	South Western University, Philippines	Completed
		Bachelor Of Medicine And Bachelor of Surgery (MBBS)	Cebu Institute of Medicine, Philippines	Ongoing

6.6: Dola's Strength-Social capital

There is something in life called "Social Capital. The people you know; the people who know you and how they know you. This is an aspect Dola taught us all…relating well with everybody. People are the best resource you have.

6.7: Siblings:

a. All about Dr. Odero Ong'ech by Mwalimu Ochieng' Ong'ech (Brother).

It is not often that families are blessed to have outstanding personality from humble background who possess positive traits that later emerge as a hero, a model, mentor, sharing common insight, development oriented and finally a pillar and supportive to nuclear family level and entire community at large. The preamble is all about Dr. Odero Ong'ech who is a male adult born in 1966. He is the fifth born child in the family of seven children to Mama Sipora Achieng and Mzee Ong'ech Ogola, grew up in humble background, started schooling 1974 and went through 7-4-2-3 system of education. He exemplary performed well in his Education from Primary School to the University.

Dr. Odero Ong'ech as family knows him has displayed generosity, love to all and has a lot of humility. He is a firm believer in **hard work, academic excellence**. He has sustained **positive relationship** which has earned him respect. For those school going students, he understands their challenges be they parental, peer pressure, low self-esteem, money worries and so forth. He has cherished the idea of democratic free society and leadership development where all persons live together in harmony and with equal opportunities and progress. This has brought together all the great Ong'ech family.

He has approached his professional duties with great dedication, diligence, boundless courage and energy which earned him many awards and honour. In his own words among the dreams he hard was that more and more people be empowered and maximize the talents for individual/ family success in life so that they are able to enjoy comforts. His little efforts in supporting people and generous contribution were some of the happiest and fulfilling moments of his life. Those he has indeed supported and ongoing supporting.

1. **Family**: Parents and their relatives.
2. **Brother :** Mr. Ogola Ong'ech Family
3. **Brother** : Mr. Ochieng' Ong'ech Family
4. **Sister** : Mary Atieno Family.
5. **Sister** : Margaret Auma Family
6. **Sister** : Benter Aluoch Family
7. **Sister** : Grace Akoth Family.

COMMUNITY

Kamhore

- Obiero Family
- Ka Sipem Family
- Ka Akungu Family
- Ka Guda Family
- Nyangera – Kamhore
- Kamhore Manyala

LEARNING INSTITUTIONS.

- **Majengo secondary school**
- **Usenge High School**
- **Bar-Kanyango Secondary School.**
- **Nyamonye Girls Secondary School**
- **Ragak Primary School**
- **Kasau Primary School**

HEALTH SECTOR

- **Ogam Dispensary**
- **St. Gorety Nyamonye Catholic Dispensary**
- **Bondo Sub-County Hospital.**

CHURCH / RELIGION

- **A.CK Nyamonye parish**
- **A.C.K Bondo Dioceses**
- **Catholic Nyamonye.**

WATER/ SANITATION.

- PENWA Water Project
- Opondo Dam - Excavating the Dam and put it for community use.

SICK AND BEREAVED FAMILIES

- Generous support across board.
- ✓ His able leadership has enable him be engaged.
- ✓ Gives inspiration talks in several schools.
- ✓ Funding alumnae activities that was formidable in nature at Usenge high school.
- ✓ Research and presentation of various papers at different levels. He meticulously used his time to do part time lectures to Medical Students university of Nairobi.

In conclusion on behalf of myself and the entire great Ong'ech family I wish to thank you for the commitment and effort for turning round and face lifting the Socio Economic Level of the family. Your public relation and networking has built strong foundation for family prosperity. Your **deep connection** has never broken as it led to successful sendoff of our late DAD **JEREMIAH ONG'ECH OGOLA ON 26/02/2021**.

LONG LIVE DAKTARI! LONG LIVE GREAT ONG'ECH FAMILY!

Written by Brother Mwalimu Ochieng' Ong'ech

b. Caren Ogola:

I am Caren Ogola, I was born in Kano Kobura Ong'eche School. I was raised up and taught right on how to live with people. I am a Christian by religion ACK church. I met Dr .John Odero Ong'ech when I visited my husband Dalmas Ogolla Ong'ech. By that time Dr. John Odero Ong'ech was in std five (5) at Majengo primary school. He was quiet and loving child. He was punctual in everything that he was doing both at school and at home. Despite the challenges people meet as they struggle with life to be on a better place I would like to acknowledge the effort of Dr. John Ong'ech who has been there for me and my family in every situation I was down he would come and help me carry on to easen the burden. Dr. John Ong'ech is a God fearing, very social determined and updated with current information among other things he likes change, education and development. Dr. John Ong'ech and Dr. Roselyne Ogolla Mwangale consulted themselves and joined hands together and build a house for my husband and me. Thank you for your loving and caring heart and sacrifices you always make. You will always be my hero and all forever be identified with such a great shemeji. **Your legacy and memories lives forever in my heart. Caren Ogola.**

c. Mary Atieno Special tribute to my brother Dr. John Odero Ongech.

Dr. John Odero Ongech is the fifth member of the late Jeremiah Ongech Ogola family with I being the third out of seven members. Through his hard work and perseverance we've seen him rise from humble background to where Almighty God has brought him. (Aruba Jadaho) nickname that came from Kamhore of Nyangera clan as we call him is one generous man I have ever seen in my life. In early 90's when I lost my husband, he organized

Harambee for construction of my house and managed to construct a Mabati house when I was still living under a 10X10 grass thatched house.

Support for Education and Community Projects: Through our Dad's philosophy I have enjoyed a cordial relationship with my brother that have seen him assist both the nuclear and extended families and the community at large as far as education is concerned. The latest is my grandchild (Eugene) is a beneficiary. He has not only looked upon his family members but also the needy within the community and its environs. Giving back to the community he has steered different development projects e.g. Ogam Dispensary. My sisters and I have benefited from his kitty through educating our children to the highest level they are in, hence will make them self-reliant in future life. May God grant you strength to continue lifting up the educational standards of both the family, the needy and the community at large.

Social Welfare: Through the cordial relationship we've had with my brother and his family, he has built trust in me. He has always trusted me with handling his finances wherever required/needed:-

i. Oversaw the dowry payment for my sister in law (Mrs Beatrice Odero) whereby he sent me money to my account to purchase and organize the function to success.
ii. School fees payment for all the beneficiaries within my reach. The trust in handling his finances is not regrettable.
iii. During his home trips he usually calls me to draw out budget for entire period of his stay in the expense of catering that would sustain the family and his visitors.

Doc is a great friend of mine and a confidant to me. Anything he wants to do he shares out with me and seeks for my advice whenever he needs/requires. He is the only man that has made me step into an airport. And when I finish the duties assigned to me by him, he always order his driver to take me home and wherever I wish to visit till my doorstep. During his home trips, he always calls me to pick him up at the airport, making me curious about aeroplanes. I know one day "nitapanda Ndege" through his invitation. During the COVID-19 Pandemic Daktari had put me on cash transfer stipend on monthly basis that helped me sustain my family members. "Asante sana nimeshukuru sana efforts zako" - Aruba Jadaho.

Health: I thank the family of Daktari especially his wife **Mrs Beatrice Odero (Mama Zippy**) for her support in ensuring the greater Ongech's family health matters is looked upon. Aruba has always introduced me to his friends. Most of them are doctors. He even allows me to seek medical attention at his friend's clinic in Kisumu, **(Dr. Otedo)** without asking for payment. May God bless you and your family as they prosper in their day to day achievements. A great leader is born in you.

Long live brother and Mama Jerry and Zippy. **Mary Atieno Ong'ech**

d. Margaret Auma Ong'ech

Dr. Ong'ech is my immediate follower we literary grew up competing for everything just like every other siblings in every family. The good old days were tough for our family and we were united in love as one family. I remember the good old days that we used to visit our late father in town and the two of us would collect used magazines and resell to buy foodstuff for our family. Father was working but hardly earned enough to take care of the family. While back in the rural, you and I could also get up early, go to the ''shamba'' weed and then come back prepare for school and you could run so fast for about 5km and be in school in time since you were the time keeper too. I believe the pain and suffering back then drove him to work harder and harder to achieve all these.

My brother was very hardworking in school and this made me push harder too coz I never wanted to share a class with him or beat me to a class as he was the most intelligent boy back in the days. His brilliantness pose a threat and a challenge to me as I was thinking my younger brother will find me in my class and probably beat me to join the next class. I had to prove myself worthy too. He left history in every school he stepped in and until to date he is a celebrated scholar.

My brother has a heart of Gold, when he started working, he took it upon himself to lift up ***The Great family of Mzee Jeremiah Ong'ech*** right from single handedly taking care of our parents to taking care of our children's school fees. After being a widow barely 3 years into my marriage, Daktari has always been there for me, he took in my first son James Omondi paid for his mechanical training and also made sure my last born Jackie went through her university education with ease without asking me for a single cent. He also gave my son his first job and also helped my daughter Jackline get a job that she currently at which intern I have being seeing and enjoying the fruits of his labour since I'm currently living in a permanent house built by her that I never knew one day I will have. This has brought me back in 2005 when I was seriously sick, you took me to Nairobi and struggle to help me get better. I would have died if it wasn't or you. You extended your good heart to even non relatives, we have seen several people you have helped in the past and currently doing so and it's evidently that majority of those who passed through your mentorship are doing well.

Dr. Ong'ech my beloved brother, I love you so much I would trade my life for you if I have to. You have done so much for me that I cannot exhaust it all on paper, I wish I can retaliate but I promise to keep on praying for you and your family has I have been doing on a daily basis.

From your loving sister Margret Auma Ong'ech

6.8: Nephews and nieces

a. Vincent Ochieng

You remain an inspiration to the Great Ong'ech Family, being one of the top academic giants for the family and a true family leader. During your school time you baby-sat me as I was a young baby. You demonstrated care towards me during my growing up as a child and this never stopped as you fully supported my academic milestone through University Education where you ensured I attained my first degree under your individual sponsorship. During this time that I noticed the things you stood for and held so high during the mentorship time. They include integrity, discipline, honesty, hardwork, focus and finally generous. The above traits formed part of me as I went through my University Education and has remained part of me to date. I sincerely thank you for the full support and more specifically for the 5 years since this largely impacted my life and shaped me to whom I am today.

"Ajuoga" as we referred to you in the education camp centre, your legacy shall remain for the other generations to come as you have extended your generosity to many people making impact on their lives across Kenya through various fronts but more specifically to ALL your siblings academics path and their well-being. This is a true reflection of what my late Grand Father Jeremiah Ong'ech had envisioned, a society free of poverty.

As to Mwalimu Ochieng' Ong'ech home where am the first born child you have supported all my six siblings where 4 of us have managed to attain First academic degrees in various disciplines with one of them finalising prestigious course of medicine at The University of Nairobi. The others are trained Engineers in both electrical and water respectively where one has recently joined Top Kenya Premier League Club Gor Mahia Fc with your support. You remain a pillar of hope to the Great Ong'ech family support system.

Long Live Dr. John Odero Ong'ech
From Onyango Vincent Ochieng' Ong'ech
Msc. Health Informatics- JOOUST. Bsc. Comp. Tech- JKUAT. Dip. Project Management- Alisson. M&E Certification- Global Health eLearning Centre & AMREF ITC-KENYA

b. Lavender Ochieng:

My name is Lavender Awuor Ochieng', daughter of mwalimu Joseph Ochieng' Ong'ech and niece to Dr. John Odero Ong'ech. I am a fifth year medical student at the University of Nairobi. It is a big blessing to have the most amazing uncle in the whole world and I thank God so much for him. My encounter with him has been the best and I feel so lucky to have him in my life. First of all my uncle is so intelligent and bright, from his exemplary academic performance in high school that I was shown by my dad to joining medical school in the best university around. He loves education so much that he will offer support to anyone who wants to go to school and will make sure you get the best education. I remember when I was still in primary school and high school and was performing well he would give me amazing gifts. This really motivated me to work more hard in school. As a child and even now I have had my imaginations of who and what I want to become and one person who has inspired me a lot and I would like to be like is my uncle. I look up to him as my role model.

Secondly my uncle's kindness and generosity is out of this world. He is such a selfless man who has not only touched everyone's life in the great Ong'ech family but also in Ogam village at large and even outside the village. My uncle is the one sponsoring my university education. He has given me the best life one could ever imagine not even ask for. He has been more than an uncle to me; he treats me like his own child and encourages me to work hard.

He offers me guidance in my medical training journey since he has been there before. Thank you so much uncle for all you have done for me.

My uncle loves those who excel and make progress in life and will support you fully no matter the field or area you are excelling in. If asked to describe my uncle in one sentence I would simply say he's a wonderful man, loving, compassionate and generous.

c. Mercy Okoyo

Mercy Okoyo first born to late Grace Akoth, over the past 20 years Dr. Ong'ech has been supporter, adviser, counsellor, educator, mentor, a man of honor and integrity. I take this moment to express my extreme gratitude to him, he has been so incredibly supportive of my education upto College level. He is a true role model for everyone in a position of education. He ensured that after finishing my training at the Nursing School, I secured a job at Coptic Hospital and then Kenyatta National Hospital where I currently work. **Mercy Okoyo (Late Grace Akoth Ong'ech Daughter)**

d. Walter Okeyo:

Mother's brother you took me in as your son and filled the place of my father. No questions about your loyalty. As many would call you Daktari...I prefer calling Ajuoga which translate to a doctor. For many years have known you u always wanted the best for me from school, career and personal life. I gained a lot from you for the years that have been next to you discipline, hard work, integrity and character has stuck with me till today and am grateful to you because they gift the cannot be taken away. The love, care and support have received from you can't be quantified and I will forever be grateful. You have seen through education, career development and sharing your wisdom and insights about living a good life I owe you a lot of gratitude. Thank you, Uncle, for all you do for me. I know it takes time away from your obligations and I want you to know how much I appreciate you.. God bless you and your family.

Walter Okeyo

e. **Triza Awiti/Benta Aluoch Ong'ech**

On behalf of Benter Aluoch's family, my heart is filled with respect and gratitude to my uncle Dr. John Ongech Odero for great support you've offered unto our family. Given anybody who was willing to learn an opportunity to go to school by paying our fees, business opportunities and even financial support. Truly you are a great mentor who is hard to find, difficult to part with and impossible to forget. Words are certainly not enough to express my gratitude towards your kindness to our family..May God bless you abundantly together with your family as you continue wearing the shoes of our Great grandfather; Jeremiah Ongech

Triza Awiti/Benta Aluoch Ong'ech.

f. **Jackline Onuko**

To Dr. John Onge'ch

In a world full of uncles, I was so lucky to get you, I admire your achievements and aspirations, and every time I see a post about you, I feel proud to be associated with such great mind. Every soul you have touched would agree with me that you should be on ***the world Guinness book of records*** for being the best Uncle in the world. I feel such a special closeness to you. I always have, I guess it's because from the beginning, you have been there for me, encouraging me, offering a listening ear in times of troubles and cheering me on along the way. I never had the privilege to grow up with a Father but I'm grateful you stepped in at some point when I thought my life is over and held my hand. You gave me a shelter, food and paid my tuition fees. I have always dedicated my First class Honors to you since you made it possible by providing avenues.

My uncle is known for being harsh and strict and anybody who happened to live with him at some point would not dare cross is path, we feared him like ***"a simba"*** a lion king of the jungle. Hehehe this takes me back to the good old days when everyone could run and disappear at the sight of him, in fact just by hearing his car enter the compound the likes of Dan, Vinny, Apela and I would run to the bedroom and close the door, then they would say and I quote "Jackie you go and open the door for Ajuoga you know you are in his good side of the book" I would then open the door and let him in, he would check of everyone's welfare and probable stay for the rest of the afternoon that would again give us headache since we didn't want to be quarreled. As we grew older we came to understand the significance of His behavior as it impacted on our lives positively. We all became who we are today due to his strict nature.

Through the years that he natured me, Dr. Onge'ch taught me so much that if I have to write them all down then I will come up with a whole book if not series of books, I would mention just a few for the sake of this autobiography. He was the first to teach me how to wash clothes by the way. I started living with him when I barely knew how to wash, I remember the first time he gave me clothes to help him wash, and I washed them dirty. He came and shared step by step on how to clean a shirt and since then I was good to go.

Discipline and integrity are fundamental values that Dr. Onge'ch held close to his heart and passed to me. Daktari has always preached to us that without discipline you cannot prosper and excel however much intelligent you are as a person, without being disciplined you are nothing, I grew up seeing how disciplined and dedicated he is to what he puts his hands and heart in. he is always advising me to work hard, be disciplined and I will make it in life. I remember one of those fine days that he was in a good mood Walter and I joked with him to join politics, he smiled at us and said he don't want to be corrupted, we asked why and he said people might force him to give tenders to undeserving individuals and he wouldn't want to be a party to such then I said to myself, this man's integrity is on another level and when I grow up I would wish to be like him. Some of the virtues and values that I learned from daktari are:

- Time management; he always say time wait for no one and time is money.
- Honest and straight forward individuals; he borrow this from his late father
- Integrity
- Courageous
- Compassion and many more…

My uncle is my True hero, my great role model. When I'm asked to name one thing that I'm proud of, I always say, my uncle. You took a responsibility of taking care of me when my clan was laughing at my mother and us, it's like they had an hearing on behalf of my family and made judgement that no child born of my mom will ever go to the University, every time I remember that one phone call you made to my mother on her sick bed offering to help me through university that changed my life to date, I cry in pain and happiness at the same time as the reflection of my life back then and now is something to celebrate. Thank you so much for your kindness.

From your loving niece Jackline Onuko

6.9: Chapter pictorials:

Mzee Ongech family in early days

Left: Mzee Ongech with the Ogola Ongech family;
Right: Mzee in his duol

Dr Ong'ech with mother Siporah

Left: The Ongech Ogola sons; Middle: The great grandchildren of Mzee Ong'ech Ogola (USA citizens), grand Children of Mwalimu Ogola Ong'ech, having a light moment with Grandpa Odero Ong'ech in their home in USA, Michigan; Right: Mzee Ongech with his eldest son, ogola

Mzee and part of his family in 1981

6.10: Fulfilling Mzee's Dreams & last wishes: The Dalmas Ogola Home

The Ongech brothers celebrating the new Ogola Ongech house

The house completed in a record of 3 months. On May 2021 they able start living in the house in Yimbo Ogam.

Ogola Ong'ech's new housing structure being official opened. With him are brothers Ochieng and Dr Odero, the wife Nyakano and his sister in law, Beatrice Odero

6.11: Keeping Family Unity:

6.1.1.1: In solidarity with Mercy Okoyo in Kano for burial of her uncle

The Ongech Daughters with their niece; Centre: Family unity: Japuonj Ochieng Ongech leading the family condole with Mercy Okoyo in Kano after the death of her uncle. With him are with his sisters, children, nieces and nephews; Right: Family unity after Mzee Ong'ech demise- supporting Mercy Okoyo (In blue; Mzee grandchild burry uncle in Kano)

Supporting Margaret Auma on losing her mother in law

10/23/21, 9:40 AM - Dr Ongech O J: 👍Family supporting Margaret Auma Ong'ech when she lost her mother in law- family unity post Mzee Ong'ech demise still intact

6.10.4: The family in support of the Ogola Ong'ech loss his brother in law at Kano Kobura;

The family unity is shown here on 11.9.2021…the family came together and supported the Ogola Ong'ech family during the loss of his brother in law at Kano Kobura;

CHAPTER 7: WORK LIFE EXPERIENCES

Prelude

"The key is not to prioritize what is on your schedule but schedule your priorities" Stephen Covey
"Be steady and well- ordered in your life so that you can be fierce and original in your work". Gustave Flaubert
"Once you stop thinking that you don't have money, and start thinking of ways to access it, your world will change" Kathy Fettke.
"You will never feel truly satisfied by work until you are satisfied by life". Heather Shuck
"We think, mistakenly, that success is the result of amount of time we put in at work, instead of the quality of time we put in" Arianna Huffingtom.
"The bad news is time flies. The good news is you are the pilot." Michael Altshuler.
"You can have it all. You just can't have it all at once." Oprah Winfrey.

7.1: My Public Working life

The story of my work life experiences starts immediately, I finished form six at Kericho high school. We finished exam in late November 1986. In January 1987, armed with form 6 mock results, I applied for teaching job at Barkanyango Secondary School. I was immediately hired by Okech Odiembo, the headmaster on merit but he was also the brother in law to Mr Ochieng Ong'ech, my brother. I remember him saying one month later when my form 6 KACE results came out (I scored 16 points, 3 principals + One subsidiary) that his instincts were right and the school is lucky he hired me.

Anyway I taught Biology at Barkanyango form 1-4. I was immediately made the Head of the Department, there was no other Biology teacher in the School. I also taught Mathematics in a few classes. I was later joined in the school by Owino Obara (now late) and Lumumba Midiwo (now a high school principal). The two taught arts subjects. We shared a house and had fun together. We were passionate and energetic. We produced very good results and many students joined the university and other colleges.

In June 1987, I went to the University of Nairobi to study medicine but left students with enough study notes as they did not have Biology teacher. The story is told of how these notes were shared amongst many schools in the region and produced good results during the national examinations. 1988, during vacations, I went back again to Barkanyango Secondary School and taught Biology. My last teaching experience was at Usenge High School in 1989. This was special to me because it was my former Secondary School, (Form 1-4). I was hired by the headmaster Mr Andiki. The school did not have a Biology teacher, so they desperately looked for me. My former Maths and physics teacher Mr Vincent Odhiambo was very happy with my come back. He decided to accommodate me in his house without contributing to any expenses. I taught Biology from Form 1 to 4 (the whole school). I was Head of Department of Biology. There were many brilliant students in the school especially the form 4 class of 1989 led by now Eng. Dick Omondi Ndiewo and Advocate Robert Oyiembo.

The students performed exceptionally very well in the national examinations. This was very fulfilling experience. The connections I established with students at that time like Dick Omondi Ndiewo, Robert Oyiembo, CPA Oduol (former Siaya Governor Aspirant), Dr. Ouko Okumbe, Deputy Governor Siaya county etc. remains to date. Being a teacher is very fulfilling experience especially if your students do well.

In 1991, at the end of my fourth year at medical school, we had a long holiday of over 6 months. I applied to Dr. Badia Willis to hire me to gain experience under his supervision. Dr. Badia hired me and posted me as clinician in charge of one his hospital. This was Mt. Sinai Maternity and Nursing Home in Bondo. I had not finished Medical School yet, but Dr Badia Willis entrusted me with this enormous responsibility. I took up the challenge and managed the place very well. Dr Badia Willis would come every week to supervise my work and he was very satisfied. This exposure would later influence my specialization choice as a Gynaecologist. An Earlier exposure by Dr. Hayanga GT during my medical School 1st year and 2nd year in Machakos Provincial General Hospital (during my holidays) also contributed significantly to this.

In 1992 during my 5th year in Medical School, I also worked in Oruba Maternity and Nursing Home in Migori, facilitated by my friend Dr. Benard Odhiambo Odoyo and Luke Kodambo (then Nursing Officer in charge at the facility). This was also another good exposure to the field of Obstetrics and Gynaecology. The doctors at the facility were great mentors- (Idagiza, Migoye and Okumu).

In 1993, when I qualified from University of Nairobi with Bachelor of Medicine and Surgery, I was posted to New Nyanza Provincial hospital Kisumu, as Medical Officer II (Intern), under ministry of health. Before taking up this appointment, I worked briefly at Miwani Sugar Company Hospital and Clinic. I took up the Ministry of Health appointment in January 1994 and worked at New Nyanza Provincial Hospital for one year up to 1995. I worked as Medical Officer Intern for 3 months each in the following departments:

(1). Obstetrics and Gynaecology under Dr Chris Oyoo and Beatrice Bonyo.
(2). Surgery- Under Dr. Omanyo and Raburu.
(3). Internal Medicine under dr GP Ogutu.
(4). Peadiatrics under Dr. Chomba and Muga.

The hospital overall boss then called Medical Superintended was Prof Richard Muga. We worked round the clock, taking calls daily, rarely sleeping and gained a lot of clinical experience. Although whenever we got off duty, we would experience the Kisumu night life- live music show by Okach Biggy and Ramogi were our favorites. In 1995 at the end of my internship, I took some time off and worked at Misikhu Mission Hospital in Webuye,

Bungoma County. This was a connection done by my great high school/ medical school friend Dr. Benard Odhiambo Odoyo, now the head of Mombasa county Orthopaedic services (The lead Knee replacement Orthopeadic Surgeon in Coast). They wanted to hire me for a permanent employment but I declined. I came back to Kisumu to a rude shock. Dr Richard Muga had posted all the doctors who had finished internship to hardship areas ranging from Wajir to Mandera etc. I had been posted to Wajir though on promotion as District Medical Officer of Health to take over from Dr. Moresh. Dr. Muga had vowed to discipline us for participating actively in the national doctors strike of 1994 led by Dr. Ateka that grounded services in the country but later earned us a small salary increase from a tough talking President Moi who had intimidated us thoroughly (we were thrown out of Government houses, hunted by police for arrests- I had to hide in Usenge Market running small clinic there for my survival) and stopped our salaries.

This was a tough moment in my life. I had to make a serious decision that would shape my future. Wajir was full of Bandits and once posted there, being released for further studies was impossible. There was no formal safe transport to Wajir, So Dr. Moresh arranged for me Kenya Air force Chopper to take me there. I rejected this posting and resigned from Ministry of Health. I was now jobless. Most of my colleagues were heading to South Africa. All you needed was to do an exams in Nairobi, get work permit and posting in one of the hospitals there. So as I planned to travel to Nairobi to register for this exams, Dr. Amos Otedo gave me a call the night before my travel that KNH was recruiting Medical Officers. He recommended that I try my luck there first. Then I remembered Advocate Benjamin Odhiambo Onianga (then a District Magistrate at Nyahururu) had introduced me to a friend of his called Makanda, then heading telephone services at KNH. I called Mr. Manas Makanda that I am coming to search for a job at KNH. Mr Manas Makanda told me that he would consult the CEO, Prof Meme on this. We talked the next day and he told me there were vacancies. He told me to apply immediately which I did. When I arrived in Nairobi, he arranged for me an interview directly with the CEO Prof Meme (Normally it would be the Deputy Director Clinical Services Dr. Muita who would do the interviews and recommend employment). Prof. Julius Meme interviewed me alone in his office, he was impressed and he hired me immediately with instructions that I must also be housed. This was implemented immediately. So on 23/10/1995, I was employed as Medical Officer I at KNH Causality/Accident & Emergency department at a salary of Ksh. 13,120 per month. This money was not enough for life in Nairobi. I had to supplement by doing low Cum/part time practice at AAR Health Services and Mater Hospital whenever I was off duty.

The hospital housed me in a 2-bedroom apartment at Nairobi west (Beverly hills apartment belonging to Hon Nyanja George, then Limuru MP). I performed very well as a Medical Officer at KNH Accident and Emergency department. The Deputy Director called me to his office to congratulate me. He was called Dr. Muita. He asked me to bring one of my friends who is a good worker like me. I nominated my Usenge High School/ Medical School long term friend Dr. Philemon Owino Oduor. He was employed immediately he availed his papers without an interview. He had been a victim of Dr.Mugas radical postings and was pondering what to do next with his life. The hospital was happy with the performance of my clinical work and I was asked to choose an area that I would like to pursue for my Postgraduate. I chose Obstetrics and Gynaecology.

To my surprise, the hospital posted me to work in the wards for obstetrics & Gynaecology for one year before starting my Maters. This had never been done before and was only done for me and a few others. It was never done again to any other person or group. Clinical experience in Obstetrics & Gynaecology department was very nice and fulfilling. It provided me with opportunity to be a head of others when we finally started our Masters

Program in 1999. On 13/10/1999, I was promoted to be senior medical officer III. Between 1999 and 2003 I worked as registrar in the department of Obstetrics and Gynaecology at KHN. I was also appointed Chief resident in charge of all the Postgraduate Doctors. I took advantage of one-year elective term in 2001/2002 and I applied for full bright scholarship to USA. In USA, I did Clinical attachments at Tulane Medical Centre and Louisian State University Hospital. This gave me a USA perspective of Clinical Care and practice. I also studied International Health (Public Health) at the same time. On 16/4/2003, I was promoted to Senior Medical Officer II. When I finished my Postgraduate later in September 2003, I was re-designated to Medical Specialist II on 16/9/2003 but without salary increase because I had risen to the equivalent as a senior Medical Officer.

So from 16/9/2003, I started providing Clinical services as Obstetrician and Gynaecologist at KNH at the level of Medical Specialist II. On 11/5/2010 I was promoted to Medical Specialist I and on 12/10/2010, I was appointed the Head of the Department of Obstetrics and Gynaecology. On 18/12/2012 I was promoted after Vigorous Board of management interview to Senior Medical Specialist, scoring the highest marks amongst all those interviewed across other disciplines. The board developed interest in me from this point and on 4/12/2015, I was appointed Senior Assistant Director (later designated as Deputy Director) in charge of all Surgical Services in the hospital (60% of all Clinical Services in the Hospital) on 26/4/2017. After another vigourous board interview, I was promoted to be Chief Medical Specialist in Obstetrics and Gynaecology. This is the highest level and by default, the Chief Gynaecologist in Kenya. This is a position equivalent to Full University Professor at the University. During my employment in KNH from 1995 to 2017, there had only been 2 other people who reached this level before me in Obstetrics and Gynaecology (Prof. Omondi Ogutu who also was my Mentor in Clinical work and the late Dr Njoroge Waithaka- who I took over from us HOD Obs/Gyn upon his death). Reaching this level was very fulfilling to me. We went to Mombasa South Coast for celebrations with my ever supportive wife Mrs Beatrice Odero.

My performance at the hospital was at its peak. The KNH board of management, Ministry of Health and the Country at large was aware of my good performance. In 2013 I had received the COYA (Kenya Institute of Management) Manager of the year award and in 2015, the grand leadership award by Kenya Obstetrical and Gynaecological society. I was also a great teacher (part time lecture) at the University of Nairobi school of Medicine where I had also won a lot of research grants from International bodies that I was implementing. I was also acting on and off in the offices of Director Clinical Services and CEO whenever either was out of the office. It is therefore, not surprising that in March 2018, the top leadership in Kenya appointed me to be the CEO of KNH (without consulting me). I rejected this appointment to the surprise of many. KNH budget is huge, almost Kshs. 20 billion (5 counties) but cartels and corruption on the institution is not a joke. The political interference is another stumbling block to good performance. Upon consulting my late father Mzee Ong'ech Ogola, I rejected the appointment (in the dreams of my father).

The subsequent leadership in the institution in 2018/2019 saw me as threat. So in 2020 I decided to take early retirement at KNH at the age of 53 years to follow my passion on Women Health Care in Private Practice. I was able to perform Clinical Work, Research, Lecturing and Leadership successfully and received many awards and recognition. I also mentored many people.

7.11: Public Health Programs

2003 University of Nairobi-CDC-Kenya; Designed PMTCT Training package for Intrapartum HIV testing, trained health care workers and implemented the first Intrapartum testing for PMTCT program in Africa

2004 Intrahealth international-Kenya (USAID funding); Designed PMTCT training
package for private sector, trained health care workers and initiated the first PMTCT program in private sector in Kenya
2004 Intrahealth International -Ethiopia (USAID funding); Designed the PMTCT training package for National Master Trainers, trained the first PMTCT National
Master Trainers for Ethiopia. Monitored the cascade of trainings in the region
2005 KCMC/EGPAF-Tanzania- Design PMTCT training package for Intrapartum HIV
Testing, trained staff, mentored them and initiated the first PMTCT Intrapartum HIV testing program in Tanzania at KCMC in Moshi
2008 HLSP (UNICEF Kenya funding); Evaluation of the safe motherhood project in
Kenya
2009 USAID AIDS Population Health Integrated Assistance (APHIA) II E; Midterm
Project evaluation (HIV/AIDS, PMTCT, Reproductive health, TB, Malaria and MCH services project)
2009 International HIV alliance-Government of Sothern Sudan (GOSS) - PMTCT Project- Adapting PMTCT training materials in the GOSS context using the first
PMTCT national guidelines for Southern Sudan, training health workers in Juba (from several states) and Wau (from several states), providing technical support in implementation and supervision in several PMTCT sites in Southern Sudan.

2010 UNICEF Southern Sudan -Government of Southern Sudan- UNICEF Southern
Sudan consultant;
-Developed the country first PMTCT training package and the Country National
PMTCT guidelines and strategic framework.
-Lead consultant in adapting the WHO 2009 PMTCT and ART guidelines in the

Southern Sudan Context
-Trained Master National PMTCT Trainers for all the states
2010 Somali- UNICEF Somali Consultant- Developed the country PMTCT policy,
Clinical guidelines, Training package, implementation plan, Monitoring and
Evaluation Tools
2010 UNAIDS-Kenya Government -UNAIDS Kenya Consultant for Universal Access Report development
2010 UNAIDS-Kenya Government- UNAIDS/TSF Consultant for developing 2010
Kenya HIV/AIDS epidemic update
2010 FHI-Kenya Government- FHI Consultant for developing minimum package for HIV- Reproductive Health integration
2010 CDC-Government of Kenya, Ministry of Public Health and Sanitation -
Consultant for updating Kenya National PMTCT guidelines and Training curriculum
2010 CAFS-TSF-IGAD Inter Governmental Authority Development- CAFS- Consultant
For capacity building on HIV-ART Protocol harmonization
2010 AB2000-NACCTOWA project- Capacity building for PMTCT Psychosocial support
Group, GIPA and quality assurance
2011 CAFS-NACC Kenya- Consultant for developing training Curriculum on GIPA and
Conducted Trainings targeting all key stakeholders nationally
2011 Tanzania- UNAIDS/UNICEF/TSF-Consultant for developing national guidelines for elimination of mother to child transmission of HIV
2011 Kenya Government-MSH consultant for developing devolved structure for
Reproductive Health.

7.12: Completed Research Support

2013-2019 Concern Worldwide /Philips Foundation/UNICEF-Innovation for Maternal, Newborn and Child health-MAKER Project. Role: PI, John Ong'ech. USD 600,000

4/15/2011-4/15/2014WHO-2011/141603-0/C6-TSA-024/FCH/CAH (PI, John Ong'ech)
Mobile phone technology for prevention of mother to child transmission of HIV;
Acceptability, Effectiveness and cost Role: Principal investigator, USD 500,000

20/11/2011-20/12/2012 and WHO-A65769 (PI John Ong'ech). Enhancing the capacity of pharmacist and pharmacy workers to offer information and referral services on Misoprostol for use in post abortion care in Nairobi, Kenya
Role; Principal investigator; USD 150,000

9/30/04 - 3/31/10 CDC –U62/CCU024526-01 (PI, James Kiarie), Capacity Building in the implementation of a comprehensive program to prevent mother to child HIV transmission at the University of Nairobi teaching hospitals. The overall goal of this program is to create a sustainable and quality PMTCT program in Kenyatta National Hospital and Pumwani Maternity Hospital that is be a national model for service provision and training. Role: Senior Technical advisor in charge of program implementation, coordination, performance management and quality improvement, USD 1 678 700

9/30/04 - 3/31/10 CDC –U62/CCU024526-01 (PI, James Kiarie), Impact evaluation of the Kenya National PMTCT program. The study aims to determine the extent to which the PMTCT program in Kenya in Kenya is meeting its aims of preventing transmission from infected Mothers to their infants, preventing unwanted pregnancy among HIV positive women, preventing HIV infection among young women and linking HIV infected women, their infants and families to long term care and support. Role: Co-investigator in charge of study coordination and implementation; USD 1 500 000

2008-2010 EGPAF- (PI, John Ong'ech), Operations Research Grant award

USD 250,000. The study investigated the Provision of services and care for HIV exposed infants; A comparison of the maternal and child health (MCH) clinic and the comprehensive care clinic (CCC) models.

Role: Principal investigator

2008 IPAS-Private Funding (PI, John Ong'ech).

USD 200,000 the study evaluated the status of Misoprostol drug in Kenya

Role; Principal investigator

9/30/07 - 3/31/09 CDC -U62/CCU024526-01 (PI, James Kiarie) USD 250,000. How late is too late? Timeliness to scheduled visit as an anti-retroviral therapy adherence measure in Nairobi, Kenya and Lusaka, Zambia. Role: Co Investigator

9/1/02 - 09/30/08 CDC - program announcement 02074 (PI, Ruth Nduati), Impact of HAART on MTCT and Mothers' Health USD 2 000 000. This study aimed to determine whether providing women with anti-retroviral therapy during breastfeeding protected their babies from HIV infection. Nested within it was a study to describe the impact of HAART on quality and quantity of passive immunity conferred on the infant. Role: Co investigator

7.13: International Conference Abstracts/Presentations/Posters

Ong'ech J, Oyieke J, Gachoki A, Machoki J, Mbori-Ngacha D, Kiarie J. Prevention of mother to child transmission of HIV; a multi-pronged testing approach to improve program effectiveness in Kenyatta National teaching and referral hospital. Abstract presented at XV International AIDS Conference, Bangkok, Thailand, 2004.

Ferguson L, Kielmann K, Grant A, Watson-Jones D, Vusha S, Ong'ech J, Ross D. Reasons underlying client attrition between testing HIV positive in antenatal and delivery services and accessing HIV care and treatment services in Kenya. Abstract presented at 6th International AIDS Society Conference, Rome, Italy; July 2011.

Ferguson L, Grant A, Ong'ech J, Kielmann K, Watson-Jones D, Ross D. Linking women who test HIV positive in maternity services to HIV care and treatment services in Kenya: missed opportunities. Abstract No. WEPDE105 presented at 18th International AIDS Conference, Vienna, Austria, 18-23 July 2010.

John Odero Ong'ech; Maximizing reproductive possibilities and choices for women living with HIV - pre-conception care and the prevention of unintended pregnancies, Oral Presentation at XIX International AIDS Conference in Washington, D.C., USA 25th July 2012.

7.14: Publications

1. John Ong'ech , Richard Ayah, Edwin Mbugua, Katie Waller Irene Inwani, Khadija Abdalla, David Gathara, Rose j. Kosgei. Effectiveness of a locally produced suction machine: an open -label pragmatic, randomized controlled non inferiority trial in national referral facility in Kenya: Journal of Obstetrics & Gynaecology of East & Central Africa Vol 1: Issue 3 June 2021

2. Richard Ayah, John Ong'ech, Edwin Maina Mbugua, Rose Chepchumba Kosgei, Katie Waller, David Gachara: Responding to maternal, neonatal and child health equipment needs in Kenya: a model for innovation ecosystem leveraging on collaborations and partnerships. BMJ Innov 2020; 0:1-7doi:101136/bmjinnov-2019-000391

3. Moses M.Obimbo, Yan Zhou, Michael T. McMaster. Craig R. Cohen, Zahida Qureshi, John Ong'ech, Julius Ogengo and Susan J. Fisher. Placental Structure in preterm birth among HIV Positive versus HIV Negative women in Kenya, J Acquir Immune Defic. syndr. Volume 80 number 1, January 1, 2019.

4. Seble G. Kassaye, John Ong'ech, Martin Sirengo, Judith Kose, Lucy Matu, Peter McOdida, Rogers Simiyu, Titus Syengo, David Muthama, and Rhoderick Machekano. Cluster-Randomized Controlled Study of SMS Text Messages for Prevention of Mother-to-Child Transmission of HIV in Rural Kenya. Hindawi Publishing Corporation AIDS Research and Treatment Volume 2016, Article ID 1289328, 8 pages http://dx.doi.org/10.1155/2016/1289328.

5. L.P. Parmar, G.N Mwango, M.N. Wambugu, J.O. Ong'ech ;The umbilical artery Resistive index and the cerebro-placental Ratio as a predictor of adverse Foetal outcome in patients with hypertensive disorders in pregnancy during third trimester; East Cent. Afri. Surg 2013 Vol 18

6. L. Jennings, J. Ong'ech, R. Simiyu, M.Sirengo, S. Kassaye; Exploring the use mobile phone technology for the enhancement of the prevention mother to child transmission of HIV program in Nyanza Kenya; a qualitative study; BMC public Health 2013; 13; 1131

7. Laura FERGUSON, Alison D. GRANT, Deborah WATSON-JONES, Tanya KAHAWITA, John O. ONG'ECH, David A. ROSS ; Linking Women who Test HIV-Positive in Pregnancy-Related Services to Long-Term HIV Care and Treatment Services: A Systematic Review; Tropical Medicine & International Health;2012;17(5);564-580

8. Laura FERGUSON, Alison D. GRANT, John O. ONG'ECH, Sophie VUSHA, Deborah WATSON-JONES, David A. ROSS; Prevention of Mother-to-Child Transmission of HIV - Understanding Reported Coverage of

Maternal Antiretroviral Prophylaxis and Vertical Transmission Rates ; British Medical Journal, Sex Trans Infect 2012;88;120-124

9. Laura Ferguson, James Lewis, Alison D Grant, Deborah Watson-Jones, Sophie Vusha, John O Ong'ech, David A Ross; Patient attrition between diagnosis with HIV in pregnancy-related services and long-term HIV care and treatment services in Kenya: A retrospective study; J Acquir Immune DeficSyndr 2012; 60: e90-97.

10. R.J. Kosgei, P.MNdavi, J.Ong'ech etal Symptom screen; diagnostic usefulness in detecting pulmonary tuberculosis in HIV infected pregnant women in Kenya. Public Health action; 2011;http//dx.doi.org/10.5588/pha.11.004

11. Dao CN, Peters PJ, Kiarie JN, Zulu I, Muiruri P, Ong'ech J, Mutsotso W, Potter D, Njobvu L, Stringer JS, Borkowf CB, Bolu O, Weidle PJ. Hyponatremia, hypochloremia, and hypoalbuminemia predict an increased risk of mortality during the first year of antiretroviral therapy among HIV-infected Zambian and Kenyan women. AIDS Res Hum Retroviruses 2011; 27:1-8.

12. Ong'ech J O, Hoffman HJ, Kose J, Audo M, Matu L, Savosnick P, Guay L. Provision of Services and Care for HIV-Exposed Infants: A Comparison of Maternal and Child Health Clinic and HIV Comprehensive Care Clinic Models. J Acquir Immune DeficSyndr. 2012 Sep 1; 61(1):83-9.

13. Blacher RJ, Muiruri P, Njobvu L, Mutsotso W, Potter D, Ong'ech J, Mwai P, Degroot A, Zulu I, Bolu O, Stringer J, Kiarie J, Weidle PJ. How late is too late? Timeliness to scheduled visits as an antiretroviral therapy adherence measure in Nairobi, Kenya and Lusaka, Zambia.AIDS Care 2010; 22(11):1323-31.

14. Stringer JS, McConnell MS, Kiarie J, Bolu O, Anekthananon T, Jariyasethpong T, Potter D, Mutsotso W, Borkowf CB, Mbori-Ngacha D,

Muiruri P, Ong'ech JO, Zulu I, Njobvu L, Jetsawang B, Pathak S, Bulterys M, Shaffer N, Weidle PJ. Effectiveness of non-nucleoside reverse-transcriptase inhibitor-based antiretroviral therapy in women previously exposed to a single intrapartum dose of nevirapine: a multi-country, prospective cohort study. PLoS Med 2010; 7(2):e1000233.

15. Beard JH, Ndegwa S, Farquhar C, Ong'ech JO, Govedi F, Kiarie JN. Mode of delivery decisions among HIV infected mothers at an urban maternity hospital in Kenya. East Afr Med J 2010; 87(1):14-19

16. Judith Kose, John Ongech, Peter Savosnick ;2010; Using Laboratory Networks to increase access to Pediatric HIV Care and Treatment; HabanaHaba Technical bulletin 2010 March vol.1 issue 3;13/20

17. Ong'ech J, Omondi-Ogutu O, Machoki M, Khisa W, Kiare J. Knowledge, attitude and practice on perinatal HIV transmission and preventive measures among antenatal mothers at Kenyatta National hospital, Kenya. J ObsGynae East Central Afr 2005; 19:1-11.

18. Ong'ech J, Omondi-Ogutu O, Machoki M, Khisa W, Orero SO. Post abortion care services at Kenyatta National hospital, Kenya.J Obs/Gynae East Central Afr2005; 18:98-106

7.2: Media Links with Dr John Odero Ongech

A rich professional contribution to society

7.21: Women's doctor with gifted hands
https://www.businessdailyafrica.com/bd/lifestyle/profiles/women-s-doctor-with-gifted-hands-3280112

BUSINESS DAILY, FRIDAY FEBRUARY 05 2021

Nairobi Reproductive Health Services chief medical specialist gynaecology and obstetrics Dr Ong'ech John O. during the photo session at his office on February 3, 2021. PHOTO | DIANA NGILA | NMG

When *JACKSON BIKO* calls Dr John Odero Ong'ech, an obstetrician and gynaecologist, to set up this interview, there is rhumba dripping in the background. In his office at Nairobi Reproductive Health Services where he is the CEO, he plays it at low volume. Dr Ong'ech is a voluminous character, full of mirth, and tales. He is a well-respected fertility doctor, having worked extensively in the public sector, his last posting at Kenyatta National Hospital as a Deputy Director, Surgical Services, and Chief Medical Specialist in Obstetrics and Gynaecology.

He has worked in dozens of missions in Africa as a consultant, authored books, research papers on maternal, and child health. He has two Master's degrees in Public Health (International Health), Tulane University, New Orleans and in Obstetrics and Gynaecology from the University of Nairobi.

What has been your best decade in life?

Interesting. In my 30s, things were shaping up, I was finishing my Master's programmes in Kenya [Obstetrics/ gynaecology] and in New Orleans [International Health] I had two children, now I have five. The future was shaping up nicely. My 40s started very well after laying a good foundation in my 30s. My career was set on a firm road. I was doing a lot of research, traveling all over the world with international collaborations. I felt I was on top of the world. Perhaps my 40s were my best years so far.

Was that your tipping point?

I climaxed in the 50s – I'm 54 now. I think I've arrived now, I've stabilised. I get to choose the things I want, like turning down the Kenyatta National Hospital offer wouldn't have been possible if I was younger. Financially, I'm secure. My children are grown, one has finished university, I can also see my daughter doing medicine.

How old are the children now?

My eldest is 21, my youngest two and a half.

How do you find fatherhood now as you compare to 21 years ago?

It's different. Twenty one years ago, I feared failing as a father. In fact, I thought if my son failed then that would be my failure. So I was extremely strict, I raised the rod a few times. Now I'm more compassionate and flexible.

Tell me the story of this lovely painting in your office. [A picture of a cottage by a river, framed by mountain range] What does it mean to you? It looks like it comes with a story. I love nature. This was a gift from one of my clients who had lost four pregnancies before seeing me. Now they have two babies. I think through talking– I talk a lot with my patients– they realised that I love nature. If I had it, that could be my dream place to stay in. I have built a small home in the village and planted a lot of trees. I love orchids.

Do you believe as a fertility doctor God works through you?

Indeed. I have many women who come here unable to conceive but end up getting babies. I feel that it's a calling and God has given me some special gift in my hands. To prove that point, not that I judge women, but I won't terminate a pregnancy. I'm pro-life but not in a dogmatic way. I mean, a woman would make their choices, but I would not use the same gifted hands to take away a life. My hands aren't for destruction. That's a decision I made a long time ago.

Did you always know you wanted to be a gynaecologist?

No. The person who mentored me in this profession was the late Dr George Hayanga. He was a big influence in my choosing this path.

What would you say is the biggest misconception of your profession?

With gynaecology obstetrics, we're dealing with the sacred area in human reproductive tracks. So it is the place where people don't talk. The mystery, I think, is that you can be able to navigate this area of medicine and still lead a normal life with your partner, and maintain professionalism. Some people always ask me, maybe jokingly, if I got into this profession because I like women, but come on, women are so many, how many can you like? (Laughs)

Now that we're here. When you spend the whole day looking at what you call the sacred areas, does it affect your marital life at home?

(Chuckles) No, no. You have to distinguish that work is work and home is home. When I'm here I approach it like a dentist approaches a mouth. When I leave work I switch off completely and when I get home I'm a husband. That balance is very important.

How was your childhood?

Aaah. The usual. I was born in Siaya County, Bondo sub-county, in Yimbo. My dad who is now 97 years old fought for the British in World War II. My mother was a stay-at-home mom. We had enough to keep us going. I wore my first shoe in Form One. I was always the brightest student in my school, so I was popular because of that, students wanted to be my friend and teachers had a soft spot for me. Then I just worked hard and doors kept opening; from Yimbo to the US and back.

What's your biggest struggle now as a 54-year-old?

(Laughter) To stay healthy. I am gyming morning and evening. I have bought a treadmill, bicycles, gym equipment... They're all in my penthouse upstairs. I'm keen on what I eat. I make sure I do low carbs, less fatty foods. I don't smoke. I stopped taking alcohol 10 years ago. But don't read me wrong, I can do champagne if I'm in a celebratory mood but it must be a high-class champagne, Dom Pérignon. I also avoid stress.

How do you avoid stress?

I let things pass. What I can't deal with, I say let it pass. It's never too serious. When I was younger, I'd want to be in control of everything, to be on top of everything but you grow older and learn that you can't.

When did you attain financial independence?

Do you ever? But I think it's when I finished paying my mortgage and things eased up. The mortgage was a killer. (Laughs). When it was done, I felt released. I don't have loans now, I'm not under pressure, business is thriving but I'm still a work in progress. I'm now free to focus on my legacy; give direction to my children, make sure I don't impose my values on them. I've built a hospital for my community and a water dam. How will I be remembered is my biggest question now.

Who is your favourite Rhumba artist?

Franco Lwambo, who else? Has there been anybody better? I love rhumba, the music of my youth and now of my adulthood. I listen to it here in my office, in my car and at home. At the hospital when I go into the theatre, they play for me Rhumba. My life is surrounded by rhumba.

What do you fear?

One, poverty. Oh, poverty isn't nice at all, Biko. The second thing is death. I don't want to die. (Chuckles) I want to live long to see my legacy that stands the test of time.

On a scale of 1 to 10, what's your level of happiness at this moment in time?

I'm ten. There's nothing I'm worried about. I'm very happy with my marriage, I'm very happy with the way the family is coming along. I only hope they live to achieve their dreams. I'm happy with the medical practice, my health is very good. I have some savings if it starts raining very hard. And I have Rhumba. (Chuckles)

7.22: City's top gynecologist wins award

http://www.nairobireproductivehealth.org/index.php/publications/category/7-awards?download=19:alumniofthemonth

https://www.standardmedia.co.ke/entertainment/thestandard/2000114481/citys-top-gynecologist-wins-award

The Standard Entertainment

The Standard: By Gardy Chacha | 8 years ago

Dr John Ong'ech

One of Nairobi's leading reproductive health specialist has won an award for his sterling performance this year. Dr John Ong'ech was awarded with The 2013 Kirit Dave Manager of the year award. Dr Ong'ech received the award at a gala dinner held at the Safari Park Hotel on November 8 and organised by Company of the Year Awards (Coya).

The gynecologist is the assistant director of reproductive health at Kenyatta National Hospital. The Kirit Dave award is a memorable tribute in honour of the late Kisumu businessman. The award ceremony was graced by Industrialisation Cabinet Secretary Adan Mohamed. Coya is an annual event meant to recognise Kenya's best performing organisations using the Organisational Performance Index (OPI) business excellence model.

Dr Ong'ech is a frequent contributor to The Nairobian's health questions.

7.23: **KNH Doctor Wins 2013 Manager of the Year Award**

https://m.facebook.com/media/set/?set=a.581819851891590&type=3&comment_id=582209921852583

KNH DOCTOR WINS 2013 MANAGER OF THE YEAR AWARD

by Kenyatta National Hospital

Dr. John Ong'ech, Assistant Director Reproductive Health at Kenyatta National Hospital was awarded 'The 2013 Kirit Dave Manager of the year award' during the Company of the year awards (COYA) gala dinner held at the Safari Park Hotel on 8th November, 2013. Kirit Dave award is a memorable tribute in honour of the late Kisumu businessman. He was eulogised as a great inspiration to many.

The occasion which was graced by Mr. Adan Abdullah Mohamed, Cabinet Secretary, Ministry of Industrialization and Enterprise Development, is an annual event designed to recognize Kenya's best performing organizations; private, public or non-profit using the Organizational Performance Index (OPI) business excellence model. The event also recognizes industry leaders and managers with an indisputable track record of success in turning strategy into action and continually improving their organization's performance.

In this year's COYA evaluation, twenty-five (25) large companies participated and for the first time fifteen (15) small and medium-sized enterprises (SMEs) contested the Small Medium Company of the Year Award (SMOYA). SMOYA which was officially launched during the gala dinner is intended to highlight the growing co-dependence between large firms and mid-sized companies. In attendance were Hon. Gerald Githinji Gakuha, Deputy Governor Kiambu County and Mr. Kinuthia Wamwangi, Chairperson of The Transition Authority.

147 Comments3 Shares
14 people like this.
3 Shares
Sasia Simon
Kudos Dr. Ong'echi, you deserve it.
8 yrsLikeReply**More**
Tumpeyo Baari
Congrats in order to Dr. Ongech!
8 yrsLikeReply**More**
Simon Kanyoro
Congratulations Dr.Ong'ech!
8 yrsLikeReply**More**
Alice Injeni
congrats Dr.ongech God bless u
8 yrsLikeReply**More**
Sally Mwikali
Congrats
8 yrsLikeReply**More**

Odhiang B. Okach

Congrats. Dr Ong'ech is a really good Doctor.

8 yrsLikeReply**More**

Bisharo Hassan
Cngrats.
8 yrsLikeReply**More**

Medic beats corporates to scoop top leadership award

BY JOANNE WANJALA

He was recently named the 2013 Kirit Dave Manager of the Year during this year's edition of Company of the Year Awards (COYA) organised by the Kenya Institute of Management (KIM) and various partners. This is none other than reproductive health specialist Dr. John Ong'ech, who is also the Head of Reproductive Health Department at the biggest teaching and referral health facility in the country, Kenyatta National Hospital.

The award was introduced in remembrance of the late Kirit Dave, a successful businessman and a member of KIM Board of Fellows. This was after a thorough evaluation of Dr. Ong'ech's leadership and governance at the hospital and how his contribution has transformed the mode of operations in the organization in promoting its vision and mission.

The award has not only elevated his managerial skills but has also raised the bar for KNH, the oldest and biggest health facility that has saved the lives of many people from the entire region since its inception in 1901.

"Although I believe in transformational leadership and culture change for the better, I least expected that I could beat the more than 10 competitors mostly drawn from the corporate world," Dr. Ong'ech says during an interview with the Standard.

"Our strive is to be a world class training, research and referral Hospital. My department has for instance already set up systems to ensure that all our operations are patient-centred," notes Dr. Ong'ech.

Dr. John Ong'ech

TRANSFORMATIONAL LEADER

He says since he took over leadership as the Head of Department at the Gynecology and Obstetrics Wing in 2009, change has been evident.

"We have managed to shorten turn-around time especially in the labour wards and reduced maternal mortality by 15 per cent through several interventions," he reveals.

Some of his achievements include:

Enhancing quality service delivery in reproductive health: Has contributed significantly in improving Maternal newborn Health through introduction of the now famous Prevention of Mother to Child Transmission (PMTC) of HIV program in 2003, an initiative that has improved maternal health and minimized mother to child transmission of HIV.

Innovations and Research: Last year, KNH pulled a first by introducing the PartoPen and Partograph technology that is used in determining the progress of a pregnancy until the time of delivery.

This was in partnership with the University of Colorado, which now enables staff in the labour ward to use paper-based system in monitoring maternal labor, which has helped reduce life-threatening complications in pregnancy in low-resource environments.

"This software tool is one of its kind and has never been used anywhere in Africa. It has contributed to quality of care and timely decision making, which is of essence in this section," says the Doctor.

Currently, KNH's labour ward has 20 of such pens and each comes with a charger.

Kenyatta National Hospital

The department also introduced a Hotline number in Labour ward to enhance effective communication and facilitate early referrals to KNH, thereby reducing late referrals and maternal deaths.

The Organizational Performance Index (OPI): He also chairs the hospital's OPI committee which has developed performance tools that to guide the hospital in enhancing competitiveness.

"Through these guidelines, this facility has improved its operations in various sectors. Several major departments have now embraced open leadership and strive towards customer satisfaction. We have also submitted our operation standards for external validation to the Joint Commission International (JCI), the highest hospital accreditation that only few hospitals in Africa have achieved," Dr. Ong'ech reveals.

OTHER AWARDS

He has also been honoured with other prestigious awards. He was the first Kenyan to receive Hubert Humphrey alumni impact award in recognition of his community contribution in Health, Education, mentorship and leadership.

He is the Alumnus of the coveted US Government sponsored training program dubbed Hubert H Humphrey (HHH) Fellow, becoming the first Kenyan recipient of such.

In addition, Dr. Ong'ech is also the recipient of the World Health Organization (WHO) Best Practices award after he pioneered the introduction of Intra-partum HIV Testing in 2003.

As COYA's Manager of the Year, he hopes to influence other managers especially within KNH to make the facility a model hospital and fast-track efficient service delivery.

"I believe in creating solutions to challenges. With commitment and goodwill from all, we can achieve so much."

The Board of management, management and staff of KNH congratulate Dr. Ong'ech for the award for this great honour.

KNH

Certificate of Recognition and Appreciation

Presented to

Dr. John Ong'ech

for emerging the Manager of the year - COYA 2013

SAD, Human Resource and Administration

Chief Executive Officer

7.24: Doctor declined plum job as "being too risky"

https://reject.awcfs.org/article/doctor-declined-plum-job-as-being-too-risky/

Unfiltered, uninhibited.... just the gruesome truth
Reject
Media Diversity Centre

BY · APRIL 19, 2018

A top doctor who turned down an appointment to replace the suspended Kenyatta National Hospital boss Lilly Koros in an acting capacity has spoken out on why he rejected the offer. Dr John Ong'ech, a chief specialist at the hospital said he declined the offer because the job was one of the most dangerous in the country. Health Cabinet Secretary Sicily Kariuki sent Koros on compulsory leave after an embarrassing and deadly mix-up in which doctors performed a delicate brain operation on a wrong patient.

The neuro-surgeon who performed the operation and a team that helped him were also sent on forced leave to give room for investigations.

This sparked protests from other doctors who went on strike to demand the reinstatement of their colleagues. Kariuki had announced that Ong'ech would oversee the management of the hospital in an acting capacity. She also appointed Dr Thomas Mutie as an acting director of Clinical Services.

The board had to go back to the drawing board after Ong'ech turned down the offer. In an interview with *Reject,* Ong'ech noted that this was a plum position that is enviable for many especially in a country where unemployment remains a big concern. Even though picking individuals for such positions remains a major headache for the appointing authorities because of intense lobbying by various players who want to be considered for the revered positions, Ong'ech says there is more to a job than just perks.

"I requested the board to allow me to decline the appointment. I have a lot of respect to and thank the country's health leadership for believing in my ability to serve this great county," said Ong'ech without regret.

He said that the position had a lot of challenges from cartels in procurement and politicians.

"This is a job of managing a budget of almost KSh13 billion per year and 4,000 staff. It also has unlimited access to power and influence but I declined based on the past history of the previous chief executive officers who never had a good ending," he explained. He cited an incident where a former CEO was allegedly picked from his house and shot. His decision took many by surprise, sparking off a heated debate on social media platforms.

While some lauded him as principled and of high morals, others chided him for wasting a golden job opportunity. To some, the incident pointed to the intrigues at the referral hospital. The hospital's chief gynaecologist is, however, unmoved by the criticism and says he would make a similar decision again under such circumstances. Ong'ech styles himself as a stickler for probity and accountability in public governance.

"Others may relate my decision to being rigid but this appointment could be a graveyard for my promising career," he explained, adding that making a change at the hospital that is riddled with a lot of challenges is a tall order.

Ong'ech, who believes in hard work and honesty, said he will still serve in his capacity to improve the lives of women and children. "In my opinion, service to our people is an honour and privilege which I continue doing even without being the CEO," he said. However, in a statement, the board chairman Mark Bor said Thomas Mutie, would be the acting Chief Executive officer and Peter Masinde acting Clinical Services Director.

7.25: Dr. John Ong'ech: My job is to keep women healthy

https://www.standardmedia.co.ke/evewoman/amp/article/2000185155/dr-john-ong-ech-my-job-is-to-keep-women-healthy

The Standard

EVE WOMAN

By GARDY CHACHA | 6 years ago

Dr. John Ong'ech ***Photo: Courtesy***

Dr JOHN ONG'ECH believes his is a call to serve women, he talks to GARDY CHACHA about the highs and lows of being a gynaecologist and what his wife thinks about his profession

Who is Dr John Ong'ech to a Kenyan who is yet to read or meet you?

I am a gynaecologist who is very passionate about women's health. I am also a mentor to young and aspiring doctors. Is that enough?

Your undergraduate was in medicine and surgery. How did you chose to specialise in gynaecology?

As a student in medical school my mentor was a gynaecologist. I have to attribute this to him. But I had also witnessed lots of problems around child birth and women's health. I knew I could make an impact and improve the situation.

Didn't you feel awkward that it was a 'female' field?

Gynaecology is not a female field. It is the clients who are female.

And by the way you treat men too?

Yes. I treat men. Sometimes I treat a couple – husband and wife.

What kind of gynaecological conditions do men come to you with?

Men come with issues of infertility, reproductive tract infections, and erectile dysfunction. That said, I still recommend that men always accompany their wives when they visit gynaecologists.

At any point in your career did you ever feel shy when a female patient knocked at your door?

No.

We recently heard of a gynaecologist who took advantage of his patients, what's your take on that?

I don't and have never looked at my clients as women. They are my patients. When I am within these walls I am here to treat and save lives.

Ideally, when female patients need to see a gynaecologist, how should they prepare?

They should be well prepared emotionally and psychologically. Gynaecological check-ups touch on the core of privacy.

Anything else?

They should avoid visiting gynaecologists when they are on menses. It makes check-ups a bit messy. Other things we can deal with.

Has your wife ever complained that you 'see' lots of women at work?

Pass. I can't speak for her.

Being a doctor people would imagine that you didn't feel the anxiety that new fathers feel when their wives are going into labour. What was it like for you?

It was probably worse because I was not only anxious as a new father but also as a medic. I thought of everything that could go wrong. With the first born it was tough.

The most difficult thing about your career?

These women like calling. They will call even at the most unholy of hours and you must answer all the calls. Maintaining your cool as you address their issues, even when it is something that could have waited till morning, is difficult.

Why don't you then switch off your phone?

You can never switch off your phone as a gynaecologist unless you want to go out of business. It has to be on and in high volume, 24 hours, round the clock.

How easy would it be to treat your own wife?

It is not the norm to treat your own wife. You let your colleagues do it. There are situations though that will force you to act. It is difficult though having to play doctor and husband at the same time.

If you never became a doctor, which profession do you think you would have preferred?

I would have pursued finance. That is where all the money is. Plus, it is a career that affects every other career.

Having experienced gynaecology, would you wish that your son followed in your footsteps?

I do. It would be easy for him now that his father is one. But my son does not want to be a gynaecologist.

When your kids ask, 'Dad, what do you do?' how do you answer?

They are already taught a lot in school. I tell them that I handle reproductive health in women. And I avoid going into the descriptive details.

When a female patient shows interest beyond coming to you for treatment what do you do?

The rule is to stay focused. I make it clear that we are here for a purpose - which is medical. Any other thing is not welcome.

7.3: Some U-Tube Media interviews

Below are some of my media interviews links available on YouTube

https://youtu.be/0tL9Rjck7UI
https://youtu.be/ipG8kQfjmbE
https://youtu.be/rq4QLy9t_OQ
https://youtu.be/qnisX594IcE
https://youtu.be/DyoYUjSjsZg
https://youtu.be/SkYmdN3jSR0
https://youtu.be/kudu7reU6cY
https://youtu.be/v8yzxPnNaQE
https://youtu.be/UojAQgipnEg

https://youtu.be/5QXXX_TaRkk
https://youtu.be/G8A6eJDQ8jw

7.4: USA embassy features Dr Ong'ech:
https://youtu.be/BEHX-urBUn8

7.5: Dr Ong'ech supports Mrs Margaret Uhuru Kenyatta during the launch of beyond zero campaign

https://youtu.be/im7Yjqxo_oc
https://youtu.be/ZCOv0GwAKOY
https://youtu.be/TD7zS9zcjA0
https://youtu.be/1LzXXv3RDVY

Alumni of the Month

March 2009

A publication of the U. S. Embassy Nairobi

DR. JOHN ONG'ECH

Many of us may not know Dr. John Ong'ech; and even if we do, we may not know him as an alumnus of a U.S. government sponsored program. He's humble, as a visit to his office demonstrates. It's a little office amongst others within the precincts of Kenyatta National Hospital, which would easily go unnoticed. However humble, Dr. John Ong'ech is proud of his exchange program experience. When I ask the doc; "What it was like as a Hubert H. Humphrey (HHH) Fellow in the U. S.?" he instantly has a glow on his face.

"Thanks for uplifting my spirit this morning," quips Dr. Ong'ech, "That was one of my favorite experiences in life… Not only did I have a wonderful time in the U.S., but I was also the first Kenyan recipient of the Hubert H. Humphrey Alumni Impact Award after my program." The award, which provides funding for projects that will impact an alumnus's country, enabled Dr. Ong'ech to build a dispensary in his home village. "It was for me a way of saying thank you to the community that brought me up and also showing the HHH program that my experience was the entire community's gain." The dispensary has since been taken over by the government and gazetted as a community health center.

Ogam dispensary

A 2001 HHH fellow, Dr. Ong'ech is economical with words about himself, and it takes two visits to his office for me to realize just how active he is in the community. An Obstetrician/Gynecologist, Dr. Ong'ech is the head of HIV training and research at Kenyatta National Hospital. With two masters degrees, he is also an honorary lecturer at the University of Nairobi's Obs-Gyn department where he is also the Prevention of Mother to Child Transmission (PMTCT) technical advisor.

Children having their meal on the feeding program

The list of Dr. Ong'ech's publications is endless. He has published numerous books and papers on his research findings. A winner of the 2007 Elizabeth Glaser Pediatric Aids Foundation (EGPAF) award, Dr. Ong'ech is also the principal investigator in the Perinatal HIV transmission studies funded by the Bill Gates and EGPAF foundations. He is a member of several professional associations, including the Kenya Country Team, which implements reproductive health best practices in Africa, a WHO initiative. Due to his rare expertise, Dr. Ong'ech is in demand from several local and international organizations. He is currently a consultant with EGPAF (USAID funding), Intra-health (USAID-CDC funding), IPAS, HLPSP (UNICEF funding), AB2000 (US department of state funding) in the area of HIV/AIDS and reproductive health project design, implementation, monitoring and evaluations.

Back in his community, he has initiated various projects for poverty alleviation and HIV/AIDS widows and orphans support. His organization AB2000 provides pediatric care, psychosocial support and counseling for the community through ***Kaluoch Widows and Orphans Group***. It also supports an outreach VCT program, provides supplies for early childhood education, and bought water tanks for the widows with which they harvest water and sell as an income generating activity. As a food security measure, AB2000 has trained the widows in farming skills and bought them dairy goats.

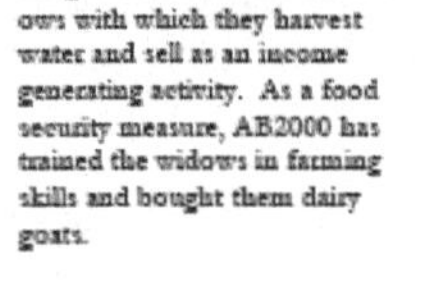

One of the dairy goats bought for the women's group

The orphans have benefited from an AB2000 run feeding program, while the widows have also received bicycles, which the community health workers use for home visits for people living with HIV/AIDS and taking the sick to hospital.

A community health worker ferries a sick child to hospital using a bicycle provided by AB2000

"I do these projects because it makes me happy to help my community," says Ong'ech. "I am glad that my area MP recently saw the benefit and installed electricity at the health center through the rural electrification program." Dr. Ong'ech continues to say that one of his challenges is lack of funding to help this program. "I always have to pump in my own money. For every consultancy payment I get, I spend about 30% on the community projects."

Dr. Ong'ech's is yet another success story from Kenyan state alumni. More on his work with AB2000 is on the net. http://www.ab-2000.org

7.6: U-Tube previews:

Preview YouTube video Youth group changing Kenya's back street abortion trend

Preview YouTube video Studies show junk food contributes to low sperm count

Preview YouTube video Curse of twins: Small clan ostracise women who give birth to first born twins

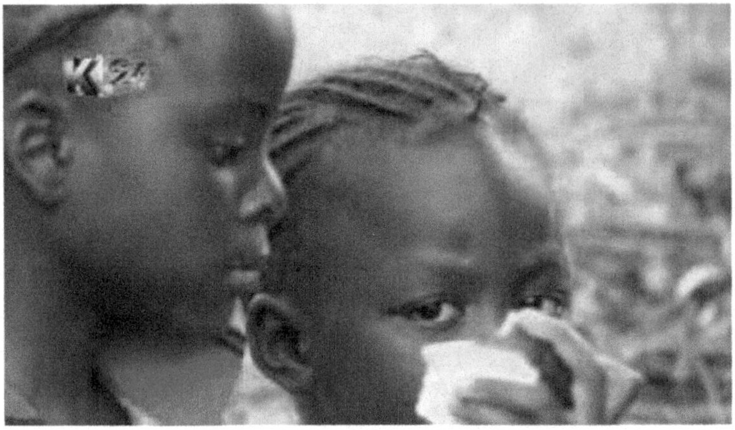

Preview YouTube video The Two Types Of Menstrual Pain And How To Treat It

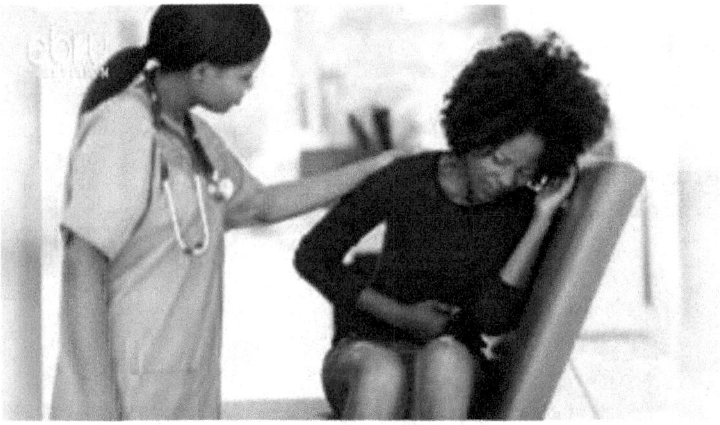

Preview YouTube video Your Health : Focus on methods that women use for family planning

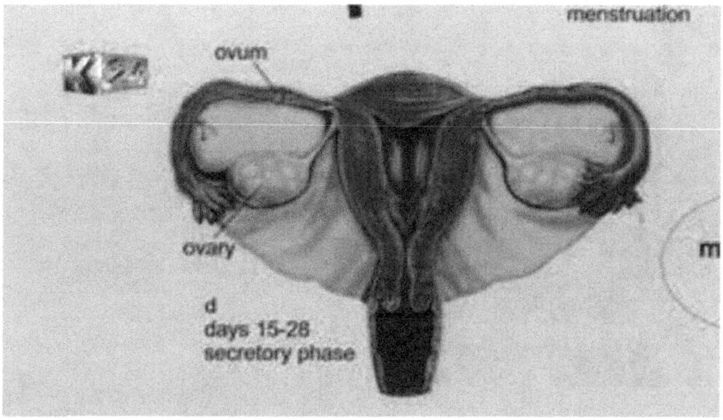

Preview YouTube video Your health: Focus on Endometriosis

Preview YouTube video Rai Mwilini: Kupoteza Mimba

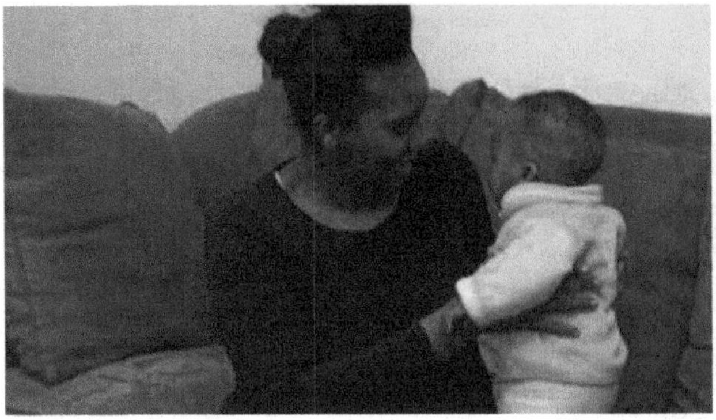

Preview YouTube video Rai Mwilini : Masaibu ya unyevu usio wa kawaida kwenye sehemu ya siri ya mwanamke

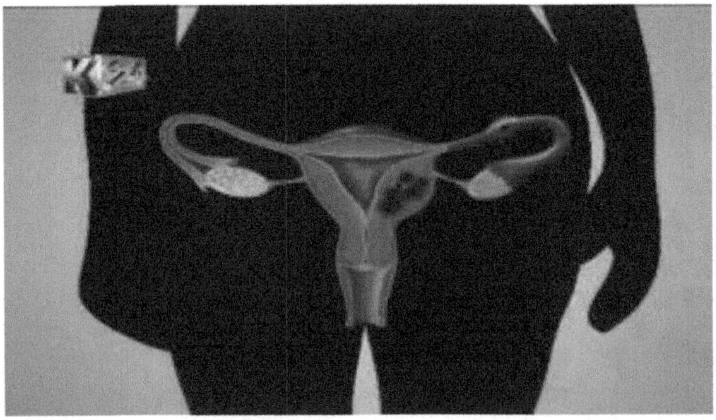

Preview YouTube video Your Health: Women in their 30s, 40s with symptoms of Menopause

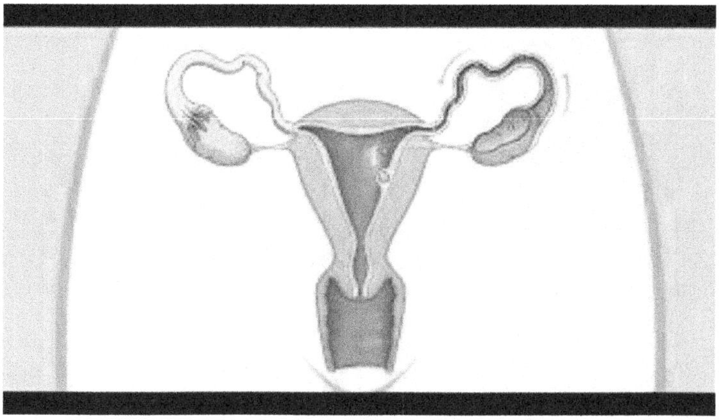

Preview YouTube video Dr. John Ong'ech

Preview YouTube video Dr. John Ong'ech - Happy moms are a good thing!

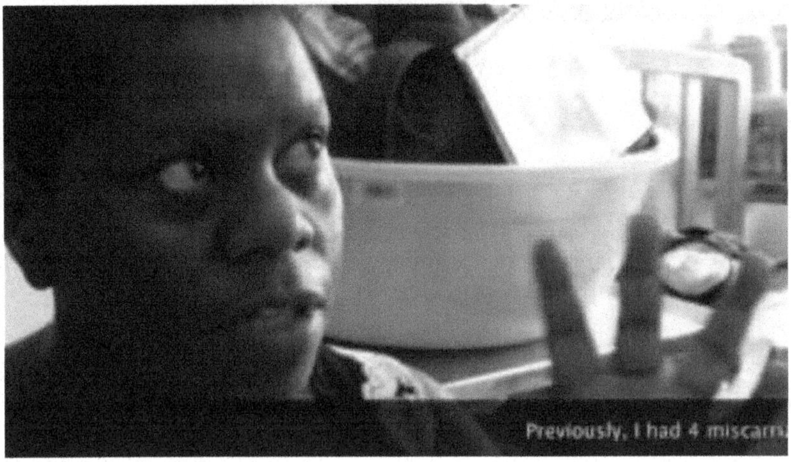

Preview YouTube video New Beyond Zero video

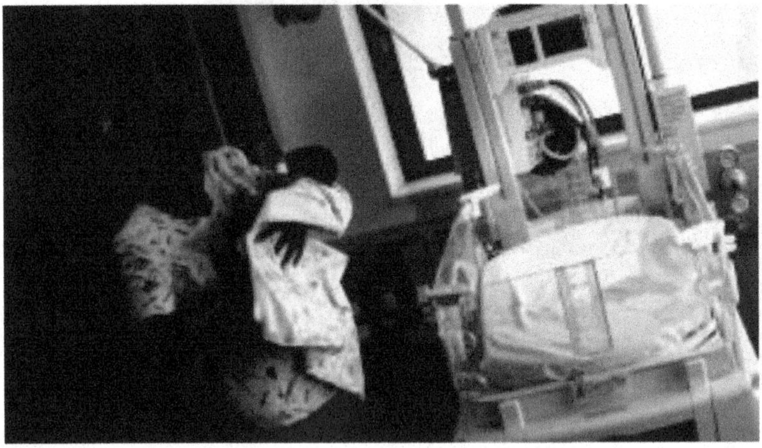

Preview YouTube video Power Breakfast Interview with Dr.John Ong'ech-Head of Reproductive Health,KNH

Preview YouTube video MATERNAL HEALTHCARE

Preview YouTube video Public health crisis interview with Dr Ong'ech Odero from Kenyatta National Hospital

Preview YouTube video Your health- On Morning Express:STDs

7.7: Honors & Awards

2015 Grand Leadership Award by Kenya Obstetrical & Gynecological Society of Kenya on improving women health care in Kenya.

2013 Manager of the year (Company of the year awards-COYA-Kenya Institute of Management)

2009 US Embassy, Kenya, Alumni of the Month of Mach 2009, www.alumni.state.gov

2004 WHO Implementing Best Practice Initiative in Reproductive Health in Africa-

Grand prize award for best PMTCT Program and Poster Presentation;

June 19-24 2004, Entebbe Uganda.

2002 Hubert Humphrey Alumni Impact Award, Institute of International Education (IIE), Washington DC, USA - HIV/AIDS Prevention and stigma reduction project.

2001 Hubert Humphrey Fellowship Award from the US Department of State

7.8: Professional Affiliations

2011 - 2019 Member of the Kenyatta national Hospital-University of Nairobi Ethics Research Committee

2008 -2010 Member of Data Safety Management Board (DSMB) for Valacyclovir in Pregnancy study.

2004-2008 Member of Kenya Country Team, Implementing Reproductive Health, Best Practices in Africa, a WHO initiative

2003-2018 Member of Technical working Groups at the Ministry of Health's NASCOP for PMTCT and HIV care and Treatment

2002-2008 Member of Hubert Humphrey Fellowship (Fulbright Scholarship), Selection l Panel at USA Embassy, Nairobi, Kenya

2001-2005 Member of America Public Health Association (APHA)

2003-2009 Member of Africa Centre for Clinical trials (ACCT)

1998- TO DATE Member of Kenya Obstetrical and Gynaecological Society (KOGS)

1993 –TO DATE Member of Kenya Medical Association (KMA)

7.9: Mentorship by Dr. Ong'ech 27th Oct. 2021

I think if I was allowed to truly write down everything I probably would end up writing a whole book because once Dr. Ong'ech focuses his lenses on you its wave after wave of commitment to you until you succeed and this has spanned over 24 years in my case. Today I will just give highlights and some of the highlights may or may not make it to the book.

My first encounter with daktari that I recall (he may have seen me in diapers I may not know) was around 1997 I was in class 5 (I was 9 years old) and I was to be pillow boy (bearer of the wedding rings) at his wedding, I for some reason really loved this task not knowing that it would be the beginning of his mentorship. I enjoyed riding on stage coach to go to town (I was on school holidays) so that I can make it to the venue we used to use to rehearse along valley road. I had never attended a wedding in my then short life, leave alone have everybody look at me walking down the aisle with the ring. For him to believe in me that much to not buckle under pressure with cameras all focused on me I may never know. My parents were late to come to pick me one day, it got dark at the rehearsal venue and in fear, I started crying. However, the bride and groom to be comforted me. I thereafter felt loved, and from here I learnt two lessons: (i) all children are the same; all they need is an adult to reassure them all is well; and (ii) the confidence daktari had in me to carry his rings. Years down the line while organizing my own wedding, I came to understand how expensive wedding rings can be and for daktari to entrust me to carry them was an honor and privilege.

I joined the UoN medical school in 2005, my father always told me that everyone has a mentor in life; someone to aspire to be- . And he told me "it's Dr. Ong'ech that I should follow". He had seen Dr Ongech's discipline, skills, work ethic and achievements, and equated him with a professional star and pride. My father would occasionally organize a trip or two in either the village or in Nairobi so that Dr. Ong'ech would give me nuggets and words of wisdom and this he never lacked on how to go about medical school and many more tips on life and way of living. I graduated in 2010 from the University of Nairobi and my mentor Dr. Ong'ech took time off his busy schedule to attend my evening graduation dinner at the intercontinental hotel. It was a really big deal for me. He not only gave me words of wisdom, but also welcomed me to the profession at the time I really didn't have anyone to look up to as I prepared for internship and life as a doctor. He generously shone his light in the seemingly dark path and I have gladly and gratefully followed. We kept in touch during my internship and life as a medical officer and whenever I had patients who had suffered from gynecological issues I sent them to him and they were always happy he also delivered babies for some of my friends, relatives. I remember one cousin coming back from Botswana where she delivered her first baby through caesarean section (CS) and she was expecting a second baby. The previous CS experience scared her and asked me to help her with a doctor who would deliver her. I didn't think twice in sending her to Dr. Ong'ech. To be honest, he shaped my decision to pursue a specialization in Obstetrics and gynecology.

In 2013 I wanted to join the University of Nairobi to pursue a Masters in medicine Obstetrics and Gynecology. I turned to daktari for advise. He was always welcoming and I remember showing up at his busy clinic thinking would be too busy he have time to see me. Of course its daktari Ong'ech he always had time he had taken time to get together a big bunch of past papers for revision he handed them over to me and told me to try my best and to use them to revise just to get a feel of entry exams. I got selected and proceeded to complete my course in 2017. During this time, there are many occasions that I turned to him for advice, and never even once did he disappoint; he always created time and even went ahead to trust me to run his clinics when he was away or engaged elsewhere. I had never In my life sat in a private obstetricians clinic and through daktari I once again got the opportunity that sometimes comes once in a lifetime of attending to his clients and he trusted me to do a good job.

Dr. Ong'ech continues to mentor me up to date. He brings me along during his major surgeries and during his ward rounds and I have learnt a lot including how to relate with different patients both at clinic and wards. Doc, you are truly in a class of your own and indeed a rare gem.

Dr. Vitalis Okola, consultant obstetrician and gynaecologist, KNH, Nairobi.

Left: Dr Ong'ech mentoring Dr Okola, now a consultant Gynaecologist at Kenyatta national hospital
Right: 2019-receiving certificate as a fellow, college of Obstetrician & Gynaecologist, East, central and Southern Africa (FCOG-ECSA)

7.10: Documentation of Profesional growth

Below is a list of correspondence of professional development (promotion) in chronological order from earliest to the most recent

The Government
of the United States of America

awards this certificate to

John Odero Ong'ech

in recognition of the successful completion of a one-year program of graduate study and professional development at

Tulane University

as a participant in the Hubert H. Humphrey Fellowship Program established in memory of an eminent American statesman

2001-2002

Secretary of State
United States Department of State

President
United States of America

s: "MEDSUP", Nairobi
e: Nairobi 726300
lying please quote -
....KNH/BA/PERS/VOL 2(2140)
and date

KNH BETTER HEALTH FOR ALL

KENYATTA NATIONAL HOSPITAL
P.O. Box 20723
NAIROBI.

(2)

23rd Oct 1995

DR. JOHN ODERO ONG'ECH
P.O BOX 84
NYAMONYE - BONDO

Dear Sir/Madam,

RE: OFFER OF APPOINTMENT

With reference to your application for employment dated 16/10/95, I am pleased to inform you that the Kenyatta National Hospital Management Board has offered you employment in the position of MEDICAL OFFICER I in the Department of CASUALTY on the following terms:-

1. Salary and Salary Scale
The salary scale attached to this position is in the Scale K. 7 viz: K£5622 x 255 — K£6337 x 300 — 10,137 x 333 — 11,136 per annum. Your commencing salary will be K£ 3629/7872 per annum. Your future incremental date will be determined if you accept this offer and report for duties in accordance with the Board's Terms and Conditions of Service.

2. Housing/House Allowance
You will be entitled to housing accommodation if and when available or to payment of house allowance in lieu at the rate of KShs. 3620 p.m. payable in arrears together with your monthly salary. (Married female Officers are only entitled to this facility on certain specified circumstances).

3. Annual Leave
You will be entitled to annual leave at the rate of 30 days per calender year, subject to the exigencies of the service, which shall exclude Saturdays, Sundays and Public Holidays.

4. Medical Benefits
You will be entitled to free in-patient and out-patient treatment for self and your family, subject to the provisions and limitations laid down in the Board's Terms and Conditions of Service.

5. Probation Period and Letter of Appointment
You will be require to serve a probationary period of 12 months, during which the services could be

terminated by either party giving the other one calender month's notice or one month's salary in lieu of notice. On successful completion of the probationary period you will be confirmed in your appointment and admitted to the Board's permanent establishment. This offer of appointment and your acceptance, duly signed and witnessed as indicated, constitute your letter of appointment.

6. Staff Superannuation Scheme
You will be required to join the Staff Superannuation scheme in operation in the Hospital. This is a contributary scheme where you will contribute 5% of your monthly salary while the Board contribute 10% of your monthly salary towards the scheme.

7. Conditions of Offer
This offer is subject to the conditions set herein and other provisions and/or limitations now in force or which may be promulgated from time to time. The offer is also subject to the following:-

   a. Satisfactory reports being received from your referees and/or your previous employer(s) (if any).

   b. Production of your original certificates and/or documentary evidence in support of your qualifications.

   c. Production of a Medical Certificate of fitness.

8. You are therefore requested to signify your acceptance of this offer within fourteen days by returning the attached copy, duly signed and witnessed, and affixing your passport size photograph.

Yours faithfully,

J.P.M. CHURI.
PERSONNEL & TRAINING MANAGER
KENYATTA NATIONAL HOSPITAL

ACCEPTANCE/~~REJECTION~~ OF OFFER

I. DR. JOHN ODERO ONG'ECH .... accept/~~do not accept~~ this offer on terms and conditions indicated in this letter.
I will report on .... 15th NOVEMBER 1995 ....
Signature.. [signature] .... Date........ 24-10-95
Witness: Full Name.. DR. ODHIAMBO J. OKUTHE ....
Address ....
.... BOX 20723 NAIROBI
Occupation .. MEDICAL PRACTIONER
Signature .. [signature] .... Date 24.10.95.

Tel.: 726300/726450/726550
Fax: 725272
Telegrams: "MEDSUP", Nairobi

KENYATTA NATIONAL HOSPITAL
P.O. Box 20723, Nairobi

Ref. KNH/531269/44

Date 13th October, 1998

Dr. John Odero Ong'ech

Thro'

The Head
Casualty Department
K.N.H.

Forwarded with compliments.
21/10/98

Dear Sir,

RE: PROMOTION

I am pleased to convey the decision of the Hospital Management that you should be promoted to the grade of Senior Medical Officer III with effect from 22nd September, 1998. The salary scale attached to this post is Job Group K6 viz Kenya Pounds 10473x330 - 10803x372 - 12663x399 - 14259x450 - 14709 per annum. You will enter this scale at Kenya Pounds 11547 per annum and your future incremental date will be 1st October.

I take this opportunity to congratulate you on this achievement and at the same time to wish you success in the service.

Yours faithfully,

J.P.M. CHIURI
PERSONNEL & TRAINING MANAGER

1998 (2)

Telegram: "MEDSUP," Nairobi
Tel.: 2726300-9
Fax: 2725272

KENYATTA NATIONAL HOSPITAL
P.O. Box 20723- 00202-KNH
NAIROBI

Ref.: KNH/ 531269/102 Date: 16th September 2003

Dr. John Odero Ong'ech

Thro',

The Head,
Obs. & Gynae,
KNH

RE: RE-DESIGNATION

Following your successful completion of Masters Degree in Obs. & Gynae, I am pleased to convey the decision of the Hospital Management that you should be re-designated from the grade of Senior Medical Officer II, Job Group K5 to the grade of Medical Specialist II, Job Group K6 with effect from 29th August 2003.

Please note that the re-designation is a change of title and **not a promotion**. You will therefore retain the same salary, salary scale and related allowances attached to Job Group K5.

Yours faithfully,

J. K. ONG'AYO (MRS),
For: **Personnel & Training Manager**

SALARY SCALE K£ 12291 x 372 – 12663 x 399 – 14259 x 450 – 16059 p.a.

SALARY KSH. 26,765.00
HOUSE ALL – 40,000.00
EXTRANEOUS – 15000.00
MEDICAL – 2220.00
TRANSPORT – 1370.00
NON PRACTISING 40000.00
RISK ALL. – 5000.00

Current Salary
85474

Scale 1/12/2005
K5 max:
pounds 31611 pa in
Scale pounds (minimum) 27561
to pounds (max) 31611

2003 (3)

TEL.: 2726300 - 9
FAX.: 2725272
Telegram: "MEDSUP".NAIROBI

KENYATTA NATIONAL HOSPITAL
P.O. Box 20723 - 00202, KNH
NAIROBI.

Ref: KNH/PERS/39/(29)

Date: 12th October 2010

Dr. John O. Ong'ech
Medical Specialist I

Thro'
The Deputy Director (CS)
KNH.

15/10/2010 Forwarded DDCS

RE: APPOINTMENT AS HEAD OF OBS/GYNAECOLOGY DEPARTMENT

You have been appointed to head the Department of Obs & Gynaecology with effect from **13th October 2010.**

As the Head of Department, you will be responsible to the Deputy Director (Clinical Services) for the planning, organization, control and co-ordination of all clinical and administrative services in the department to ensure delivery of quality service. You will also be expected to liaise with other Heads of Department both in the Hospital and the University of Nairobi (College of Health Sciences) in all matters aimed at quality service delivery.

In addition to your regular earnings, you will be paid the following office-related allowances attached to the position:-

	Category		*Amount per month (Kshs)*
i.	Telephone Allowance	-	4,000
ii.	Responsibility Allowance	-	2,200
iii.	Entertainment Allowance	-	680

Attached are two (2) copies of your duties and responsibilities as Head of Department. Kindly sign and return one (1) copy to the Human Resource Manager.

I wish you success as you discharge duties of the higher office.

Dr. J. N. Micheni
CHIEF EXECUTIVE OFFICER

Cc: P/File - 531269

2010 4)

KENYATTA NATIONAL HOSPITAL
P.O. BOX 20723, 00202, Nairobi

Tel.: 726300/2726450/2726550
Fax: 2725272
Email: knhadmin@knh.or.ke

Ref: KNH/531269/(209) **Date: 18th December 2012**

Dr. John Odero Ong'ech

Thro'
The Senior Assistant Director,
Surgical Services Division,
KNH

Dear Sir,

RE: PROMOTION

Following the interview you attended on 27th November, 2012, I am pleased to convey the decision of the Hospital Board of Management that you should be promoted to the position of **Senior Medical Specialist (Reproductive Health), Job Group K4** with effect from 6th **December, 2012.**

The salary scale attached to **Job Group K4** is **Kshs.89,748 x 4,487 - 94,235 x 4,712 - 98,947 x 4,947 - 103,894 x 5,195 - 109,089** per month. You will enter this scale at Kenya Shillings **103,894** per month and your future incremental date will be **1st December.**

All the allowances remain the same.

I take this opportunity to congratulate you on this achievement and wish you success in the service.

Yours faithfully,

Dinah Kirwa (Mrs)
SAD, HUMAN RESOURCE & ADMINISTRATION

2012 (5)

KENYATTA NATIONAL HOSPITAL
P.O. BOX 20723. 00202 Nairobi

Tel.: 2726300/2726450/2726550
Fax: 2725272
Email: knhadmin@knh.or.ke

Ref.: KNH/531269/(242)

Date: 4th December, 2015

KENYATTA NATIONAL HOSPITAL
RECEIVED
13/01/2016
DEPUTY DIRECTOR
CLINICAL SERVICES
P. O. Box 20723-00202, NAIROBI

Dr. John Ong'ech

Thro'
The Deputy Director (CS),
K.N.H

RE: **ACTING APPOINTMENT TO THE POSITION OF SENIOR ASSISTANT DIRECTOR, SURGICAL SERVICES**

In line with the revised Hospital structure meant to facilitate the Hospital's realization of its mandates, positions of Senior Assistant Directors were created to provide leadership and direction in transforming services in the Hospital. As part of the implementation of the new structure, officers in clinical areas who are already on substantive permanent and pensionable terms of service may from time to time be called upon to perform administrative duties on a rotational tour of duty arrangement.

Accordingly, you are hereby appointed in acting capacity as a **Senior Assistant Director (SAD) - Surgical Services** effective from **7th December, 2015**. Subject to continued satisfactory performance and/or any necessary administrative adjustments in line with the prevailing Hospital establishment, you may either be confirmed in the position or the position subjected to internal competition in which case if you are not successful, you shall revert back to your substantive clinical position.

The position you have been appointed to carries heavy responsibility. In this respect, you will be paid a Special Duty Allowance (SDA) at the rate of 10% of your basic salary, Responsibility Allowance of Kshs.20,000 and an Entertainment Allowance of Kshs.5,000.

On behalf of Management, I take this opportunity to welcome you to Surgical Services, assure you of Management's support and wish you the very best in your new role.

The duties and responsibilities of the position are herewith attached. Please sign and return a copy to the SAD, Human Resource & Administration for record purposes.

Yours faithfully,

Lily Koros Tare
CHIEF EXECUTIVE OFFICER
Encl.

2015 (7)

KENYATTA NATIONAL HOSPITAL
P.O. BOX 20723, 00202 Nairobi

Tel.: 2726300/2726450/2726550
Fax: 2725272
Email: knhadmin@knh.or.ke

Ref.: KNH/531269(383) Date: 26th April, 2017

Dr. John Odero Ong'ech
Reproductive Health

Thro'
Director, Clinical Services
K.N.H.

Forwarded and Congratulations 3/5/17.

KENYATTA NATIONAL HOSPITAL
RECEIVED
27 APR 2017
DEPUTY DIRECTOR
CLINICAL SERVICES
P. O. Box 20723-00202, NAIROBI

Dear Sir,

RE: APPOINTMENT

With reference to the interview you attended for the position of Chief Medical Specialist (Reproductive Health) on 6th April 2017, I am pleased to convey the decision of the Hospital Board of Management that you have been appointed to the position of **Chief Medical Specialist (Reproductive Health), Job Group K1 with effect from 6th April, 2017**

The salary scale attached to job Group K1 is Ksh.190, 075 x 31,441 - 252,957 x 31,442 - 378,725 pm. You will enter this scale at Ksh.190,075 pm and your future incremental date will be 1st April.

You will be entitled to the following allowances;

i.	House Allowance	-	Kshs 80,000
ii.	Out-patient Allowance	-	Ksh. 2,490
iii.	Non- Practice Allowance	-	Ksh. 60,000
iv.	Transport Allowance	-	Ksh.16,000
v.	Extraneous Allowance	-	Ksh. 40,000
vi.	Emergency Call Allowance	-	Ksh. 30,000

I take this opportunity to congratulate you on this achievement and wish you success in the services.

Yours faithfully,

PP **LILY KOROS TARE**
CHIEF EXECUTIVE OFFICER

16/4/2012 (8)

KENYATTA NATIONAL HOSPITAL
P.O. BOX 20723, 00202 Nairobi

Tel.: 2726300/2726450/2726550
Fax: 2725272
Email: knhadmin@knh.or.ke

Ref No: KNH/531269/357 **Date: 8th October, 2019**

Dr. John Odero Ong'ech

Thro'

HOD, OBS & GYNAE,
KNH

Wishing you the best in endeavours
Forwarded 23/10/2019

Dear Sir,

RE: RETIREMENT FROM THE SERVICE UNDER THE 50 YEAR RULE

Reference is made to your letter dated 1st October, 2019 requesting to be allowed to retire under the 50 year rule. This is to inform you that your request has been accepted. Your retirement therefore takes effect from **1st January, 2020**. Accordingly, you will proceed on **twenty eight (28) days** earned leave for the year 2019 with effect from **23rd October** to **29th November, 2019** and thereafter you will continue with your **one (1) month** Special Terminal Leave with effect from **1st December**, up to and including **31st December**, 2019, during which period you will be entitled to Salary, House, and Out-patient medical allowances only. You are advised to take your previous earned leave and/or off days before the start of your **Terminal** leave to avoid forfeiture.

On retirement, you will be entitled to Retirement Benefits under the Kenyatta National Hospital Staff Superannuation Scheme and Age benefits under the National Social Security Fund (N.S.S.F). You will also be entitled to Medical treatment for five (5) years after retirement as outlined in Personnel Circular **Ref.KNH/PERS/4/85** of **19th July 2000**. In this regard, you are advised to continue contributing towards **National Hospital Insurance Fund (NHIF)** to qualify for the service. You are also advised to ensure that all **Hospital liabilities** and **personal commitments** if any are fully settled within the notice period.

Please sign and return to this Office the enclosed Official Secrets Act Declaration Form, Declaration of Income, Assets & Liabilities and Bank Details. Also, have the attached Clearance Certificate duly completed in the relevant areas and return the same to our office to enable us process your dues as per existing Retirement Benefits Authority rules.

On behalf of the Hospital Management and Staff, I thank you for the service you have rendered to the public during your tenure with the Hospital and wish you a happy retirement and success in your future endeavours.

Yours faithfully,

Dr. Evanson Kamuri
Ag. Chief Executive Officer

2019 (9)

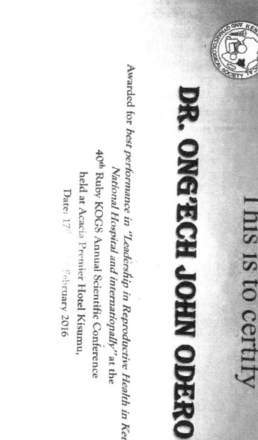

This is to certify

DR. ONG'ECH JOHN ODERO

Awarded for *best performance in "Leadership in Reproductive Health in Kenyatta National Hospital and internatiopally"* at the
40th Ruby KOGS Annual Scientific Conference
held at Acacia Premier Hotel Kisumu,
Date: 17[illegible] February 2016

Dr. Anne Beatrice Kihara	Dr. Benjamin Elly Odongo	Dr. Kennedy Onyango
Chairperson, KOGS	Honorable Secretary KOGS	Chairman, Western Branch

KENYATTA NATIONAL HOSPITAL
P.O. BOX 20723, 00202 Nairobi

Tel.: 2726300/2726450/2726550
Fax: 2725272
Email: knhadmin@knh.or.ke

Ref: KNH/ADM/CR/40 **10th September, 2015**

Dr. John Ong'ech
AD, Reproductive Health
KNH

RE: <u>CONGRATULATIONS</u>

Reference is made to a letter Ref. CHS/CESM/BNM/37/2015 dated 28th July 2015 appointing you as a member to the Pumwani Maternity Hospital Management Board for a period of three (3) years with effect from 1st September to 31st August 2018.

I take this opportunity to congratulate you on your appointment and wish you success.

Congratulations.

Lily Koros Tare
CHIEF EXECUTIVE OFFICER

C.C. SAD, HR & Administration

CHAPTER 8: RETIREMENT FROM PUBLIC SERVICE AND FULL TIME PRIVATE MEDICAL PRACTICE.

Prelude

"Don't act your age in retirement. Act like the inner young person you always have been"Unknown

"Retirement: a time to enjoy all the things you never had time to do when you worked" Catherine Pulisfer.

"Retirement mean doing whatever I want to do. It means choice". Dianne Nahirny

8.1: Retirement process and experience: in my own words

When I retired from KNH in 2020, I was 53years. My colleagues from the department of Obstetrics and Gynaecology organised for me a big party at a Five Star Hotel led by HOD Dr. Owiti Maureen and they made really nice speeches on my leadership, department transformation and being visionary. They also talked a lot about my mentorship. Then they gave me gifts. But one gift was outstanding and touched me. It was a nice portrait of a Giraffe. They explained that it symbolizes my vision of always seeing far. This has been mentioned a lot even by dear wife Beatrice Odero. So it must be true. I actually started preparing for early retirement from 2010.

Initially I was very active in doing consultancies implementing Public Health Programs and Research. I was doing very little in Private Clinical Practice. Then the vision came to me that these Donor fundings are not sustainable and I am not in control. The only thing I would be in control of is a robust Private Clinical Practice that one day will help me in retirement. So I quickly put up a strategy to build my Private Medical Practice. I needed a good practice environment, so I moved out of KNH Doctors Plaza to Nelson Awori Centre. Here I set up a system of for good private medical practice which is customer focused. To augment this, I activated my admission rights in all the major Private Hospitals in Nairobi. Private Medical Practice is controlled by the Insurance Industries and Cooperates. It was easy for me to be accepted in the industry because of the brand name I had built over time. Within a short time, I was included in the panel of providers for most Insurances and Companies. Currently I am in the following panels:

GDC, KRA, NSSF, Heritage, KPLCo AON MINET, SAHAM CIC, FIRST ASSURANCE,JUBILEE, BRITAM, KCB, PACIS APA, NCCK, CO-OPERATIVE,MADISON, NATIONAL ASSEMBLY,
RESOLUTION INSURANCE, AAR, UAP, PACIFIC, PARLIAMENT SERVICE COMMISSION
KENGEN, PACIS, SANLAM, LIAISON, KENYAN ALLIANCE, HENNER, CIGNA, EQUITY.

My Private Medical Practice became busy within a short time. Meanwhile my predictions on Public Health Programs Consultancies and Research by foreign Donors came to pass. Many people became jobless. So by the time I retired from KNH, my Private Medical Practice was thriving and I just transitioned to it. I now have more time for it. My patients in my Private Medical Practice now receive more quality care and I am more available. I am enjoying what I am doing and I feel happy that I am not stealing time from an employer as I used to during my days in KNH. Private Medical Practice also pays very well. I have been able to do many things due to financial stability. I feel satisfied and fulfilled. I am able to give my family quality Life and Education. I also have more time for holidays with my family. Currently I am focusing on Succession Planning which is not easy in Private Medical Practice but I will make it happen. Dr. Vitalis Okola whom I have mentored since he was in Primary School, through High School and through Medical School has proven to be just the right person for this.

On 5/3/2021, the Kenya Medical Practitioners and Dentists Council appointed me to the panel of experts for review of Disciplinary and Ethics matters in the field of Gynaecology and Obstetrics in the country. So I serve in the Disciplinary and Ethics Committee. This is a fulfilling appointment as it enables me to bring some sanity and integrity to the practice of medicine which has been deteriorating very fast in our Country. I am also exploring other areas in Occupational Health since I also hold a Master's Degree in Public Health (International Health).I recently received a license as a Designated Health Practitioner in the Directorate of Occupational Safety and Health Services(DOSHS) in the Ministry of Labour and Social Protection. The principal secretary in the ministry, Eng. Peter K. Tum gave me very high recommendation. These will open for me new doors as Company Health Advisors in top Cooperates in Kenya.

8.2: The private clinic staff, Awori House

The entire Nairobi Reproductive Health Services are sincerely grateful to have a director like you. We are very grateful for the far you have brought us.

We would like to thank you for your encouragement and support over the years. You are an exceptional boss who always has his employees' best interests in mind, and your leadership qualities and support have earned you much-deserved respect.

Thank you for being the friendly and open-minded boss that you are. Your support has furthered our career beyond measure, and your generosity will remain in our hearts forever. We appreciate your help so much.

Thank you for giving us an opportunity to work with you.

Be blessed.

Staff of Nairobi Reproductive Health Services (Name of Dr Ongech's clinic

MINISTRY OF LABOUR AND SOCIAL PROTECTION
STATE DEPARTMENT FOR LABOUR
OFFICE OF THE PRINCIPAL SECRETARY

Tel: +254 (20) 2729800
Fax: +254 (20) 2726222
Email: ps@labour.go.ke
When replying, please quote:

Social Security House,
Bishops Road
P.O. Box 40326-00100
Nairobi, KENYA

Ref. No. ML&SP/L/42/1

24th September, 2021

TO WHOM IT MAY CONCERN

RE: RECOMMENDATION LETTER – DR. JOHN ODERO ONG'ECH

Dr. John Odero Ong'ech is a respected leader in the medical/ health care sector in Kenya and internationally. He is a licensed Designated Health Practitioner (DHP) in the Directorate of Occupational Safety and Health Services (DOSHS) in the Ministry of Labour and Social Protection. Dr. Ong'ech is a valuable resource to the Ministry and has my highest recommendation.

Any assistance accorded to him will be highly appreciated.

Eng. Peter K. Tum, O.G.W
PRINCIPAL SECRETARY

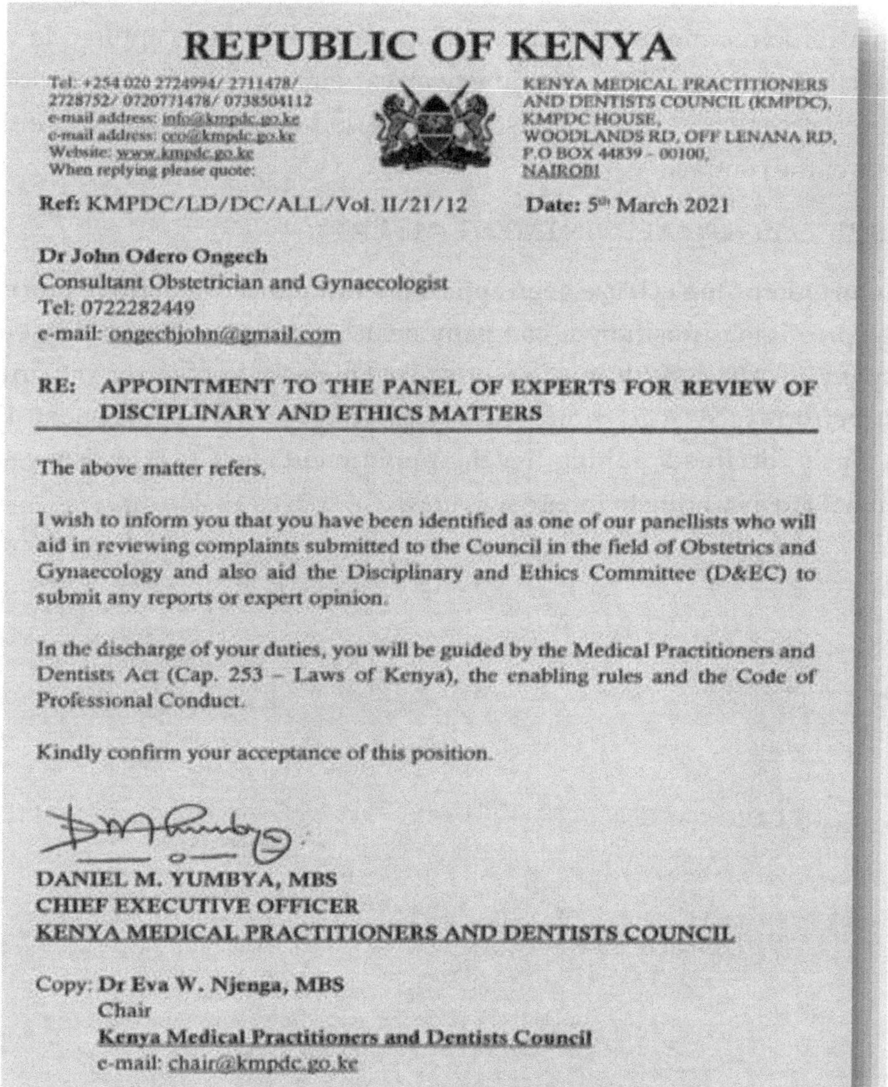

REPUBLIC OF KENYA

Tel: +254 020 2724994/ 2711478/ 2728752/ 0720771478/ 0738504112
e-mail address: info@kmpdc.go.ke
e-mail address: ceo@kmpdc.go.ke
Website: www.kmpdc.go.ke
When replying please quote:

KENYA MEDICAL PRACTITIONERS AND DENTISTS COUNCIL (KMPDC),
KMPDC HOUSE,
WOODLANDS RD, OFF LENANA RD,
P.O BOX 44839 - 00100,
NAIROBI

Ref: KMPDC/LD/DC/ALL/Vol. II/21/12

Date: 5th March 2021

Dr John Odero Ongech
Consultant Obstetrician and Gynaecologist
Tel: 0722282449
e-mail: ongechjohn@gmail.com

RE: APPOINTMENT TO THE PANEL OF EXPERTS FOR REVIEW OF DISCIPLINARY AND ETHICS MATTERS

The above matter refers.

I wish to inform you that you have been identified as one of our panellists who will aid in reviewing complaints submitted to the Council in the field of Obstetrics and Gynaecology and also aid the Disciplinary and Ethics Committee (D&EC) to submit any reports or expert opinion.

In the discharge of your duties, you will be guided by the Medical Practitioners and Dentists Act (Cap. 253 – Laws of Kenya), the enabling rules and the Code of Professional Conduct.

Kindly confirm your acceptance of this position.

DANIEL M. YUMBYA, MBS
CHIEF EXECUTIVE OFFICER
KENYA MEDICAL PRACTITIONERS AND DENTISTS COUNCIL

Copy: **Dr Eva W. Njenga, MBS**
Chair
Kenya Medical Practitioners and Dentists Council
e-mail: chair@kmpdc.go.ke

8.3: The safaricom award

The Award winning side of daktari comes out in true colours

This book is entitled……in the dreams of my father..from humble begginings to an award winning medical doctor. This part title is best captured in the most recent past by Dr Ongech winning an extremely competitive Safaricom contract of company health advisor for a period of 3 years. Below are the details of the contract.

12/23/21, 19:10 - 😀: *APPOINTMENT ALLERT*

Dr John Odero Ong'ech has been appointed through a competitive process to the prestigious position of company health advisor for Safaricom, best company in Africa, 67th in the world. Dr Ong'ech, known for integrity, high performance, strict work ethics, has accepted the appointment. He previously declined a high level appointment as CEO of Kenyatta National Hospital due to integrity issues.

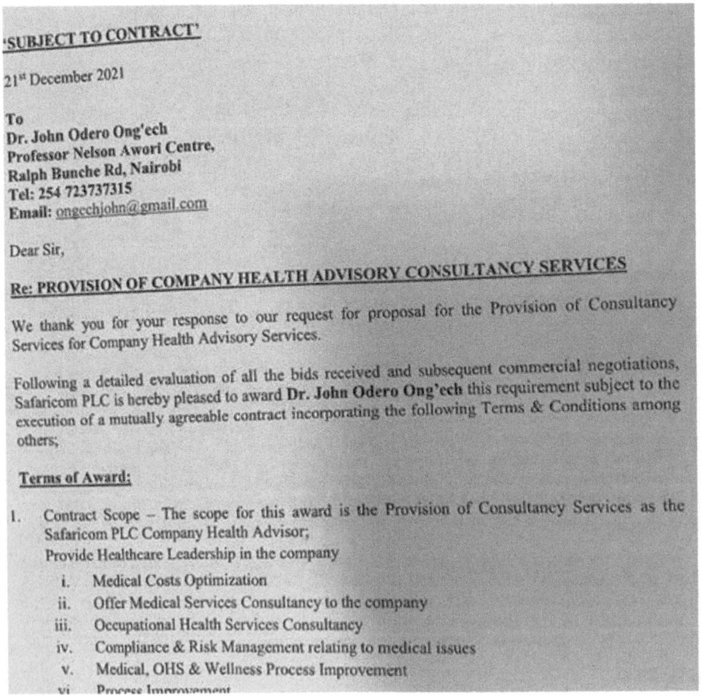

'SUBJECT TO CONTRACT'

21st December 2021

To
Dr. John Odero Ong'ech
Professor Nelson Awori Centre,
Ralph Bunche Rd, Nairobi
Tel: 254 723737315
Email: ongechjohn@gmail.com

Dear Sir,

Re: PROVISION OF COMPANY HEALTH ADVISORY CONSULTANCY SERVICES

We thank you for your response to our request for proposal for the Provision of Consultancy Services for Company Health Advisory Services.

Following a detailed evaluation of all the bids received and subsequent commercial negotiations, Safaricom PLC is hereby pleased to award **Dr. John Odero Ong'ech** this requirement subject to the execution of a mutually agreeable contract incorporating the following Terms & Conditions among others;

Terms of Award;

1. Contract Scope – The scope for this award is the Provision of Consultancy Services as the Safaricom PLC Company Health Advisor;
   Provide Healthcare Leadership in the company
   i. Medical Costs Optimization
   ii. Offer Medical Services Consultancy to the company
   iii. Occupational Health Services Consultancy
   iv. Compliance & Risk Management relating to medical issues
   v. Medical, OHS & Wellness Process Improvement
   vi. Process Improvement

Introduction-Why Dr John Odero Ong'ech for Company Health Advisory Services at Safaricom
Award winning medical Doctor and public Health expert-i) Recipient of Kenya institute of management company of the year award(COYA), manager of the year 2013 . ii) Recipient of Alumni impact award for Fulbright scholars, institute of International Education, Washington DC USA iii)other awards in the CV
Respected consultant for United Nations, US Center for Disease control and Prevention(CDC), United States Agency for international Development(USAID) on implementation of public Health programs across Africa
Well respected health care sector in Kenya-i)Member of the Kenya Medical practitioners and Dentist Council-Ethics and disciplinary committee ii) Well networked with many hospitals where I provide clinical care
Well networked in the Directorate of Occupational safety and Health services (DOSHS) in the ministry of labor and social protection with a highest recommendation from the principal secretary
I have the skills, experience , passion and vision to transform safaricom occupational health, wellness and clinical matters to global standards

Simple · Transparent · Honest FOR YOU

'SUBJECT TO CONTRACT'

21st December 2021

To
Dr. John Odero Ong'ech
Professor Nelson Awori Centre,
Ralph Bunche Rd, Nairobi
Tel: 254 723737315
Email: ongechjohn@gmail.com

Dear Sir,

Re: PROVISION OF COMPANY HEALTH ADVISORY CONSULTANCY SERVICES

We thank you for your response to our request for proposal for the Provision of Consultancy Services for Company Health Advisory Services.

Following a detailed evaluation of all the bids received and subsequent commercial negotiations, Safaricom PLC is hereby pleased to award **Dr. John Odero Ong'ech** this requirement subject to the execution of a mutually agreeable contract incorporating the following Terms & Conditions among others;

Terms of Award;

1. Contract Scope – The scope for this award is the Provision of Consultancy Services as the Safaricom PLC Company Health Advisor;
   Provide Healthcare Leadership in the company
   i. Medical Costs Optimization
   ii. Offer Medical Services Consultancy to the company
   iii. Occupational Health Services Consultancy
   iv. Compliance & Risk Management relating to medical issues
   v. Medical, OHS & Wellness Process Improvement
   vi. Process Improvement

SS **Safaricom Staff Updates** 15:01

To SAFARICOM STAFF

ORGANISATIONAL ANNOUNCEMENT

Simple • Transparent • Honest • FOR YOU

Dear Colleagues,

As we continue safeguarding the health and wellbeing of all staff, I am pleased to inform you of the following change within the Resources Division:

Company Health Advisor

Dr John Odero Ong'ech has effective **1st January 2022** assumed the role of **Company Health Advisor**.

He will work in conjunction with the Health, Safety and Wellbeing Team in providing support to our HSW strategies, compliance with occupational health and safety regulations, support staff with health concerns, and act as a subject matter expert on all issues relating to the health and wellbeing of staff. He will also serve as a member of Safaricom's Medical Board.

Dr Ong'ech brings onboard over 27 years' experience as a medical practitioner and public health expert. He holds a Bachelor of Medicine & Surgery and a Master of Medicine in Obstetrics/Gynaecology, both from the University of Nairobi, as well as a Master of Public Health (International Health) from Tulane University in New Orleans, USA.

He takes over from Dr Paul Wangai Junior, who has been our Company Health Advisor since 2016, and was instrumental in shaping our wellbeing and occupational health strategy.

Please join me in welcoming Dr Ong'ech to the Safaricom family and wishing Dr Wangai all the best as he transitions to his next role.

Paul Kasimu
Chief Human Resources Officer
I am Safaricom, I am Notoriously Customer Obsessed!

Safaricom

https://lakeregionbulletin.co.ke/2022/01/05/safaricom-picks-leading-obstetrician-as-health-advisor/

SAFARICOM APPOINTS OBSTETRICIAN AS NEW HEALTH ADVISER; FRIDAY JANUARY 07 2022

SUMMARY:
ECONOMY
NEWS
CORPORATE
LIFESTYLE
OPINION & ANALYSIS
MARKETS
DATA HUB
VIDEOS
SPECIAL REPORTS

By KABALE NASIBO
More by this Author

SUMMARY

Through a memo, the company stated that Dr Ong'ech will be working in conjunction with the health, safety and wellbeing team.

The 54-year-old medic takes over from Dr Paul Wangui who had been with the company since 2016.

Safaricom's health adviser role is part of the company's efforts to boost employee welfare.

Safaricom PLC headquarters in Westlands, Nairobi. PHOTO | DENNIS ONSONGO | NMG

Safaricom Plc has appointed Dr John Odero Ong'ech, an obstetrician and gynaecologist as its company health advisor and a member of its medical board.
Through a memo, the company stated that Dr Ong'ech will be working in conjunction with the health, safety and wellbeing team.
"He will work in conjunction with the Health, Safety and Wellbeing Team in providing support to our HSW strategies, compliance with occupational health and safety regulation, support staff with health concerns and act as a subject matter expert on all issues relating to the health and wellbeing of staff," the memo stated.
The 54-year-old medic takes over from Dr Paul Wangui who had been with the company since 2016.
Dr Ong'ech is a well-respected fertility doctor, having worked extensively in the public sector, with his last posting being at the Kenyatta National Hospital as a deputy director, surgical services, and chief medical specialist in obstetrics and gynaecology.
He has worked in dozens of missions in Africa as a consultant, authored books as well as research papers on maternal and child health.

He has two Master's degrees in public health (international health), Tulane University, New Orleans and in obstetrics and gynaecology from the University of Nairobi.
In 2018, Dr Ong'ech was picked to act as chief executive of the Kenyatta National Hospital (KNH) but declined the role for fear that standing up against cartels blamed for plunder of the referral facility could ruin his career and endanger his life.
He said there are cartels of 'tenderpreneurs' interested in controlling the institution's budget that runs into billions of shillings.
Safaricom's health adviser role is part of the company's efforts to boost employee welfare.
Many companies state that employees are one of their most valuable resources and have taken steps to enable their workers to perform well.
particularly reliant on ideas generated and implemented by their workforce.
knasibo@ke.nationmedia.com

CHAPTER 9: COMMUNITY SUPPORT AND SERVICE

Prelude:
"Alone, we can do so little, together we can do so much" by Hellen Keller.
"The greatness of a community is most accurately measured by compassionate actions of its members" by Coretta Scott King.
"No one has ever become poor by giving" by Ann Frank.
"A person's most useful asset is not a head full of knowledge, but a heart full of love, an ear ready to listen and a hand willing to help others" by Quotes Gat.
"We rise by Lifting others" by Robert Ingersoll.

9.1: A feeling of Indebtedness to my people

My father, Jaduong' Jeremiah Ongech Ogola (Dola) was a peoples person. Whereas he had a huge responsibility to keep his family going despite a meagre salary, he did not tire. He pushed all relevant facets of life using any legal route at his disposal, always working closely with and cooperating with people at work and at home. Due to his strong social network, he was able to take some of his children to school, supported directly those he could not, build and left behind an enviable and well-functioning system. His mentorship to us was directed towards building a strong system that is able to take care of one regardless of circumstances (especially on rainy days). Moreso, service to his people was a top priority, and he did it with all his might. He left this as a permanent lesson to us. It is in this respect that I have tried to live his dream in community service. This is to keep his legacy and spirit live on. In it I dare to dream.

Living the dream of Dola, providing support to my family, extended family, community and those in need has been my satisfaction in life. I believe in the quotes that we rise by lifting others and no one has ever become poor by giving. I have taken care of my parents financial and Healthcare needs. I gave my late father Mzee Ong'ech Ogola the best support I could think of. I continue doing the same to my mother Sipora Achieng Ong'ech. I believe a child gets blessings by taking care of the parents. I have extended by support to my parent's relatives. I have provided generous financial assistance to my brothers and their family (Ogola Ong'ech Family, Ochieng Ong'ech family) and my sisters' family (Mary Atieno, Margaret Auma, Benter Aluoch and Late Grace Akoth families). In some cases, I have extended my assistance to their relatives. In my Kamhore clan, I have provided financial assistance to many families, like Obiero Sigar family, Sipem Sigar family, Akunga Sigar family, Dima Ngore Family and Guda Omwanda family. These are Kamhore from Ogam-Lwala. I have supported Kamhore from Nyangera, Kamhore from Manyala and Kamhore from Mago. I have extended my support to many people from yimbo, from Bondo sub-county, from Siaya County, from Nyanza and from Kenya. I have provided financial support to many learning institutions. Some of them include: Majengo Primary School, Majengo Secondary School, Barkanyango Secondary School, Nyamonye Girls Secondary, Ragak Primary, Kasau Primary School, Nyabondo Primary School, Usenge High School amongst others.

I have provided support to many churches, some of them include: ACK Nyamonye Parish, ACK Bondo Diocese, Nyamonye Catholic Church amongst others. Access to clean water has been a big challenge to my community since my child hood. I supported Komolo/Opondo pond/dam excavation. I also support the PENWA water project that brought clean piped water to my village. This has since been tapped by many villagers contributing to access to clean water.

I have contributed enormously in the health sector to assist my community. I pioneered the construction of Ogam Dispensary which I have also support through supplies of medicines and equipments. I linked the international NGO's to Ogam dispensary and they have continued to provide support.

The late John Alaru Obiero donated the land for Ogam dispensary construction for free. My father late Mzee Ong'ech Ogola was the first chairman for the Ogam dispensary committee. He later handed over to my bother Ochieng Ong'ech. I have remained the patron for Ogam Dispensary since inception to date. I financially supported the construction of St. Gorety Nyamonye Catholic dispensary. My brother Ochieng Ong'ech is currently a member of the dispensary committee. I have also supported Bondo Sub County hospital with medicine supplies. I have conducted several community health outreach programmes throughout Yimbo. I have also worked closely with Prof. PLO Lumumba to support the community health outreach programmes.

I formed an NGO called AB 2000 around the year 2000. It was operational for ten years. I got grants from TOWA- NACC and used it to support orphans and vulnerable children throughout Nyanza province. I also conducted a lot of capacity building in the fight against HIV/ AIDS. I have provided Education and social support to those in need including assisting in acquiring others employments. Some of the beneficiaries are:

a. Jeremiah Ong'ech Ogola memorial Scholarship beneficiaries

- David Otieno Owuor
- Dr. Roselyn Ogola Mwangale
- Vincent Onyango Ochieng
- Jackline Onuko
- Walter Omolo
- Ruth Amina Ochieng
- Julius Guda
- Lavenda Awour Ochieng
- Seline Atieno Ochieng'
- Lucas Onyango Awiti
- Irine Akinyi Ochieng
- Triza Awiti
- Bethi/Christine Okeyo
- Rhoda Awuor
- David Owino Ochieng
- Maurice Badia
- Jack Audi
- Elvis Okoth (C/O Mary Aongo Mang'ana)
- Kevin Okoth Onyango
- Susan Akinyi

- Christine Anyango Okeyo
- Dan Obera
- Moses Apela
- Mercy okoyo
- Jairus Onyango Sipem
- Sons of Oginga Akungu
- and many others- the list is long

I initiated the Jeremiah Ong'ech Ogola Memorial Scholarship fund after the death of my father. I have personally contributed Kenya shillings One million to the fund. It has supported many students to pursue education – **this again is in the dreams of my father.**

9.2: The Jeremiah Ong'ech Ogola Memorial Scholarship Fund

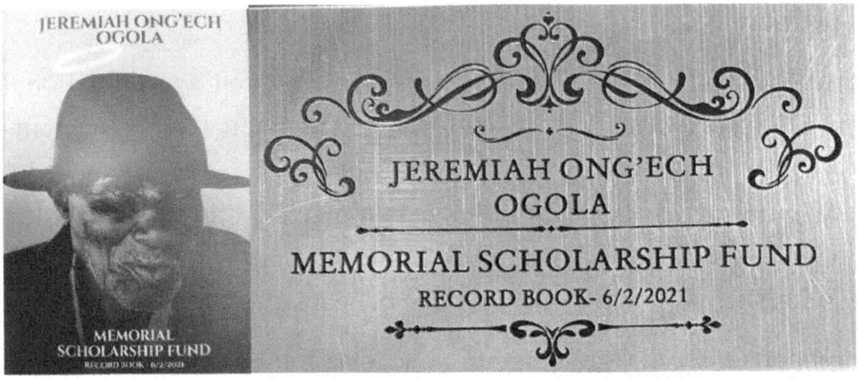

This is a facility established by the Dola family, led by Dr John Odero, as an academic support and bursary to the needy. It has to date sponsored a number of children in secondary and college levels. A total of Kshs 1,000,000 has been used, largely contributed by Dr John Odero Ong'ech. Under this facility, a number of Mzee grandchildren have been supported to make it through their education. Whereas some are done, others have upgraded, and others are still ongoing. The following have been beneficiaries:

1. Eugene Okeyo---Form 1-4; Sponsored in Majengo secondary school for 2 years.
2. Eugene Otieno Ochieng': This was the top KCPE candidate in the whole of Rarieda Sub-county in the 2020 (March 2021) KCPE exams. This was a

desperate case whose situation quickly spread in social media. Dr Odero picked this case and he has been sponsored to the tune of Kshs 41,000 in Usenge high school. He is on a 4 year full sponsorship.

3. Michael Dache Form 1-4--- Otieno Oyoo secondary school;
4. Wanda Angel Triza: has a form 3 and 4 fee sponsorship in Furaha girls' high school. A total of Kshs 90,000.
5. Elizabeth Achieng' Onyango: Sponsorship of form 4 fees worth Kshs 15,000 in Nyamira girls secondary school;
6. Lavender Awuor Ochieng'; Bachelor of Medicine and Surgery.
7. Seline Atieno; B 3.5 years Com (Banking and Finance) @ Egerton University;
8. Irine Akinyi; Fundraising to support her joining Moi University for a Bed (Arts);
9. Ishmael Onyango: Kshs 20,000 for medical (MBChB) degree Masinde Muliro University;
10. Brian Apudo Owino: Kshs 45,000 Laptop purchase to assist in studies for medical degree at Uzima University (See pictorials below);
11. Stephen Ouma: Kshs 10,000 fee support for a degree of Bachelor of Medicine and Bachelor of Surgery in Kenyatta University;
12. Kshs 10,000 for Kevin Okoth Onyango college Education, clinical medicine at Bondo Medical Training college
13. Susan Akinyi (ASU). This is Mzee's granddaughter and the immediate former caretaker in his duol. Asu was admitted to Nyamonye girls as Mzee had instructed. Her full four year fee has been fully paid by the fund (see picture below).
14. Others.

10/23/21, 10:13 AM - Dr Ongech O J: Mzee granddaughter and care taker, Susan Akinyi (ASU) joins form one at Nyamonye Girls secondary School as per his wishes

9.2.1: Tributes from Fund beneficiaries

Eugene Otieno Ochieng: A case study of Jeremiah Ongech sponsorship;

Below is an exceptional End term, Term 1, 2021 result for one of the top beneficiaries of the Jeremiah Ongech Fund. At end of his term 1 in Usenge high school, Eugene has shown his intentions very clearly. And he is raring to go. We wish him well in his 4 year journey and beyond. Here are his term 1 Form 1 results. Usenge High School- Jeremiah Ong'ech Ogola memorial Scholarship fund beneficiary

NAME: Ochieng Eugene Otieno: ADMNO: 6437; FORM: 1 Ibadan

Mean GRADE: A; MN MKS: 85%; TT MKS: 942 / 1100; OVRL POS: 2 / 379; STRM POS: 1 / 63

Subject performance:

ENG: 82 A; KIS: 93 A; MAT: 87 A; BIO: 75 A-; PHY: 83 A; CHE: 93 A; HIS: 81 A; GEO: 89 A; CRE: 87 A; AGR: 87 A; and BST: 85 A

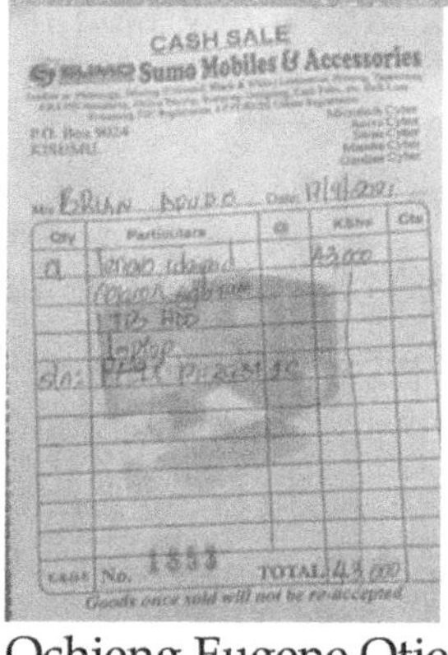

Ochieng Eugene Otieno with Dr Ongech Right: Brian Apudo Owino

Picture 1: Eugene Otieno Ochieng of Usenge High School, with Dr John Ongech, the chief sponsor, 2021

Pic 2-3: Brian Apudo Owino, a beneficiary of the Jeremiah Ongech Ogola scholarship, with his newly acquired laptop courtesy of the fund

9.3 Sponsorship testimonies from fund beneficiaries:

On 9/17/21, 5:51 PM – a beneficiary wrote:

My name is Ishmael Onyango, former student of Usenge High School class of 2020. And now am a student of Masinde Muliro University of Science and Technology pursuing Bachelor of medicine and bachelor of Surgery (MBChB). I would like to sincerely thank Jeremiah Ong'ech Ogola Memorial Scholarship for their support of Ksh. 20,000 towards my school. This support made the foundation of my dream of pursuing MBCHB. May God bless you abundantly as you continue to support other students.

On 9/17/21, 5:58 PM – a second beneficiary wrote:

My name is Brian Apudo, Former Student of Usenge High School KCSE 2020, I have been admitted to Uzima University to study Bachelor of Medicine and Bachelor of Surgery degree (MBChB). I hereby thank the Jeremiah Ong'ech Ogola memorial scholarship fund for sponsoring my laptop at 45000/= to help me with my studies. .May the living God favour the family more.

The communication below gives further details:

8/18/21, 18:49 - Dr Ong'ech O J: Hi Prof, as you write Mzee book post humus, I want to bring to your attention on Jeremiah Ong'ech Ogola memorial Scholarship fund which so far I have supported single handedly. We have spent Kshs 1,000,000 on Education for needy children. I will bring the record book on beneficiaries and leave at Mzee resource center this Friday 20.8.2021. You can make reference to it if you want.

7/9/21, 10:03 - Dr Ong'ech O J: I will be presenting the above awards (Dr Odero Ong'ech Award's) to best KCSE 2020 performance at my former school-Usenge High School on 31.7.2021

7/9/21, 10:03 - Dr Ong'ech O J: Through my motivation initiatives, the school this year has produced 2 students who have been admitted to the university to do Medicine. The School has not seen that in a long time. This has been my dream for the school to produce more people like me

7/9/21, 13:04 - 😀: Excellent and impeccable record and work doc.

7/9/21, 13:04 - 😀: A well-deserved honor worth Mzee's efforts and contribution.

7/9/21, 13:06 - 😀: Keep it up. A permanent record...shall go a long way motivating more students

7/9/21, 14:06 - Dr Ong'ech O J: Thanks

9.4 Tributes from community support beneficiary organisations

a. Bishop David Kodia

To Dr John Odero Ong'ech: Today 7.11.2021, marked the end of our long journey mobilizing for funds to complete our synod project. It had not been easy but we thank God that you were there for us. You prayed with us at a time when all appeared gloomy and irredeemable, you stood with us at a time when some could not even pick our phone calls. Yes, by God's grace you contributed to your last ability. As your servant i couldn't be more proud of having you in my prayers for making our day a success. May God bless you and your family for doing such a marvelous work for the sake of his name. You forever remain a hero in our ministry. Just in case it escaped your attention as the guest of honour we raised 1.2m with total collection raised being 10m + to God be the glory. **Bishop David Kodia, ACK Bondo Dioceses**

b. Sister Domician Odero

To Dr John Odero Ong'ech (16TH NOVEMBER, 2021)

The entire Nyamonye Mission Hospital is extremely indebted and sincerely grateful for your generous contribution to help set up the Pharmacy. May God bless you and your Family: Sister Domician Odero, Incharge, St Mary Goretty, Nyamonye Mission Hospital

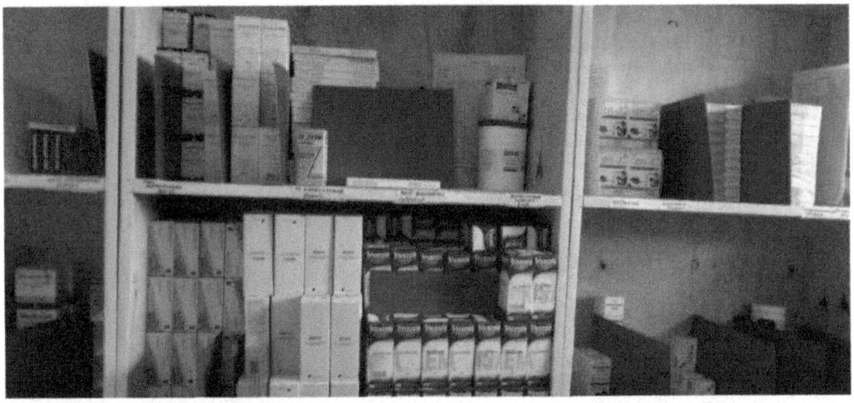

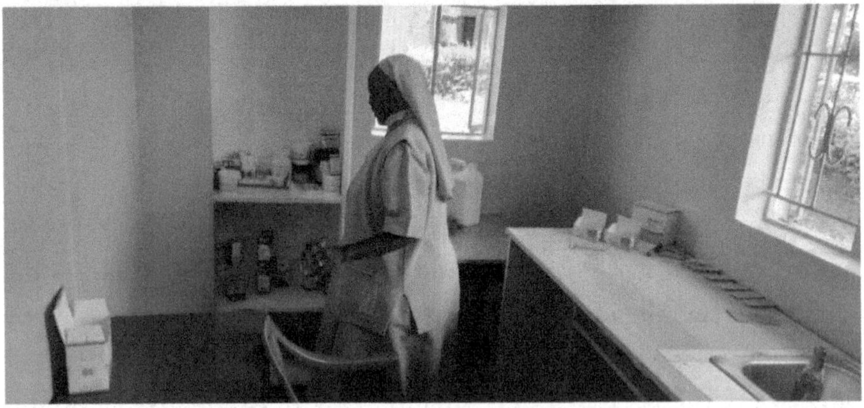

Sister Domician Odero, St. Mary Goretty, Nyamonye Mission Hospital

ST. MARY GORETTY NYAMONYE
MISSION HEALTH CENTER
P.O BOX 34-40632, NYAMONYE.
TEL. 0748169186

Dear Dr. John Ongech,

REF: LETTER FOR APPRECIATION.

The entire Nyamonye Mission Health Centre Board and Management is extremely indebted and sincerely grateful for your generous contribution to help set up the facility pharmacy. The structure is operational and effectively used.

May God bless you and your family.

Yours faithfully,

Sr. Domiciana Odero.

Administrator.

RIARA

CERTIFICATE

OF APPRECIATION

IS PROUDLY PRESENTED TO

Dr. John Ong'ech

In recognition of your diligent service to the KCPE Class of 2019 as a committee member of The Riara Primary School Motisha 2018/2019 Club.

Presented On 1st November 2019

HEADMISTRESS

DIRECTOR

RIARA PRIMARY MOTISHA CLUB

2018/2019

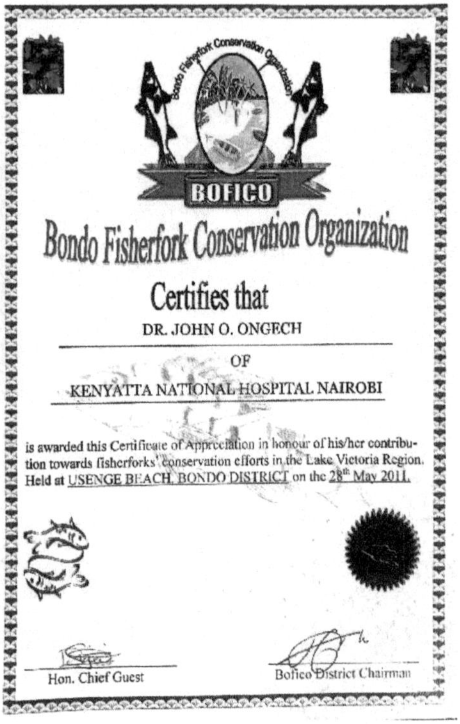

BOFICO

Bondo Fisherfork Conservation Organization

Certifies that

DR. JOHN O. ONGECH

OF

KENYATTA NATIONAL HOSPITAL NAIROBI

is awarded this Certificate of Appreciation in honour of his/her contribution towards fisherforks' conservation efforts in the Lake Victoria Region. Held at USENGE BEACH, BONDO DISTRICT on the 28th May 2011.

Hon. Chief Guest

Bofico District Chairman

USENGE HIGH SCHOOL

P.O. BOX PRIVATE BAG, USENGE
Email: usengehigh@gmail.com

Our Ref: UHS/L.O.SPT/01/21

Your Ref: ....

Date: ....09/09/2021......

TO WHOM IT MAY CONCERN

RE: LETTER OF SUPPORT FOR DR. JOHN ODERO ONG'ECH, ID NO 8974561

This is to confirm that Dr. John Odero Ong'ech, Patron for Usenge High School Alumni Association has been supporting the school tremendously. He has provided financial support for:

1. Teachers' capacity building.
2. Students' performance improvement by sponsoring academic awards ceremonies, motivational speakers and purchase of books.
3. School infrastructure improvement by supporting laboratory equipment purchase, dormitory construction and classrooms repairs and tilings.
4. School fees for needy students.

Currently he is paying school fees for:

a. Ochieng Eugine Otieno Form 1
b. Ishmael Okulo a first year student at Maseno University taking Bachelor of medicine and surgery from Usenge High School.

Any assistance given to him will be highly appreciated.

Regards.

CHIEF PRINCIPAL
USENGE HIGH SCHOOL
PRIVATE BAG, USENGE.
Date............Sign...............

Mr. Daniel Mirumbe
Chief Principal
Usenge High School
Telephone Number: 0712828680

THE ANGLICAN CHURCH OF KENYA
ST PAUL`S PARISH, NYAMONYE
DIOCESE OF BONDO
"Founded On The Gospel Of Christ"

FROM THE PARISH VICAR,
REV : LABAN O. ONDURU
10TH SEPTEMBER 2021

TO WHOM IT MAY CONCERN

REF: LETTER OF SUPPORT FOR DR. JOHN ODERO ONG,ECH. ID NO 8974561

Greetings .

Dr . John Odero Ongech is a dedicated member of Anglican Church of Kenya, St Paul Parish Nyamonye, a member easily approachable and willing to serve GOD within his ability.
He is very steady in providing generous financial support to the Parishes' Project since 2018 to date (2021) .
The activities are:

- **Covid – 19 protocols**
- **Flood victims**
- **Orphans and vulnerable children**
- **Widows**
- **Food donation for those in need**
- **Medical care for those in need.**
- **Medicine purchases for Ogam Dispensary.**

Kindly, any assistance given to him will be highly appreciated,
Regards

ST PAUL'S PARISH NYAMONYE P.O Box 95 NYAMONYE VIA BONDO DATE 10.09.2021 ANGLICAN DIOCESE OF BONDO

Lotien

Rev laban O. Onduru
Vicar,St Pauls Parish, Nyamonye

P.O BOX 95 .40609, NYAMONYE, PHONE: 07 21874070
email: otienolaban@yahoo.com.

APPOINTMENT

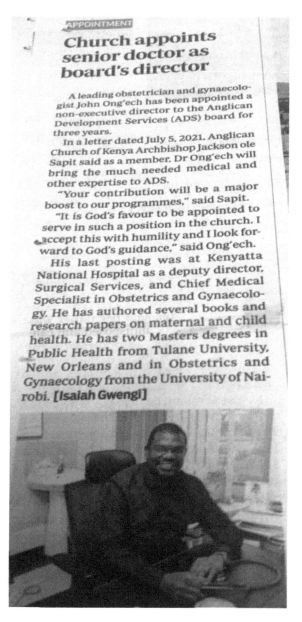

Church appoints senior doctor as board's director

A leading obstetrician and gynaecologist John Ong'ech has been appointed a non-executive director to the Anglican Development Services (ADS) board for three years.

In a letter dated July 5, 2021, Anglican Church of Kenya Archbishop Jackson ole Sapit said as a member, Dr Ong'ech will bring the much needed medical and other expertise to ADS.

"Your contribution will be a major boost to our programmes," said Sapit.

"It is God's favour to be appointed to serve in such a position in the church. I accept this with humility and I look forward to God's guidance," said Ong'ech.

His last posting was at Kenyatta National Hospital as a deputy director, Surgical Services, and Chief Medical Specialist in Obstetrics and Gynaecology. He has authored several books and research papers on maternal and child health. He has two Masters degrees in Public Health from Tulane University, New Orleans and in Obstetrics and Gynaecology from the University of Nairobi. [Isaiah Gwengi]

It is significant to note that immediately after we buried Mzee Ong'ech, I received those 2 important appointments…some blessings from Jaduong.

9.5: Dr John Ong'ech pictorial story:

Below are the current photos of Usenge School where Dola learnt from. The high school later became the school of his two children, retired teacher Dalmas Ogola and Dr John Odero. On 10/30/21, 7:29 AM - Dr Ongech O J observed as follows: 'The following is the pictorial form of my life story. Hopefully at 55 years, my autobiography will be ready- the age at which our fathers retired'. We have worked hard to make this come to a reality. Our draft I was delivered in November, with a sit in on 20th December. The second draft is to be ready by 31st December birthday. We shall strive to deliver. Here goes the pictorial story of dakatri.

Left: 10/30/21, 7:31 AM - Dr Ongech O J: 14 years old Form one at Usenge High School 1981
Middle: 10/30/21, 7:31 AM – Dr Ongech O J: 15 years old Form 2 at Usenge High School 1982
Right: 1983, 16 years old, with Form 3 classmates Usenge High School

Left: 17 years old, Form 4 at Usenge High School, 1984
Centre: 18 years old Form 5, Kericho High School 1985
Right: 19 years Old , Form 6, Kericho High School 1986

Left: 10/30/21, 7:31 AM - Dr Ongech O J: 21 years old , Medical School year 1, UoN, 1987
Centre 10/30/21, 7:31 AM - Dr Ongech O J: 22 years old , Medical School year 2, UoN 1988
Right: 7:31 AM - Dr Ongech O J: 24 years old medical student year 4, working at Mt Sinai hospital, Bondo 1991

Left: 24 years old, Medical School year 4, UoN 1991
Middle: 25 years old, Medical School, Year 5, UoN, 1992
Right: 26 years, old, 1993. Social event for Philemon Oduor

Dr Ongech and Mzee(in a cap) at a fundraising for a community project. With teachers: Obat (diseased), Okech (Kasau) , Okulo (now retired), Onyango Spem and Dr Odero (sitting down)

Left: 1991: UoN Medical school; right: 1988: 21 year old UoN Medical school

Left: 1990: Bondo S Mt Sinai hospital; employer-Dr Badia; right: 1990: UoN Medical school

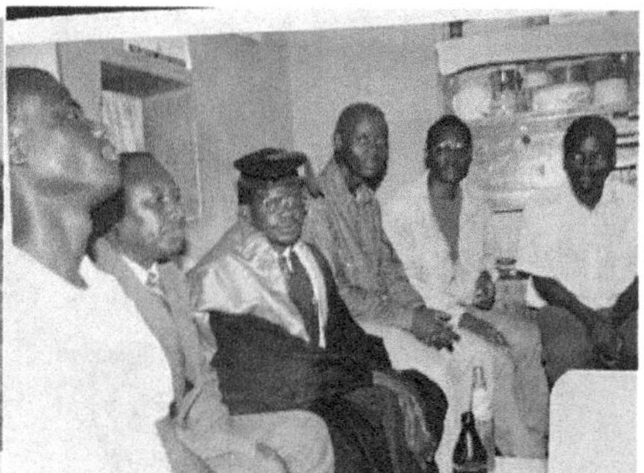

Dr Ongech graduation party: Right: 1993: 26 year old graduation party-bachelor of medicine and surgery;

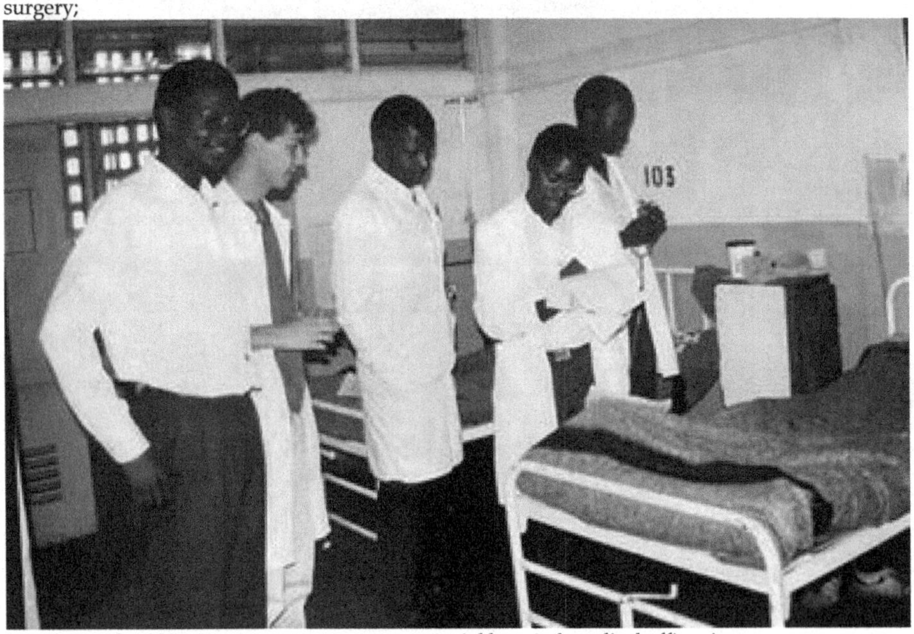

Last foto right: 1994: Kisumu new nyanza provincial hospital medical officer intern

Left: 27 years old, graduating with Bachelor of Medicine and Bachelor of Surgery, UoN, 1993
Middle: 27 years old, Medical officer intern at Nyanza Provincial General Hospital, Kisumu 1993
Righr: 28 years old, Medical officer intern at Nyanza Provincial General Hospital, Kisumu

Left: 29 years old, Medical Officer at Nyanza Provincial Hospital, 1995
Middle: 34 years old, studying international Health, Tulane University, USA 2001
Right: 35 Years Old, Studying international Health, Tulane University, USA 2002

Centre: 36 years old, graduating with Master of Medicine in Obstetrics and Gynaecology, University of Nairobi, 2003
Right: 38 years Old, Medical Specialist 2, Kenyatta National Hospital, 2004

Left: 40 years old , Medical specialist 1, launching annual Dr Odero Ong'ech Trophy 🏆 for best student at Usenge High School 2007.
Centre: Occasion Chief Guest at Usigu Division Education day held at Usenge High School 2007
Right: 45 years old, Senior Medical Specialist and HOD Obs/Gyn Dept, KNH, 2012

Left: 48years old, Senior Medical Specialist and HOD Ob/Gyn , KNH , 2014
Centre: 49 years old, Senior Medical Specialist, Deputy Director (Surgical services), KNH, 2016
Right: 49 years old, 2016

Left: 50 years old 31.12.2016, celebrating at UAE- Dubai & Abudhabi

Middle: 51 years old, Chief Medical specialist in Obstetrics & Gynaecology, KNH, celebrating in Mombasa South Coast beaches 2017; Right: 52 years old, 2019, Chief Medical Specialist, Obs/Gynae KNH

53 years old, 2020, Full time private Practice (Retired from KNH) in Obstetrics & Gynaecology

31.12.2020-54 years old. Relaxing at my Lavington Home, Nairobi.

9.6: Community service and family history with Usenge

A history of partnership in Mzee's dreams:

On the 7/9/21 at 10:01 am, Dr Ong'ech O J gave me some important Facts on Usenge High School and the great Ong'ech Family 1. Late Mzee Jeremiah Ong'ech Ogolla went to Usenge Primary School from 1935-40 (The primary school which was later upgraded to Usenge High School in 1972) 2. Dalmas Ogola Ong'ech went to Usenge High School from 1972-75 and posted the best results in Mathematics in his form 4 class of 1975 3. John Odero Ong'ech went to Usenge High School from 1981-84 and posted the second best form 4 results in the history of the School to date. 5. Usenge High School is managed by the Anglican Church of Kenya 6. The Ong'ech II passion for education has gone real deep, into the family. Dr Odero Ong'ech and Mwalimu Ogola Ong'ech were both Educated at Usenge High School. How Odero got to Usenge is the best example of Dola's love for the school. Odero joined in 1981, the year of Dola's retirement. According to Mzee, when Odero passed class 7 CPE exams, he got a form 1 admission to Chianda High School in Rarieda Sub county. But Mzee didn't like Chianda. According to him, children there were spoilt, and Mzee wanted Odero to learn in Usenge secondary, a school he was sure of, where even Odero's brother Ogola learnt. He talked to the late senior principal, Warom who gave Odero an automatic admission. At that time, Only Ogola had finished college studies in Kisii, but Ochieng was till in college. Knowing fee would still be a challenge, Mzee needed a place close enough, with someone whom he could easily approach and bank on his support and understanding to sort school fees issues. Warom offered this support. The understanding of Mzee's financial position and his willingness to pay full school fees given time and alternative options by Mr Warom made Mzee have even more liking for Usenge, over and above his childhood attachment. It is in Usenge secondary where Odero did wonders, leaving an impeccable academic record which stands to date.

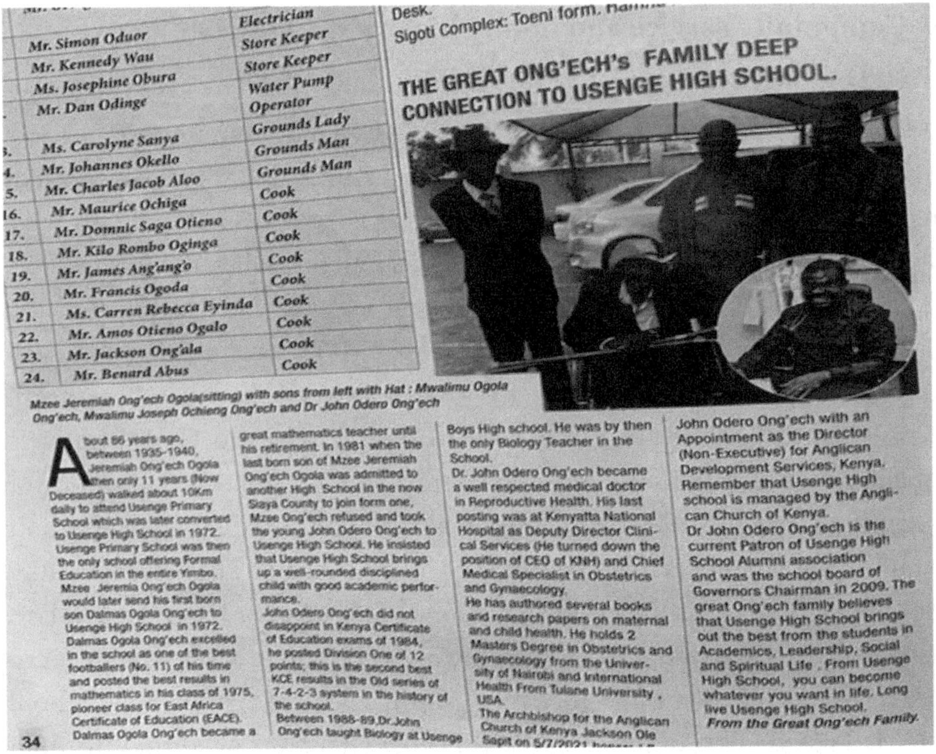

Desk.
Sigoti Complex: Toeni form. ...

	Mr. Simon Oduor	Electrician
	Mr. Kennedy Wau	Store Keeper
	Ms. Josephine Obura	Store Keeper
.	Mr. Dan Odinge	Water Pump Operator
3.	Ms. Carolyne Sanya	Grounds Lady
4.	Mr. Johannes Okello	Grounds Man
5.	Mr. Charles Jacob Aloo	Grounds Man
16.	Mr. Maurice Ochiga	Cook
17.	Mr. Domnic Saga Otieno	Cook
18.	Mr. Kilo Rombo Oginga	Cook
19.	Mr. James Ang'ang'o	Cook
20.	Mr. Francis Ogoda	Cook
21.	Ms. Carren Rebecca Eyinda	Cook
22.	Mr. Amos Otieno Ogalo	Cook
23.	Mr. Jackson Ong'ala	Cook
24.	Mr. Benard Abus	Cook

THE GREAT ONG'ECH's FAMILY DEEP CONNECTION TO USENGE HIGH SCHOOL.

Mzee Jeremiah Ong'ech Ogola(sitting) with sons from left with Hat : Mwalimu Ogola Ong'ech, Mwalimu Joseph Ochieng Ong'ech and Dr John Odero Ong'ech

About 86 years ago, between 1935-1940, Jeremiah Ong'ech Ogola then only 11 years (Now Deceased) walked about 10Km daily to attend Usenge Primary School which was later converted to Usenge High School in 1972. Usenge Primary School was then the only school offering Formal Education in the entire Yimbo. Mzee Jeremia Ong'ech Ogola would later send his first born son Dalmas Ogola Ong'ech to Usenge High School in 1972. Dalmas Ogola Ong'ech excelled in the school as one of the best footballers (No. 11) of his time and posted the best results in mathematics in his class of 1975, pioneer class for East Africa Certificate of Education (EACE). Dalmas Ogola Ong'ech became a great mathematics teacher until his retirement. In 1981 when the last born son of Mzee Jeremiah Ong'ech Ogola was admitted to another High School in the now Siaya County to join form one, Mzee Ong'ech refused and took the young John Odero Ong'ech to Usenge High School. He insisted that Usenge High School brings up a well-rounded disciplined child with good academic performance.

John Odero Ong'ech did not disappoint in Kenya Certificate of Education exams of 1984, he posted Division One of 12 points; this is the second best KCE results in the Old series of 7-4-2-3 system in the history of the school.

Between 1988-89,Dr.John Ong'ech taught Biology at Usenge Boys High school. He was by then the only Biology Teacher in the School.

Dr. John Odero Ong'ech became a well respected medical doctor in Reproductive Health. His last posting was at Kenyatta National Hospital as Deputy Director Clinical Services (He turned down the position of CEO of KNH) and Chief Medical Specialist in Obstetrics and Gynaecology.

He has authored several books and research papers on maternal and child health. He holds 2 Masters Degree in Obstetrics and Gynaecology from the University of Nairobi and International Health From Tulane University, USA.

The Archbishop for the Anglican Church of Kenya Jackson Ole Sapit on 5/7/2021 ... John Odero Ong'ech with an Appointment as the Director (Non-Executive) for Anglican Development Services, Kenya. Remember that Usenge High school is managed by the Anglican Church of Kenya.

Dr John Odero Ong'ech is the current Patron of Usenge High School Alumni association and was the school board of Governors Chairman in 2009. The great Ong'ech family believes that Usenge High School brings out the best from the students in Academics, Leadership, Social and Spiritual Life . From Usenge High School, you can become whatever you want in life. Long live Usenge High School.

From the Great Ong'ech Family.

34

The great Ong'ech's family deep connection to Usenge high school

NB: This Great Ong'ech family write-up is an extract from page 34 of the Usenge high school newsletter of 2021.

About 86 years ago, between 1935 and 1940, Jeremiah Ong'ech Ogola, then only 11, walked about 10 km daily to attend Usenge sector school, later converted to Usenge high school in 1972. Usenge sector school turned primary school was then the only school offering formal education in the entire Yimbo (now Usigu division). Mzee Jeremiah Ong'ech would later send his first born son, Dalmas Ogola to Usenge High school in 1972. Dalmas enrolled in the school as one of the best footballers (No 11) of his time and posted the best results in mathematics in his class of 1975 pioneer class for eastern African certificate of education (EACE). Dalmas Ogola Ong'ech became a great mathematics teacher until his retirement. In 1981 when the last born son of Mzee Jeremiah Ong'ech Ogola was admitted to another high school in the now Siaya County to join form 1, Mzee Ong'ech refuses and took the young John Odero Ong'ech to Usenge high school. He insisted that Usenge brings up a well-rounded disciplined child with good academic performance. John Odero Ong'ech did not disappoint in Kenya certificate of education exams of 1984, posting division 1 of 12 points. This is the second best KCE results in the old series of 7-4-2-3 system in the history of the school. Between 1988 and 89, John Ong'ech taught Biology at Usenge High school. He was by then the only Biology teacher in the school.

Dr John Ong'ech became a well-respected medical doctor in reproductive health. His last posting was at Kenyatta National Hospital [19] as deputy director Clinical services and chief medical specialist in Obstetrics and gynecology. He turned down the position of CEO of KNH in 2018 when it was offered to him. In addition, Dr Odero Ong'ech has authored several books and research papers on maternal and child health. He holds two Masters degrees from the University of Nairobi and International health from Tulane university, USA.

The archbishop for the Anglican church of Kenya Jackson Ole Sapit on 5th July 2021, appointed Dr John Ong'ech as a non-executive director for Anglican development services (Kenya). Usenge high school is sponsored by the Anglican church of Kenya (ACK). Dr John Ong'ech is the current patron of Usenge High School Alumni Association and was the school board of governor's chairman in 2009. The great Ong'ech's family believes that Usenge high school brings out the best from the students in academics, leadership, social and spiritual lives. From Usenge high school, you can become whatever you want in life. Long live Usenge high school.

From the Great Ong'ech Family.

9.7: The Dr Ong'ech Academic award

Every year there is Dr Ong'ech award (trophy, cash and certificate) for Best KCSE student at Usenge High School. This is an honor to Mzee Ong'ech love for Education and strong faith in the school. Mzee launched the award in

---

[19] This is the largest teaching and referral hospital in Eastern and Central Africa; Dr Odero Ong'ech was appointed as the CEO of this facility, a position he turned down in 2018 at the advice of his late father. Records had it that the CEOs of KNH never had a profession thereafter; they never finished well- either jailed or shot due to the many interests, tender related.

2007. This is part of meeting Mzee's dreams. Another worth-mentioning initiative is the Jeremiah Ongech Ogola respource centre in which are lots of materials for reference. This was established in his duol (Ikuli) after his demise, to keep the site where he mentored meny people in his life, alive. All part of the journey towards fulfilling his great dreams.

Plate 6: The Dr Ong'ech trophy award for Best KCSE student at Usenge High School.

9.8: The Jeremiah Ong'ech resource Centre and scholarship fund

9.9: Jaduong' Ong'ech's Twin Science Laboratory: a lifelong partnership

Construction of the twin laboratory

7/9/21, 10:09 AM - Dr Ongech O J: And Finally the principal of Usenge High School has just called me and said that new modern science laboratory which has just been constructed shall be named after late Mzee Ong'ech...it shall be Jeremiah Ong'ech laboratory. Described below is how this great name finds itself in Usenge.

On 31st July 2021, Jeremiah Ong'ech Ogola made a special visit to Usenge high school. The family was led by Japuonj Joseph Ochieng Ong'ech, in the company of Dr John Odero and Beatrice Odero. The family had taken to the school a cheque worth Kshs 100,000 as a donation towards purchase of laboratory equipment. Japuonj Ochieng Ong'ech handed over the cheque to the Board of management member and alumni chair, Eng Ndiewo. The school highly appreciated this. The laboratory is names in honour of the late Jeremiah Ong'ech.

9.10: Usenge high school alumni association[20]:

(An extract from the UHS newsletter, 2021)

In early 2016 one of us witnessed a key challenge the school faced at the time. That was gross congestion in the dormitories. He thought that if the old students were mobilized to raise funds to build at least one dormitory that might ease the congestion in the school. He reached out to one other old student who brought the idea and together they agreed to start mobilizing other old students of Usenge high.

In May 2016, they set up a WhatsApp t forum to mobilize the Usenge high old students. . Through 'member get member' approach the forum soon enlisted many others. The main objective then was to mobilize funds to build one dormitory for occupation by the start of the third term session beginning September 2016. A coordinating committee was formed as follows: patron-Dr John Ong'ech; chairman-Eng Dick Ndiewo; Vice-chairman-George Otieno; Secretary- David Wasamba; organizing secretary- Linus Sijenyi; Treasurer- John Achoki; Ass Treasurer-Aggrey ochieng; Legal Advisor-Robert Oyiembo . We needed to raise at least Kshs 2.5 million to build the dormitory.

In June 2016, we had an official alumni day in the school which was our first meeting. On that day we also laid down the foundation for the dormitory. The alumni coordinated and supervised al the construction work to completion. We utilized various professional input, by early July 2016, we

[20] Dr Odero Ongech id the reigning patron of this association.

were confident that the dormitory was going to be ready for occupation by the start of September as we had targeted. The response was quite encouraging as a number of old boys we secured their contacts contributed funds. All that was done through contributions sent through Mpesa channel and our treasurer provided daily updates of financial status. Eventually a new dormitory with a student capacity of 80 was completed in time. In early september2016, the alumni were in the school to officially commission the alumni dormitory. It was a colorful ceremony graced by the school board. The entire school community appreciated this achievement within a record time with funds that were 100% accounted for. By the alumni committee. To date the dormitory stands out as one of the buildings in the key school.

The alumni agreed that in June every year there shall be an alumni day when we visit the school on a date mutually agreed with the school leadership. This started the following year in 2017 and that has been maintained annually save for 2020 due to COVID 19 restriction on mass gatherings and visits to schools. During the alumni days we award a number of students who excelled in various subjects and other disciplines like co-curricular activities. The awards have been in the form of trophies, certificates, text books and cash. The awards was extended to include both teaching and non-teaching staff. The main focus for the awards was the form four candidates who excelled in the previous KCSE. The practice has been maintained by the alumni to date. The last award was held on 28th Feb 2021.

Other than the dormitory, the alumni also sponsored tiling and ceiling of most classrooms. That too was appreciated by the entire school community. As of now, the alumni is contributing towards equipping the newly constructed twin laboratory so that it can effectively serve at optimal level for the benefit of the students desired.

We want to thank the school leadership from 2016 to date for the warm relationship cultivated and nurtured which has enabled all that we have accomplished. We remain committed to the growth of our school and more so attaining the most competitive results every year. We also thank our alumni committee leadership ably led by the ever hard working chairman engineer Dick Ndiewo and our very supportive patron Dr John Ong'ech who always leads by example. Finally thanks to the entire alumni team who have remained true to the alumni cause. Long live UHS as we continue to aim highest. Thank you.

Mr John Achoki, UHS Alumni association.

CHAPTER 10: TRAGEDY STRUCK

Prelude:

"Do noble things, not dream them all day long: And so make life, death and the vast forever one grand, sweet song" by Charles Kingsley.

"Those who have had near -death experiences will tell you that realm is far more real than this world, more crisp, vibrant, alive." Dr. Eben Alexander.

10.1: The day hell broke loose

The black day in my life remains 11.12.2009 when some rogue pumped 4 bullets using AK47 Riffle/Gun into my body and I miraculously survived. A lot of theories have been said about this day but a lot of them is not true from my perspective. I will describe in this chapter how things did unfold. It happened that one week earlier, around 4.12.2009, I received a letter that I had been selected to join Board of Governors for Usenge High School, my former High School (Form 1 to 4). I was very excited that my dream to give back to my former school that shaped my life was finally here. I quickly booked a flight that was scheduled to arrive in Kisumu at 7 am. Since I anticipated that the activities of the day on 11.12.2009 for new board inauguration would take a whole day, I booked Imperial Hotel in Kisumu for a sleepover. I had planned to go back to Nairobi on 12.12.2009 early in the morning as I had a busy schedule in the city.

So on 11.12.2009 at 5am, I went to the Jomo Kenyatta International airport (JKIA) in Nairobi, boarded Kenya Airways, landed in Kisumu as scheduled at 7am. I was picked by a project vehicle (I was in charge of a HIV project in Kisumu District & Nyando District- the project was funded by CDC and Implemented by University of Nairobi). I Went to Imperial Hotel, and made reservation for one night (the night of 11.12.2009).

I told the drive that I will drive myself to Yimbo Usenge and he should pick the vehicle in the evening. So with my favourite rhumba music playing and in high spirits, I started my journey to Yimbo. I decided to make a brief stopover at my village, Nyamonye sub location to say hello to my parents. My mother as usual slaughtered a chicken and within 45 minutes, I was having a full meal. My father was very excited that I will be serving in Usenge High School board because of his liking of the school and the historical connections. I also inspected construction of the house I was building. At 10.30 am on 11.12/2009, I resumed my journey to Usenge High School, arriving at 10.55am.

At 11am, The District Education Office represented by Owino Kanam (Alumni of Usenge High School) convened the board inauguration meeting. 1st in the agenda was to elect the Chairman. Mr Okumu Obuogi, a retired senior education officer hailing from Yimbo, proposed my name, Dr. Mirega Othuon (a son to Hanington Mirega, a former classmate of Dola in Usenge, now late) Seconded and unanimously I was elected the board of Governors Chairman. Present was Dan Owenda amongst others.

I chaired the meeting and outline my strategies for my term. The meeting ended at 2pm after which the school offered us a late lunch and we left the school. Mr Okumu Obuogi suggested that we pass sunset hotel in Usenge (whose proprietor is Raudo Francis) I buy him one drink before we can go to Kisumu as I was to sleep in Imperial Hotel and leave for Nairobi the next day. When we arrived at Usenge sunset Hotel, I found my cousin Ongoro of Nyangera Kamhore. I ordered for them some drinks. Then Ongoro insisted that I have to escort him to Asembo the next day to pay dowry for his second wife. He insisted I must cancel my trip to Kisumu and also reschedule my flight. After a lot of push, I gave in. I called my brother Mwalimu Ochieng Ong'ech to join me. I also informed my cousin Jeremiah Oduwo who was in the Initial plan that I will join them. So we were all excited and eagerly looking forward to the trip to Asembo the next day. At 5pm, I excused myself and went inside my car for a conference call with folks in USA, the Elizabeth

Glaser Peadiatric Aids Foundation (EGPAF) research team to discuss the research we were doing. This was a 2-hour call that would last up to 7pm. Mr Okumu Obuogi excused himself at 5pm and left. After I finished the call at 7pm, I ordered chicken and assortment of other food i.e. meat and fish. We were expecting Jeremiah Oduwo and other Cousins from Nyangera Kamhore to join us. And indeed they did around 8.45pm. Then we started feasting and bonding happily. At around 9.30 pm, Ongoro left us. My brother Ochieng Ong'ech for some strange reasons started hinting to me that we should also leave. But I insisted that we stay a little.

At 10 pm, hell broke loose. A group of people walked into the makuti where we were in police jungle jackets, one of them having AK47 Riffle/Gun. They ordered all of us to kneel down and said they were policemen searching for guns. They ordered us to remove our guns and hand over to them. As we obeyed their command, I made a comment that we are just innocent Kenyan Citizens who are just enjoying our evening. I did not appear shaken and I think this rattled the fellow with the gun. He pointed the gun at me and shouted that I keep quite. I knelt down as per his command but strategically at an angle. I heard the sound of a gun fire several times but thought they were just scaring us. There was a brief period of silence. I did not feel any pain and I did not think I had been shot 4 bullets in that brief period of gun fire which lasted only a minute. Then wow, I saw blood trickling from my chest, around my heart but no pain. I told my brother Ochieng Ong'ech who was lying down next to me that I had been shot in the heart and I can die any minute. In my pocket I had Ksh. 100,000 which I was to use to pay workers who were doing construction in my rural home. I gave the money to my brother and told him that this will help during my funeral arrangements. He took the money and the next minute I saw him run past the gunman and jumped over the fence (which was quite high-stone wall with barbed wire on top). The gun man fired several shots towards his direction and for a moment

I thought he was dead. I became restless while lying on the ground and started shouting that they are killing innocent people.

I shouted, saying that they had killed me, mentioning my name, Dr. Ong'ech and my brother Ochieng Ong'ech. I told them that the same gun that they have used to kill us is the same way they will also die. There were people sleeping upstairs in the hotel, and when they heard my name, they made calls to the police post in Bondo.

Meanwhile after my brother Ochieng Ong'ech had jumped over the fence, there was some confusion amongst the gunman and his accomplishment. They started panicking and looked fearful. They quickly robbed everyone, taking cash and phones. Interestingly they did not touch me (may be they feared finger prints). Then my cousin Jeremia Oduwo started protesting that we don't deserve what they were doing to us. They fired a shot at him to keep quite. The bullet missed his head by an inch. The gangsters then disconnected the electricity in the place and fled. After about 5 minutes of silence, I started feeling pain in my legs. I dragged myself to the road in the hope that a good Samaritan would find me, while still shouting that the gangsters had shot an innocent Dr. Ong'ech. I decided to make a phone call. Seemingly, the thugs had assumed I would shortly be dead so they had not taken my phone. I called the owner of Usenge Sunset Resort, Mr Raudo Francis, and informed him on what had happed. I told him where they can locate my body in case I die shortly afterwards. Meanwhile my brother Ochieng' Ong'ech had run all the way to Usenge police post to report the issue. It was a miracle that the bullets the gangsters fired at him did not hit him.

The police at Usenge Police Post told my brother that they actually had heard the sound of gun fire, but they could not go where gangsters have guns. So they did not respond. Meanwhile Mr Raudo made desperate calls everywhere. Meanwhile, Justice Ouko William was around with his personal

Police Guards at his home, which was nearby. Upon receiving the information, he immediately rushed to the scene. He found my cousin Jeremiah Oduwo had picked me and was rushing me to a hospital in Kisumu. Policemen from Bondo also arrived at the scene following calls from Nairobi and people who were sleeping in the hotel room. Unfortunately, we were later to learn that the policemen from Usenge Police Post only came in the morning. Jeremia Oduwo drove bravely to Kisumu's Aga Khan Hospital in an attempt to save my life, desperately crying that I should not die. Our journey to Kisumu was not smooth, as the weather became very bad. It started raining so heavily that Oduwo could hardly see the road. But I cautioned him not to take me to public hospital along the way as I would just die there. We arrived in Kisumu when I was almost losing consciousness. I was now bleeding profusely from the gunshot wound in my leg, with a lot of pain. Luckily, Jeremia Oduwo had informed our cousin Dr Walter Otieno who was based in Kisumu that I was coming with gunshot wounds. Dr Walter Otieno Mobilized a team of surgeons and the entire Kisumu Agha Khan Hospital staff. This served well, as upon our arrival at Aga Khan, we found Walter and his medical team waiting. Things moved very fast. At that time I was unconscious. I was luck to have had a good medical insurance, thanks to the EGPAF project where I was working as a research consultant. I was quickly resuscitated, and a series of emergency formalities were intiated, such as transfusion, X-rays. Thereafter I was rushed to the theatre. More than 4 surgeons operated me lead by Dr. Dedan Ongong'a. Meanwhile Dr. Otieno Walter (the 2021 renowned malaria vaccine researcher and innovator) drove to Yimbo at night, organized for the project car I had to be brought to Kisumu and passed information to the rest of my family that all was well. The news of my shooting had spread very fast; it was big news in the local vernacular Radio station, Ramogi, as well as in daily Newspapers. I regained consciousness in the morning of 12.12.2009, surrounded by many relatives from as far as Kisii (Caren Ogola Ong'ech) my parents, brothers, Sisters and all close family relatives were there.

By 10am of Jamhuriday, the Agha khan Hospital Kisumu was stormed by many friends and relatives wanting to see me. The hospital clearly had difficulty in managing the anxious crowd. In the meantime, the Doctors made a quick decision that I needed a cardiothoracic surgeon to perform further surgeries on me. For this, I had to be transferred to Nairobi Hospital. EGPAF contacted AMREF flying Doctors and a plane arrived within an hour. I was airlifted to Nairobi, landing at Wilson airport. Here, I found a family friend, Mr Gerald Oyiengo Okola and his family waiting for me. Hs son and my mentee, Dr Vitalis Okola was part of this team.

I was quickly taken by an ambulance to Nairobi Hospital where Dr. Munene immediately took me to theater. It was yet another Medical team of the-who-and-who in the medical world in Kenya, including Prof. Ogola E N. As expected, some blood vessels had been raptured by the gunshots. These they repaired. Luckily, the 4 bullets did not break any of my bones or injure the vital organs. This was a miracle of some sort, for even the heart was intact, unhurt. A real miracle even the Doctors could not understand. I was in the hospital for 2 weeks. As I mentioned earlier, I had a very generous medical cover courtesy of my research body. Therefore, all my bills, including airlifting, were fully paid by EGPAF. I was discharged after one agonizing fortnight.

However, one week after my discharge, I was back to the hospital with a massive blood clot in the leg caused by a phenomenon called Deep Venous Thrombosis (DVT). I spent my birthday of 31.12.2009 as well as the New Year of 1.1.2010 in the hospital. I was in the hospital for another one week, and upon discharge, I walked with crutches for another one month. Like in Kisumu's Aga Khan, my admission at Nairobi Hospital saw a huge flow of visitors (friends and relatives) coming to see me. People came from all over the country to see me. Pastors from different churches came to pray for me.This gave the hospital difficult time to control. As such, they decided to block all the physical visits, they were only allowed to sign a get well soon book, leave flowers and cards. No one was to come to my room. However, A few people such as Prof PLO Lumumba and a Former PS Eng. Peter Wambura could not hear any of that; they made their way to my bed side.

Back in Yimbo, civil war was looming, with the youth taking up arms to revenge. Clans were accusing each other of my shooting. Accusations and counter accusations on how my shooting was well planned by my enemies was the news of the day in Yimbo. My Uncle, former councilor Obera Ombere was on the war path. I had to send a word for peace, dismissing all the theories. I told them that I was just in the wrong place at the wrong time. Fortunately, my word cooled tempers and peace prevailed.

This shooting tragedy changed my life. I made a promise that while in Yimbo, I will always be in my house by 6pm. I stopped going out at night. I became more prayerful. I adjusted many things in my life to date. Sincerely speaking, it is only God that saved my life on this black day of 11.12.2009.

Now let me allow my brother Ochieng Ong'ech to say his part.....

10.2: A black day in Dola's family: by Japuonj Ochieng' Ong'ech

An Account of the Historic Usenge Sunset Hotel Tragic Incident That Occurred On 11/12/2009

I will never forget the smile and mood we had as we gathered at the renowned hotel sunset at Usenge. We gathered here to celebrate Board of Management (BOM) chair-elect at Usenge High School, a position that was competitive. Dr. Odero Ong'ech had seemingly wielded immense support among the fellow members of the board, a spirit that made them elect him as their chair. Among those who gave him overwhelming support were Eng. Oriaro, educationist Mr. Obuogi Okumu and Dr. Othuon Mirega.

Before joining other colleagues such as Oduo Jodo, Oreno Okech, Ongoro at the hotel restaurant,,Daktari was engaged in a lengthy phone conversation spanning an hour, passing vital health information to working colleagues in America. He later joined us and together we made an order of food. While the food was getting ready, we discussed a wide range of issues and ideas, laughing and least aware of an impending terrible incident. While addressing us about his new position as BOM chair, he promised to assume the post with utmost humility, gratitude, dedication and commitment. His focus would be for academic excellence and improvement of school infrastructure. We were all happy and looked forward to him taking up the responsibility.

No sooner had he finished giving his maiden address and acceptance speech than I saw three men clad in fade uniform holding guns. The gun nozzle was pointed towards us and a deep raspy voice demanded either we all lie down or send us to our creator. At the sound of those words, my body was paralyzed with fear, becoming scared out of my wits. I realized that our life hung on a whisker and if anything could be done, it had to be done really fast with speed, precision and courage.

I whispered to daktari to hand over anything he considered vital to me silently. He then gave me Kshs 100, 000 tied with a rubber band. With my body filled with the fright-fight-flight hormone, I stealthily moved out, truck my assailant jaw with my fist and at breakneck speed, jumped over the fence, running as fast as a deer leaving dust floating in the air. No sooner had I jumped over the fence running towards the police station than I heard gunshot boom behind me. However, this did not deter me. Instead, I literally flew to the police station where I reported the incident. I was retained at the station. Tears welled up my face as I was clueless about the fate of my brother and others I left behind. I vividly remembered that as I left, he was in a state of near-despair, informing the attacker that they were taking the life of an important person in this country. All my effort at the police station bore no fruits as the policemen became so reluctant to leave the station to the scene. The night was indeed long.

Luckily arounnd 6am, I felt a sigh of relieve when our cousin, also a medic, Dr. Walter Otieno came to look for me at the police station. He wanted to drive me home to a message to my parents. He later dropped me at home and rushed to Kisumu to monitor the progress of emergency attendance Daktari was receiving. I then organized how we could travel to Kisumu with parents immediately. On reaching Aga Khan Kisumu, we found many people who had arrived queuing to see Daktari.

How Daktari won the battle for his life was a mystery engraved in many people's minds. On seeing him, he kept assuring us that all would be well. Word went round like fire, and hue and cry filled the entire Siaya County, as the incident was captured by the daily nation newspaper. Relatives' and friends were pushing the security wing to take action and come out with the source of this incident.

Later after a week I took the entire family to the scene of the horrendous incident and nobody could believe their eyes. Daktari's professional position saved him as he was flown to Nairobi for further treatment (Nairobi Hospital in particular). We had come within a whisker of death. Thanks to God we survived the terrible ordeal and I could not believe and it took me a long time to heal. An account by: Brother Retire Mwalimu Ochieng' Ong'ech

10.3: The newspaper documentation:

Mzee son short 11.12.2009

Surgeon flown to city after attack by gang

By NATION Reporter

A doctor based at Kenyatta National Hospital was at the weekend flown to Nairobi after gangsters shot him and injured several people in Usenge market in Bondo District.

Dr Odero Ong'ech, a surgeon at the hospital, was yesterday undergoing emergency operation at Nairobi Hospital where doctors were trying to remove a bullet lodged in his stomach.

Bondo police boss Josephine Barmao confirmed that the gangsters raided a bar at Usenge market on Kenya's order with Uganda where they found the doctors and friends at around 8 pm on Saturday.

Mrs Barmao said the incident was isolated but investigations are going on following a spate of gun attacks in the area.

Another man identified as Mr Otieno Radier was killed on his way from the market last month. Also last month, a Kenya Power and Lighting Company employee, Mr George Ayore, was injured when homes in the area were raided.

The surgeon was yesterday undergoing emergency operation at Nairobi Hospital

"We are trying our best because since April police have killed several gangsters and their ring leaders in the area. I am aware the doctor was shot and his friends injured during the raid at the weekend but the thugs' days are numbered. Let people not fear during this Christmas season," the police boss told the *Nation* on phone.

People who called the Nation from Bondo said the situation is getting out of hand and accused police officers at Usenge Police Station of doing little to fight crime.

Patrol boat

"We are terrified ... Our Chiefs and District Officer should be supported because it appears there is a missing link with the regular police. The DO does not have a vehicle or a patrol boat in an area next to a neighbouring country," a resident who sought anonymity for security reasons said.

When the Nation visited Dr Ong'ech at Nairobi Hospital, he said the gang raided the bar at 8 pm and demanded to know who in the crowd is "a doctor". Before they could scamper for safety, one of the gangsters shot at him as the others were beaten senseless.

He lost his documents and some cash.

A NEWSPAPER CUTTING: Adopted from MZEE 2018 BOOK, page 378

CHAPTER 11: IN THE WORDS OF OTHERS

Prelude:

Tributes from selected relatives, friends, peers: a short writeup each

11.1: Luke Juma Ogono

I feel highly honored and greatly privileged to be nominated to participate and make my maiden contribution towards this noble cause. Nothing can be more humbling for want of space and without any further ado, I will jump straight to the fundamentals of our history with reference to our primary school life experience in the 70s to date.

Dr. Ongech and I grew up in a rural village Ogam and Ragak respectively. Typical of any rural set up, we had a lot of homogeneous challenges and/or intrigues reminiscent of any such background structure anywhere else. Our primary school experience was, as expected, a mixture of fan and pain. We attended primary schools a few kilometers apart both located on Kisumu Bondo Usenge Rd. Mine was Nyamonye Primary while Majengo was for John both in the same Administrative Location then. Each one of had to cover about 1.5 kms to school on bare foot poor pathway and bad weather notwithstanding.

As young boys growing up, we discovered our common bond pretty early in life. We were posting impressive results in class work throughout our primary education consistently maintaining the lead to the finish. I vividly remember exchanging notes on weekends and periodically setting and marking exams for our respective classes interchangeably. Daktari could set and mark for us and vice versa. This was no mean feat I must say. It created and in instilled synergy between us and as fate would have it, we ended up in in one school for our secondary education. This was Usenge Boys High School. The year was 1981. I can talk about this great man time on end and effortlessly but at least a few things in him stand out and I will categorize them accordingly for purposes of clarity and record: 1: Highly Disciplined and Independent Minded; 2: Astutely Generous and Sociable; 3: Razor Sharp; 4: Development Oriented; and 5: Team Player and Great Mobilizer.

I choose not to mention everything about John because it is simply not possible here. It is not easy get one man at this time and age in possession of all this but John does. This is what makes this man different. This great man blends, connects and dines with all and sundry in the village and elsewhere. He is just his own man. His deep sense of purpose, his desire for a better society and dignified life for humanity transcends all borders. He believes in education and has been a pillar of hope and inspiration to many within and outside his family lineage He has touched and saved many a life in equal measure.

It is not easy to sufficiently describe this man because it will never be enough but I will endeavor to bring out more when, in the fullness of time, I retire to do my Memoir in which a whole Chapter shall be dedicated to this icon for posterity. I, therefore, only wish him good health together with the entire Kong'ech Family for they gave us this great man.

As I conclude, it would be inappropriate of me not to mention something which touches the very fabric of my life in a manner unprecedented. The month was March, date 27th, 2021.The place and facility were Nairobi and Coptic Hospital respectively. We had just buried Mzee Ongech aka Dola (Daktari's father in a colorful ceremony never witnessed before and whose details will not disclose here for obvious but good reasons).

I was diagnosed with cancer after several tests were done in Ksm at the beginning of March this year. Immediately this was confirmed and the result communicated to me, I didn't hesitate to share the same with Dr. Ongech who upon receipt of the same, upon thorough consultations with the relevant specialists, only had this to tell and I quote him verbatim. "Thura come to

Nairobi immediately. I will set up a team of Doctors to take care of you". That was the turning point in my life as it also came with challenges. We had to raise money, running close to a million in his estimation including post-surgery therapy/follow ups. Things were running so fast with Daktari taking the lead in mobilizing for resources from self, relatives and friends of like mind. Within a week, we had met our our initial admission target at the facility. This man took charge of this project passionately and cleared my admission process in a record time as I was seated at the admission area. When he eventually personally checked me into my room. VIP room and looking at the environment, I declared to him that I had healed way before my surgery and that was the spirit I maintained to the end. The surgery started at 11am and ended shortly after 6pm when I regained consciousness. Dr. Otieno Edwin who was my surgeon did the magic and I remember him telling me when he came to visit after surgery the following day at noon and I quote: "Luke osiep Dr Ongech, ingima ka siling". That was good news coming from your surgeon immediately after surgery.

Dr. Ongech in his uncharacteristic manner and for a good reason took photos of the resection to completion and shared the same with me in confidence. What a courage!! Besides, he personally took the resected tissues to The Nairobi Hospital for Histology at his own expense. It was after the histology report was out that my Oncologist, Professor Chite, after perusal, confided in me that everything was removed and that I wasn't a candidate for chemo.What a relief! I can't thank Dr. Ongech enough. The rest will come through in my Memoir coming soon.

SO LONG LIVE OWAD GI MARY!; LONG LIVE AKUCH KA RODI

LUKE JUMA OGONO, YIMBO, RAGAK VILLAGE

11.2: Dr. Omondi Afulo:

TRIBUTE TO DR. JOHN ODERO ONGECH.

The Ongech family is very close to the Afulo family dating back to the 1960s and even earlier when my father was the pioneer headmaster of Nyamonye primary school since 1948. Japuonj Afulo was also the pioneer of Catholicism in Yimbo and Sakwa locations. The children of Mzee Ongech were schooling at Nyamonye School. The eldest son was Japuonj Ogola Ongech who was classmate to my elder brother, Prof Engineer Thomas Odhiambo Afulo. The next son was Mwalimu Ochieng' Ong'ech who was my classmate and age mate. Dr. John Odero Ong'ech was born much later. He is age mate and classmate to my 5th follower, Prof Augustine Otieno Afulo. I came to know about the young Odero Ong'ech when I was teaching at Majengo Secondary School in 1982 after my A-levels. I was one of the pioneer teachers of the school together with Mr. John Ogola, brother to the current Bondo MP, Hon Gideon Ochanda. One of his teachers, the late James Otieno Ogutu, who was my uncle, used to talk fondly about **wuod Mzee Ong'ech matin who is very sharp especially in mathematics**. I left Majengo for Barkanyango Secondary school the following year, 1983. I never heard about John until 1988 when I was in 5th year medicine course **when I heard ni jayimbo moro odonjo timo medicine**. I enquired and found out whom he was. He was welcomed into the noble profession. John started working in consultation with me. I even advanced him some text books to start off before he could buy his own. Medical school textbooks are never given out completely since you need them even at postgraduate level. I was posted out as a medical officer to various stations in the country. I did my postgraduate training from 1993 to 1998 and then joined KNH in 1999 as a medical specialist. However, Dr. Ong'ech did not stay out for long. After his internship, he almost immediately joined KNH as a medical Officer and he worked very well until he was sponsored for postgraduate training in Obstetrics/Gynecology. He excelled in his training and qualified very quickly as a specialist. At some stage, he was appointed HOD of Obs/Gyn department while I was HOD Accident/Emergency. We worked very well as now senior colleagues in KNH. He pioneered the establishment of Ogam Health Centre which to date is helping the local community very well. He has participated in a lot of Corperate Social Responsibilities (CSRs) both at home and the country at large. These include schools, churches, school fees for the needy and many more. He took an excellent care of his father throughout his aging life till his demise. He also, to date, takes care of health and aspects of well being of his siblings, their families and the community at large. That is part of the source of Dr. Ong'ech's massive blessings. Dr. Ongech followed the footsteps of Dr. Badia Jangolo who was his mentor in obstetrics/gynecology since his medical school days to date. He followed suit by mentoring Dr. Moreen Owiti (from Kasau) and Dr. Vitalis Okola (from Orom, majengo) who are now established Obs/Gyne Consultants and leaders in their own right. Dr. Ongech has set a legacy which will live long beyond him. He is indeed living the dreams of his father

Congratulations Doc!.

Dr. G.O AFULO,

Consultant Hand and Orthopedic Surgeon.

11.3: Dr. Edwin Otieno on Dr John Odero Ong'ech

I first met Dr. Ongech at the University of Nairobi medical school in the late 1980s as a young, vibrant scholar full of energy and promise. He was indeed a loud individual but very focused. We parted ways when we qualified as doctors and were posted to do internship in different centers. However, we still kept in touch through the various professional and societal networks. To further our studies Dr. Ong'ech joined UoN to study Obstetrics and Gynecology while I crossed over to Makerere University to study general surgery. He selflessly hosted my wife and I whenever we visited Nairobi from Kampala.

When I completed my course and came back to Kenya, work was difficult to come by. At the time he was working in one of the AAR medical outlets while at the same time running a private clinic in town. I was desperately looking for some worthwhile economic activity to hook on. At the time, Dr. Ong'ech had just been awarded a full bright scholarship to the USA and was leaving in a short while. He not only influenced so that I took over his work position that he was vacating at AAR but also handed me his private practice. He also secured a job placement for my wife, who is a nurse. In one sweep of administrative and organizational genius, Dr. Ong'ech had solved our work dilemma and put my wife and I on sound financial footing. His magnanimity during our early formative years is memorable and indeed invaluable. Doc, may you be blessed.

By Dr. Edwin Otieno
Consultant Surgeon and Lecturer,

11.4: David Otieno Owuor

As a cousin, we were also friends, I would visit your home sometimes during holidays and we could go to Nyaudenge beach, Nyamonye market etc. Not forgetting bike rides from Nyamonye hill to Lwala village non-stop with me as your passenger, Hahaha. In 1994, at your graduation party extension in Githurai 44, you started by asking me what am doing in Nairobi. My reply was some menial jobs kwa wahindi on and off. This was the date my star started shinning all the way. You invited me to Kisumu while you were doing your internship, I remember you weren't earning much but you sat me down and asked me what I could do. I chose to peruse sales/marketing and driving which you paid fully for me. With your connections I was to join Coca-Cola Company through your friend Mr. Milanya who later left Coca-Cola for USA.

Later you got me a job at Pioneer Assurance company as a sales executive. Still you never gave up on me, when you went for further studies in USA, with your network you started connecting me to fly to America but unfortunately I missed one document that could not allow me to travel. Thanks so much for all that you've done- I only can return the favour by praying to God to grant you long life, I will always be thankful to you. Not only you have been a fantastic sponsor and mentor to me, but you have taught me how to mentor other people. Even the courage and English I speak now, it's due to the environment you enabled me to live in I have a lot to say but what I know for sure I'm what I am today because of you. I'm humbled and grateful, your thoughtfulness is a gift I will always treasure, I'm touched.

David Otieno Owuor, Cousin

11.5: Dan Obera, Uncle

It was a dream comes true to visit the Capital City of Kenya, Nairobi after the Easter holidays of 2014, and the time to face reality of life immediately after Secondary Education. Nervously, the journey to meet Dr. John Ong'ech who I had never interacted with before in my life started. You touched my life by your selfless and countless acts of kindness, always giving and never expecting any favours in return. For every institution you worked for, you laid path for others to succeed like me. The benefits of your hard work are a living testimony for so many men and women you took under your wings at a personal and professional level. Dr. Ong'ech you will always be an inspiration to me, my entire family and anyone who have interacted with you. You have proved that supporting another's success cannot dampen yours. May the Almighty Lord continue blessing you. Live long Ajuoga.

Dan Obera

11.6: Moses Apela, Uncle

Dr Ong'ech has been a great pillar and mentor in better part of my life as from the days of high school where he came handy to pay my school fees from form 3 and 4. In 2006 he made sure that I was enrolled in KMTC to pursue Clinical Medicine and surgery all this while he paid the required fees besides residing in his private residence.

In 2013 while at the brink of burying my late father in a foreign land, he was very instrumental in ensuring that he collected to a tune of Kshs 70,000 which at the point was the main deficit. On my employment, he made sure that I secured a chance at Nairobi West Hospital till 2018 when I joined German doctors where again he became my sole guarantor while I was traveling to Germany in 2019 for my Pediatrics specialization. Thanks daktari and may God bless you abundantly and do more to other deserving people.

Moses Apela

11.7: Prof Alfred Omenya

I first knew Dr. Ong'ech when I was s student at Majengo Primary School. I was three years behind Dr. Ong'ech but we looked forward to him, not only for the athletic prowess he demonstrated in the field, but more so for academic dominance - he was always the top student in his class. Dr. Ong'ech was also our School Bell Ringer. For some reason the school always appointed the best students as bell ringers. It is instructive that the following year, Eng. George Obara, who was the top student become bell ringer, followed by another top student, the late Peter Odida and then myself.

Dr. Ong'ech's inspiration continued even as he transitioned into high school and later to the University. He spent time teaching us pro-bono, especially Maths and Science, which he was particularly good at. Dr. Ongech was my top encourager, even as I joined Alliance High School and later on the University of Nairobi's School of Architecture. We had a network of close friends that we had built from our childhood, who only shared one thing in common- excellence. These included Eng. Dick Ndiewo and Deputy Director of Public Prosecutions, Robert Oyiembo, Agricultural Economist, Dr. Evans Owino, Erick Ouma, among others. Most of us we groomsmen in Dr. Ongechs wedding.

We teamed together to support our local schools. Dr Ong'ech was instrumental in the development of Majengo, Usenge and Nyamonye schools, supporting both primary school and secondary school. Later on the entire team was to converge as Members of the Board of Management of Majengo. This was a school of 187 students, with six classrooms and the Principal's office, when we joined the board in 2008. During our tenure in the board, the school grew to over 1000 students and become officially five streams. We built dormitories, classrooms, library, school hall and many others.

Dr. Ong'ech is a man of unimaginable principles. He was the first Kenyan to turn down a presidential appointment to head the National Referral Hospital, Kenyatta. Despite what many Kenyans saw as opportunity to become a millionaire through corruption. He quietly went on early retirement from Kenyatta Hospital but continued his leadership in the profession while running his personal clinic.

Dr. Ong'ech generousity was legendary. At a very personal level, Dr. Ongech accommodated my family in Nairobi for the entire duration that I was pursuing Masters and PhD studies in South Africa. When Ong'ech Dola, John's father, who was a giant in his right, passed on, I had the honour of chairing the committee that celebrated that great man. Dr. Ong'ech is my big brother and indeed family, in real meaning of the word.

This autobiography is therefore an important milestone, where different dimension of the life of this great man is explored: from a philanthropist with a heart of gold, a community development champion, to a professional giant globally, to a man rooted in family, community and culture; a man with great love for education of people and a principled patriot.
Prof. Alfred Omenya, B.Arch, M.Arch, PhD, MAAK (Fellow),
CEO Eco-Build Africa and Professor, University of Canberra, Australia.

11.8: Elisha Ogutu

The Fulbright Scholar (Hubert Humphrey Fellow) Alumni Elly Ogutu

It's a great honor and privilege to write a short tribute on Africa's most celebrated Fulbright Scholar (Humphrey Fellow) Dr John Odero Ong'ech. My fellow Fulbright Scholar is a very generous, resourceful, well networked and has promptly assisted many folks irrespective of their socio-economic and political status. Daktari is down to earth fellow, speaks his mind without fear or favour, even blurting out bitter truth without battling an eyelid. He provides good recommendations, follow-up referrals, proud of hardworking and focused people. **In 2001**, Dr Ong'ech was awarded the prestigious **Hubert Humphrey fellowship Award,** funded by the U.S. Congress through the U.S. Department of State. The Kenya and USA selection panelists were greatly impressed with his excellent academic records, superb professional work experience, strong leadership qualities, good record of public service, community work involvement, excellent English proficiency and confident personality.

Dr Ong'ech then travelled to USA to advance his academic and professional career at the prestigious Tulane University, School of Public Health in New Orleans, Louisiana. Tulane is one of the best Ivy League universities with excellent academic, medical & research programs, vast resources and great support for Humphrey Fellows. He utilized the valuable opportunities to enhance his academics, medical profession and leadership skills. He also travelled extensively in many US states giving lecture talks, participated in many symposiums, conferences and networked with top global health experts. The program enhanced his knowledge on American culture and broaden his global perspectives to become health a global leader. He returned home after successful completion of the graduate program

In 2002, Dr Ong'ech was one of the most brilliant Humphrey Alumni who won the most coveted **Hubert Humphrey Alumni Impact Award** for HIV/AIDS Prevention and stigma reduction project. The Award was sponsored by the Institute of International Education (IIE), Washington DC, USA. This was a major feat as thousands of Humphrey fellows & Alumni worldwide competed for the only available ten (10) slots for Alumni Impact Awards. The kind Daktari advised us (Yimbo Professionals) to apply for Humphrey's Fellowship and Alumni Impact Awards. Thanks for Daktari for guidance & support for I successfully applied and won the two competitive awards. It was a historic feat for two Kenyans (again Yimbians) to win the Hubert Alumni Impact Awards for two consecutive years (2002-2003).

In 2009, Dr Ong'ech received global landslide votes for the **Best Humphrey Alumni Award** in the world for his dedicated public service, initiating and supporting community health development projects in Kenya. The Good News was relayed by the US Embassy, which prompted huge celebrations in Kenya, especially his home city of Kisumu "Yurop" and rural Ogam-Lwala

Village where songs, sigalagala (ululations) and celebratory drumbeats rent the air all night long. Daktari has mentored many youths, motivated and facilitated many scholars who applied and won Fulbright Scholarships, travelled to USA and successfully completed their Fellowships programs including graduate studies mostly Master degrees in Public Health (MPH).

If it wasn't for Daktari, I wouldn't have known the existence of Humphrey Fellowship program which also enabled me to successfully complete MPH program at the prestigious Emory University, Rollins School of Public Health, Atlanta next to CDC Hqs office. Erohamano thura Daktari. Amor ni atimo nendi (tribute) kapod ingima. God bless you my fellow Fulbright Scholar (Humphrey Fellow) from the great Ogam-Lwala village, Yimbo.

Gordon Elisha Ogutu
Hurbert Humprey fellow 2002/3
Emory University, Rollins School of Public Health, Atlanta USA

11.9: Moses Oginga

The Kamuhore community staying at Ogam is constituted of the following homes:

1. Mzee obiero home
2. Mzee Sipem home
3. Mzee Ong'ech home
4. Mzee odung'a home
5. Mzee akungu home
6. Mzee Paul yamo home
7. Mzee Guda home

These famines as I was growing up only one family was a bit blessed and had a job with government, which is Mzee Gudah Omwanda. The community of Kamuhore was so much invisible, was as a minority within the area, and was voiceless. At the home of humble Mzee Ong'ech, a son was born, the 5th child and last born son, Dr. John Odero Ong'ech (Aruba, as was always referred to by the father). Dr. John Ong'ech I lack words to describe you. You are a God-send to the family of entire Karodi. History says that the Kowil, Wanyenjra and Dimo came together in the land of Yimbo and found Karodi already on the land. The three communities had long ago gone up and had a voice. However, it is you who has gone out of your ways to place the Kamuhore people where they are now. No any home a child have gone to school without your support. According to my analysis, you are the first person to have a degree within this community, and through your initiative and support: (i) 1. We have more than 10 degrees within these homes (Almost in every home); (2) we have electricity crisscrossing the community of Kamuhore; (3) we have a dispensary within the community; (4) we have a story to tell; we can be heard. We have a voice. Daktari. This is not your might, it's very unique, it's God's doing it in you, through you we can now sit around the tables and negotiate with other community. May the almighty God preserve you, may the God of Abraham bless the work of your hand in Jesus name amen:

Moses Owino Oginga, Yimbo Ogam, Kamuhore.

11.10: Advocate Ray Maduda Tollo

Life has never given forth a truer man: One who inspires, is brilliant and generous. The instant impression is his meticulous analysis of things, intonation that is burdened with knowledge and a gait that stands for country but this soon fades as you quickly notice his focus on integrity and zeal for social cohesion that dominates conversations. Encounter Dr. John Ong'ech and you will learn to work, give and smile.

ADVOCATE RAY MADUDA TOLLO

11.11: George Owaga

Dr John Ong'ech is a **"Woman doctor with gifted hands".** He has touched many lives by putting life at the centre of everything he does. He started from a humble beginning and through his academic and professional excellence, managed to transverse the world in pursuit of excellence. This he did without losing sight of his vision. He has finally put down the story of his life journey in this book *"dreams of my father"*. It is a narrative of his roots, of how he rose from a village boy in Yimbo and through sheer determination, getting a Fulbright scholarship (HHF) USA...to finally realising his full potential.

The writing is conversational and provides insights of his late father's knowledge of the Luo roots and the role he played in shaping his life. He has inspired lives and continues to support many people to achieve **their dreams of Jaduong Dola**. True philanthropist!

May the lord bless the work of your hands.

George Owaga

11.12: Ruth Amina Ochieng

To my community you are a black messiah but to me you are a mentor, a teacher, the person I emulate in my everyday life (a role model). You have taught me that discipline and hard work is the only way to success in this life. You have made me realize that I have so much potential as a woman. Your support both emotionally and financially have made me who I am today. You have always reminded me that am not yet there, and in my life, I just want to be like you. You have walked with me this journey from when I finished secondary school to my undergraduate and even the job market. I really appreciate. I have walked in big offices because of you, including Ouma Oluga's office, Dr Patrick Amoth's Office and many more. You have always told me that ,"Nyar kamhore you are the doctor we never had" and one day I must be a doctor… not a medical doctor but a doctor of philosophy. You are an inspiration to the whole Kamhore community. May God expand your territories and bless you in everything you do

CHAPTER 12: OPINION ON THE KENYA HEALTH CARE SYSTEM AND DEVOLUTION OF HEALTH

Prelude:

"Health Care in Denmark is Universal, free of charge and high quality. Everybody is covered as a right of Citizenship". Bernie Sanders

"Universal Health coverage is one of the most powerful social equalizers among all policy options" Dr. Margaret Chan Director General WHO.

"Universal Health Care coverage is key to building resilient Health Systems that make people and planet Healthier". Dr. Judith Rodin, President the Rockefeller Foundation.

12.1: The Kenyan health system and its blocks

A key purpose of the Framework is to promote common understanding of what a health system is and what constitutes health systems strengthening. To achieve this, clear definition and communication is essential. For health systems in whatever jurisdiction to be strengthened, it is essential to be clear and have a common understanding of the problems, where and why investment is needed, what will happen as a result, and by what means change can be monitored. The approach of this Framework is to define a discrete number of "HS **building blocks**" that make up the system. These are based on the functions defined in World health report 2000, and the building blocks are: **service delivery; health workforce; information; medical products, vaccines and technologies; financing; and leadership and governance (stewardship)**. The building blocks serve three purposes. First, they allow a definition of desirable attributes - what a health system should have the capacity to do. Second, they provide one way of defining WHO's priorities. Third, by setting out the entirety of the health systems agenda, they provide a means for identifying gaps in WHO support.

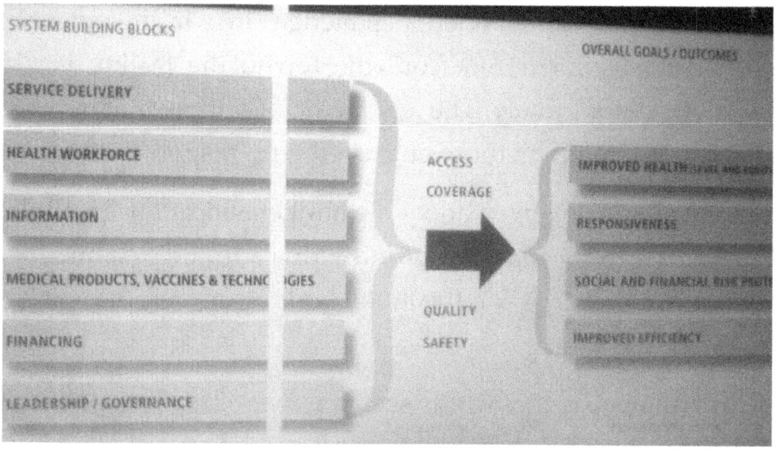

12.2: The Kenyan Health care system: do we devolve?

Access to affordable quality health care has remained a big challenge to majority of Kenyans since Independence. It has always been a priority to every Government since Independence but progress has been slow and unacceptable. Many Health Policies and strategic documents has been developed but all these remain on paper.

The current one is the Kenya Health Policy **2014-2030**. The frame work which replicates the World Organization building blocks of a good Health system namely: **Services delivery, Health Workforce, Health Information System, Access to essential Medicine, Financing and Leadership/ Governance.** There has been rapid expansion of services delivery points through the effort of many players. But many of the buildings remains a shell without medicine or equipments or Health Workers.

Kenya has a large number of well-trained **health work force**. The tragedy is that they are not employed in the Kenya Health System to provide services. We actually export them to Europe, USA and other countries while the hospitals continues to have staff shortages resulting in poor service delivery.

Access to essential medicine has remained a challenge since Independence. The supply chain system is corrupted from the top to the facility level. KEMSA has corruption scandals daily. The few medicine supply that trickles down to the facility is also stolen by those entrusted with responsibility.

The **Health Care financing** is not given adequate budget allocation. The little that is allocated is also taken by the corrupt individuals in the system. The allocation has never reached 15% of the total budget as per the WHO recommendations.

The **leadership/Governance** in the health sector is wanting. The political class does not give the technocrats space to work. The Ministry of Health is led by politicians and not Health Experts at the top. The Cabinet Secretary and Principal Secretary are not Health Experts and yet they are the decision makers in the Ministry.

The Health Care last blow was in the 2010 Constitution that devolved Health Care to the Counties. The Governors and the MCA's priorities is not in Health but to enrich themselves. The budget allocation for Health is negligible. The Health Workers are either not hired or not paid. There is no supply of the **essential drugs and equipments**. The Health Information System to generate data for planning is not responsive.

So what is the way forward in this terrible quagmire? Eliminate corruption and wastages. Health work force should not be devolved. This should be managed centrally. There should be a Health service commission to manage Health workforce. Employ locally our trained Health Work force to support service delivery in Kenya instead of exporting them out and yet a lot of money was used to train them.

The supply of essential medicines should also be centralized with a robust computerized system that eliminates corrupt practices. Adequate supervision should be in place to ensure the medicines and equipments reach the intended destinations. Encourage Public-Private partnership on equipment leasing. Hospitals could also outsource none core services.

Increased budget allocation to Health Care Financing. Allocate 15% of budget both Nationally and at the County level on health as per the Abuja declaration of 2001. Adequate system to eliminate the eating culture from the top to the facility level should also be put in place with accountability prioritize. The cartels that have infiltrated the supply chain system should be eliminated.

The Ministry of Health Top Leadership at Cabinet Secretary Level and Principal Secretary level should be Health Experts. Health information system should be reviewed to provide solutions to the challenges in the Health Care Sector. The Devolution of Health System should be reviewed. Currently there are 6 levels in Health Care System:

a. **Level1- community,**
b. **Level-2 Dispensaries,**
c. **Level 3- Health centers.**
d. **Level 4-Primary (District) referral facility**
e. **Level 5 Secondary(Provincial) referral facility**
f. **Level 6 Tertiary (National) referral facility**

Level 1-5 is currently developed with only level 6 under the National Government.

The Devolution should manage level 1-3. Level 4-6 should be managed at the National level with Semi-Autonomy. They should be managed like Kenyatta National Hospital with Semi-Automous boards, budgets, performance targets and accountability. The Universal Health Care access should be fully supported and financed. The Afya Care Pilot done in Kisumu, Nyeri, Isiolo and Machakos should be rolled out Nationally. The NHIF should have robust management with efficiency. The Government should pay NHIF to all Kenyans who cannot afford. Corruption at NHIF should be addressed. There should be information Technology solutions to some of the inefficiencies at NHIF. All Kenya Citizens deserve quality Universal Health Care as a right.

CHAPTER 13: PHOTO GALLERY.

13.0: A wonderful family pictorial collection

All About The

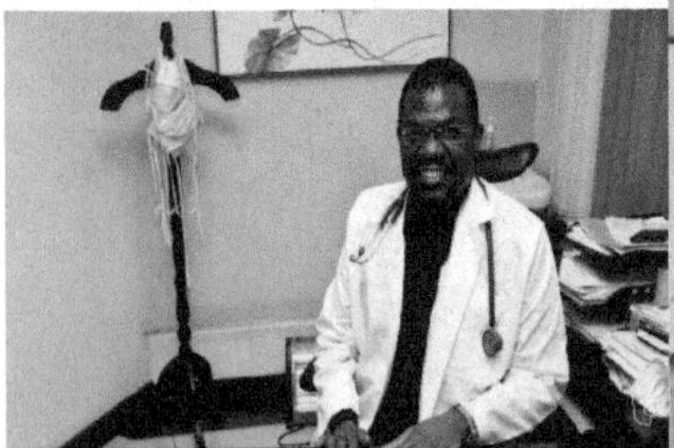

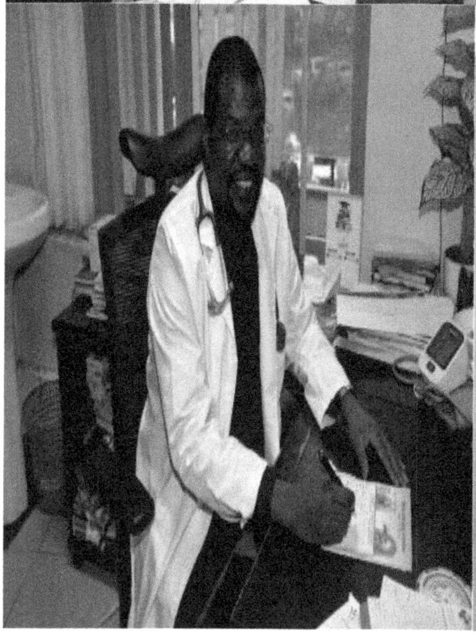

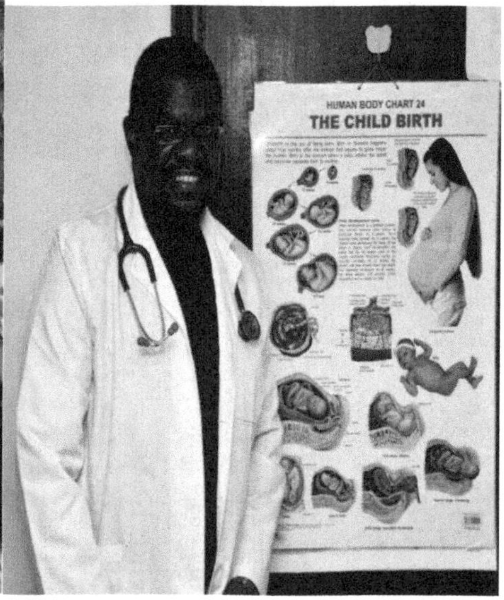
HUMAN BODY CHART 24
THE CHILD BIRTH

RADISE HOTEL MANAGEMENT WISHES YOU A

WELCOME TO SHIMBA HILLS
NATIONAL RESERVE
MAIN GATE

13.1: Celebrating Dola's life:

The setting in the venue of Dola's burial ceremony

Tributes and Proceedings on the Burial Day: 27th February, 2021:

Right: Dr Odero Ong'ech with the doctors who came to condole him at Dola's funeral

Left: Trans-Nzoia (Kitale) County commissioner, Samson Ojwang, making his remarks in honor of Dola before his burial
Right: Prof Augustine Otieno Afullo, the author of Dola's books, making his final remarks at Dola's funeral in Ogam on 27th February, 2021

The Clergy taking charge of Dola's funeral just after the end of the family tributes

Dr John Odero Ongech, Mzee's last born son, making his final remarks during Dola's burial. Right: At burial site

Blessing the grave and Prayers at the graveside The last soil by family into the grave

Remains of Dola being lowered to the grave
Laying the wreath / Laying a wreath on Mzee's grave

Dr Odero's colleagues: Medical doctors who attended Dola's funeral

Dola Funeral Committee Chairman, Prof Odhiambo Omenya, giving his tribute during Dola's final send-off in Ogam, Yimbo

13.2: The family reunion: To nyakwara ibiro chamo tong' karango? Mama Obera asks.

A section of the Usenge High school alumni who came to condole with Dr Ongech at the burial of Dola

Right: Mzee's childhood friend, Mzee Hanington Mirega (right), attending Dr Ong'ech's graduation ceremony

13.3: Mzee Dola's Final Resting Place: The Jeremiah Ong'ech Ogola Mausoleum

9/20/21, 8:17 AM - Dr Ongech O J: 1st, Family leaving Yimbo, 2nd Family arrives at Kano Kobura

13.4. Celebrating Achievement of friends

In December 2022, Prof A Afullo had visited Dr Ongech Family in their home in Lavington. He came alongside his two daughters: Zawadi Anyango and Mitchele Amani. Zawadi is a 2nd Year BSc physiotherapy student in JKUAT, and seemingly Dr Ongech had been closely following her performance and progress, including her exemplary A- performnc ein KCSE with As across Sciences. To date Dr Ong'ech has not ben comfortable that Zawadi is not doing Medicine degree. However, on tnhis particupar visit, another celebrity was on the spot. Mitchele Anmani Achienhg' a class 6 pupil in Miangeni School, had scoopted top marks in Maths and Science and overall position their time running. For thseese the school had awarded her with medals, one for each achievement. It was these medals Dr Ongech and family appreciated and gacve aher an award. These are what she is sen displaying in the photo below.

13.5: Dr Ongech Handshake with President Kenyatta on 24.8.2017

13.6: Celebrating the graduation of Jeremy Odero and Grace Odero on 25/9/21:

Jeremy: Bachelor of business information technology; Grace- BSc Biology

Left: We had graduation party yesterday, for Jeremy Ong'ech Odero, my first born son. He graduated from Strathmore University with degree of Bachelor of Business Information Technology; Grace Odero late last year had received Bachelor of Science degree in Biology (Pre-Medicine degree) which we had not celebrated, so we celebrated both degrees

13.7: Celebrating Family unity

Left: 10/26/21, 8:16 AM - Dr Ongech O J: 2. Dr John Odero Ong'ech and Wife Beatrice Odero with Jerry and Zippy
Right: 10/26/21, 8:16 AM - Dr Ongech O J: 1. Mzee last born grandchildren: Jerry Ong'ech and Zippy Achieng

31.12.21: Dr Ongech on his 55th Birthday

Left: Humphrey Dave Odero celebrating with Jeremy on his graduation; Right: Dr Odero Ong'ech children celebrating during graduation of Jeremy

13.8: Celebrating Beatrice Odero Graduatuion, MBA

Mrs Beatrice Odero graduation, MBA (UoN in December 2021)

Original Gangsta

INDEX:

ISBN: 9798793424387

DR. JOHN ODERO ONG'ECH: In the Dreams of My Father

Published on: 31st December, 2021

Prof A O Afullo (Ed)

+254722690956/ wamratechnoprises@gmail.com

Made in the USA
Columbia, SC
14 January 2022

53796285R00220